AF559939

Insurance Marketing

Insurance Marketing

Dr. Sandeep Sharma

RANDOM PUBLICATIONS
NEW DELHI (INDIA)

Insurance Marketing

ISBN 978-93-5111-449-9

Published in 2014 in India by

RANDOM PUBLICATIONS

4376-A/4B, Gali Murari Lal, Ansari Road
New Delhi-110 002
Phone : +91-11-43580356, +91-11-23289044
e-mail: randomexports@gmail.com, sales@randompublications.com, info@randompublications.com

Reprinted 2022

Type Setting by : Keystoneprintads, Delhi-110051
Digitally Printed at: Replika Press Pvt. Ltd.

Preface

Insurance is the equitable transfer of the risk of a loss, from one entity to another in exchange for payment. It is a form of risk management primarily used to hedge against the risk of a contingent, uncertain loss. An insurer, or insurance carrier, is a company selling the insurance; the insured, or policyholder, is the person or entity buying the insurance policy. The amount of money to be charged for a certain amount of insurance coverage is called the premium.

Risk management, the practice of appraising and controlling risk, has evolved as a discrete field of study and practice. The transaction involves the insured assuming a guaranteed and known relatively small loss in the form of payment to the insurer in exchange for the insurer's promise to compensate (indemnify) the insured in the case of a financial (personal) loss. The insured receives a contract, called the insurance policy, which details the conditions and circumstances under which the insured will be financially compensated.

Insurance involves pooling funds from many insured entities (known as exposures) to pay for the losses that some may incur. The insured entities are therefore protected from risk for a fee, with the fee being dependent upon the frequency and severity of the event occurring. In order to be an insurable risk, the risk insured against must meet certain characteristics. Insurance as a financial intermediary is a commercial enterprise and a major part of the financial services industry, but individual entities can also self-insure through saving money for possible future losses.

Insurance can have various effects on society through the way that it changes who bears the cost of losses and damage. On one hand it can increase fraud; on the other it can help societies and individuals prepare for catastrophes and mitigate the effects of catastrophes on both households and societies.

Insurance can influence the probability of losses through moral hazard, insurance fraud, and preventive steps by the insurance company. Insurance scholars have typically used morale hazard to refer to the increased loss due to unintentional carelessness and moral hazard to refer to increased risk due to intentional carelessness or indifference. Insurers attempt to address carelessness through inspections, policy provisions requiring certain types of maintenance, and possible discounts for loss mitigation efforts. While in theory insurers could encourage investment in loss reduction, some commentators have argued that in practice insurers had historically not aggressively pursued loss control measures - particularly to prevent disaster losses such as hurricanes-because of concerns over rate reductions and legal battles. However, since about 1996 insurers have begun to take a more active role in loss mitigation, such as through building codes.

Insurers will often use insurance agents to initially market or underwrite their customers. Agents can be captive, meaning they write only for one company, or independent, meaning that they can issue policies from several companies. The existence and success of companies using insurance agents is likely due to improved and personalized service.

I thank all members of my team who have helped in the preparation of the book. My special thanks go to "Random Publications" who have published the book.

– Dr. Sandeep Sharma

Contents

1

Insurance: An Introduction

Insurance helps protect you from financial loss when things go wrong.
For example:

- Your mobile phone could fall out of your pocket and break while you're travelling (and you need a new one)
- You might be injured in a car accident (and you have to pay for treatment and the cost of repairs to your car).

While having insurance can give you peace of mind, it's not like a savings account, where any money you pay in belongs to you. What you can claim back from the insurance company depends on what's covered in your insurance policy.

HOW DOES INSURANCE WORK

Depending on what you are insuring against, the insurer agrees to pay you money to help cover costs if that thing happens. For example, if your laptop was stolen from your home, and you had insured it against theft, you could make a claim with your *insurer* to help cover the costs of getting a new laptop. This is called a 'transfer of *risk*' because the insurer is taking the risk of meeting the cost of the loss. Without insurance, you are taking the risk that you will have to wear the financial loss if things go wrong.

WHAT CAN YOU INSURE

You can buy different types of *insurance policies* that cover a range of *risks,* depending on what you are insuring. *Insurers* offer policies with different features, so make sure you choose a policy that is right for you.

WHAT IS AN INSURANCE POLICY

You and the *insurer* agree on what is being insured. This is written in a legal agreement (contract) called an *insurance policy*.

The insurance policy sets out exactly:

- What is being insured and the risk being insured against (*terms and conditions*)

- Any *exclusions*
- How much the *insurer* will pay if you make a claim
- How much the policy will cost you (*premium*).

The *premium* can depend on things like where you live or what you and the *insurer* agree will be the cost of replacing something if it's stolen or damaged. The premium is less than the total cost of what you are insuring.

HOW CAN YOU GET INSURANCE

You can buy insurance directly from the *insurer* or from an insurance broker. Insurance brokers are not employed by the *insurer* and may be able to help you get a better deal.

If you are thinking of buying insurance from a broker, make sure they are licensed by ASIC, or that they work for someone who is licensed by ASIC.

What You	Types of Policies Insure
Your holiday	Travel insurance
Your property	*Car insurance, home insurance* and *contents insurance,* boat insurance
Your person	*Health insurance, life insurance* (including *income protection insurance, total* and *permanent disability insurance, term life insurance* and sickness or accident insurance)
Your business	Business insurance, professional indemnity and public liability insurance
Your loans	Consumer credit insurance

SOME REASONS TO INSURE

- Insurance can help you replace something you own and could not afford to replace. For example, if your home was destroyed in a fire, you would need a big lump sum to rebuild it.
- Insurance can protect you from something that might not happen, but which would be bad for you if it did. For example, if you were injured in an accident and couldn't work anymore, you would need money to live on.
- Insurance can help you pay off a debt if something you've bought with a loan is damaged or destroyed. For example, if you took out a loan to buy a car and the car was written off in an accident, you would need money to pay off the loan.

EXCESS

Some *insurance policies* include an excess. This is how much you must pay out of your own pocket on any *claim*. For example, if you have a car accident, the total cost of repairing your car might be $2,000. If you have an *excess* of $500, you would have to pay the first $500 and the *insurer* would pay the remaining amount, $1,500.

Sometimes an *excess* might be compulsory (for example, on *car insurance* for young drivers). In other cases, you can choose to pay a higher *premium* to reduce or remove the *excess*. Generally, the higher the *excess* you're willing to pay, the lower your *premium*.

WAITING PERIOD

Some *insurance policies* have a *waiting period*. This means that you must wait for a certain period of time after you buy the policy before you can make a *claim*. For example, you may have to wait 12 months before you can claim the cost of going to the dentist or having a baby on a private *health insurance* policy. You may be able to change the *waiting period* for some policies. If you choose a longer *waiting period*, you may pay a lower *premium*. You need to decide whether you can afford to wait for your insurance benefit.

VALUE

Some *insurance policies* include a value (or cost) for what you are insuring.

This is based on what the insurer will pay you if you have to claim on your insurance:

- *Agreed Value*: This means that the *insurer* will pay you a fixed dollar amount as stated in your policy. (There may be some deductions, for example, an *excess*.)
- *Market Value*: This means that the *insurer* will pay the value of the item based on its current age and condition at the time of loss (for example, cars or laptop computers may lose their value quickly and the *insurer* will only pay you much less than what it cost you to buy, or to buy a replacement).
- *Replacement Cost*: This means that the *insurer* will cover the cost of replacing the item with a new one, regardless of its current age and condition.

The value (or cost) you insure for can affect the *premium* you pay upfront. For example, your *premium* might be cheaper if you insure for *market value*.

CLAIMS

A *claim* is when you ask your *insurer* to pay for something that is covered by your *insurance policy*. You can only claim on your insurance if the thing that goes wrong is covered in your *insurance policy*. When you're shopping around for insurance, look for *claim* procedures or conditions in the policy. How the *insurer* deals with *claims* will be important to you if you need to make a *claim* later on.

Typical Exclusions from Cover	**Type of Policy (Where the Insurer will not Pay)**
Any illegal behaviour, such as driving while	Car insurance drunk
Modifications to your car (for example, the interactive)	Car insurance addition of spoilers as shown in the *Safe or sorry–Insurance*

Adventure sports such as bungee jumping, and scuba diving	Travel insurance white-water rafting, skiing
War/terrorist damage contents insurance	Travel insurance, life insurance,
Your luggage is stolen while left unattended	Travel insurance in a public place
Damage caused by floods	*Home insurance* and *contents insurance, car insurance*
Damage caused by a failure to maintain or property (for example, rain through a hole in the roof that you knew about but didn't repair)	*Car insurance, home* repair the insured *insurance* and *contents* gets into your house *insurance*
Cosmetic surgery	Health insurance

INSURANCE IN INDIA

LIFE INSURANCE CORPORATION OF INDIA

Life Insurance Corporation of India (LIC) was established on 1 September 1956 to spread the message of life insurance in the country and mobilise people's savings for nation-building activities. LIC with its central office in Mumbai and seven zonal offices at Mumbai, Calcutta, Delhi, Chennai, Hyderabad, Kanpur and Bhopal, operates through 100 divisional offices in important cities and 2,048 branch offices. LIC has 5.59 lakh active agents spread over the country.

The Corporation also transacts business abroad and has offices in Fiji, Mauritius and United Kingdom. LIC is associated with joint ventures abroad in the field of insurance, namely, Ken-India Assurance Company Limited, Nairobi; United Oriental Assurance Company Limited, Kuala Lumpur; and Life Insurance Corporation (International), E. C. Bahrain. It has also entered into an agreement with the Sun Life (UK) for marketing unit linked life insurance and pension policies in U.K.

The total new business of the Corporation during 1998-99 was ₹ 75,316 crore of sum assured under 148.43 lakh policies. LIC's group insurance business up to 31 March 1999 was ₹ 66,085 crore (provisional) providing cover to 219 lakh people.

SOCIAL SECURITY GROUP SCHEME

A Social Security Fund (SSF) administered by the LIC was set up in 1989-90 to meet the insurance requirements of the weaker and vulnerable parts of the society. As on 31 March 1999, about 49 lakh people belonging to 24 occupational groups/areas have been covered under various social security group schemes financed from the SSF. Under these schemes people in the age group of 18-60 years are covered for a sum of ₹ 5,000 on death due to natural causes, and ₹ 25,000 on death caused by accident. While the SSF subsidises 50 per cent of the premium, the beneficiary has to pay the remaining 50 per cent. Under Landless Agricultural Labourers Group Insurace Scheme (LALGI) in operation since 1987, the heads of the families in the age group of 18 to 60 years and not appearing as a land holder in the revenue records and not having inheritable right in agricultural land are eligible to be covered for an insurance cover of ₹ 2,000 payable only on death before 60 years.

Upto 1 April 1990, it was operated by LIC on behalf of the Central government which used to reimburse to LIC the premium payable by the beneficiaries. However, with effect from 1 April 1990 the entire premium payable by the beneficiaries is being met out of the SSF. At present, about 1.2 crore landless agricultural labourers are covered under the Scheme. During 1998-99, 47,122 claims were settled.

All over the country, the Integrated Rural Development Programme (IRDP) beneficiaries between the age group of 18 to 60 years are covered under a Group Life Insurance Scheme being operated by the LIC for which the entire premium is paid by the Central government. An amount of ₹ 5,000 is payable to the beneficiary in case of normal death and ₹ 10,000 in case of accidental death. During 1998-99, 5,896 claims were settled.The Rural Group Life Insurance Scheme (RGLIS), announced on 15 August 1995, is a group insurance scheme which provides a life cover of ₹ 5,000 for persons in rural areas. The premium payable is ₹ 60 per year for those who enroll up to the age of 40 years and ₹ 70 per year for those who enroll beyond 40 years and up to 50 years. The entry age is restricted to 20 years (minimum) and 50 years (maximum). Deaths occurring after 60 years are not covered. Nor is there any saving element in the Scheme.

There are two types of scheme:

1. *General Scheme*: For persons between the age 20 and 50 years where premiums are to be paid by the members in full and
2. *Subsidised Scheme*: For persons between the age of 20 and 50 years who belong to a household below- poverty line.

Only one member of such a household is eligible under the scheme where 50 per cent of the premium is shared by the Central government and State government in equal proportions. Intermediate Level Panchayats are designated as the nodal agencies for its implementation. LIC provides incentives to village level workers of ₹ 6 for enrolment of a new member and ₹ 3 on renewal of insurance cover for an existing member in the subsequent year. From 15 August 1997 to 14 August 1998, 3,09,252 persons were enrolled and 73,925 persons renewed their membership. Among them 2,98,917 and 70,183 persons were under subsidised category respectively 5,047 claims were settled up to 31 March 1999.

INSURANCE REGULATORY AUTHORITY

On the recommendations of the Malhotra Committee, Government has set up an interim Insurance Regulatory Authority (IRA), with a view to activate an insurance regulatory apparatus essential for proper monitoring and control of the insurance industry. The IRA is headed by a Chairman who is also Controller of Insurance and Chairman of TBC. The other Members of the IRA, not exceeding seven in number of whom not more than three shall serve full time, shall be nominated by the Central government.

GENERAL INSURANCE CORPORATION OF INDIA

The general insurance industry in India was nationalised and a government company known as General Insurance Corporation of India (GIC) was formed by the Central Government in November 1972.

With effect from 1 January 1973 the erstwhile 107 Indian and foreign insurers which were operating in the country prior to nationalisation, were grouped into four operating companies, namely:

1. National Insurance Company Limited;
2. New India Assurance Company Limited;
3. Oriental Insurance Company Limited; and
4. United India Insurance Company Limited.

All the four subsidiaries of GIC operate all over the country competing with one another and underwriting various classes of general insurance business except for aviation insurance of national airlines and crop insurance which is handled by the GIC. From 799 offices in 1973, the network grew to 4,208 offices as on 31 March 1998.

Besides the domestic market, the industry is presently operating in 17 countries directly through branches or agencies and in 14 countries through subsidiary and associate companies. The wholly-owned subsidiary of GIC known as India International Insurance Private Limited set up in 1988 in Singapore has grown into a leading company in the Singapore market. The gross premium income of the general insurance industry in India during 1997-98 was ₹ 7,736 crore as against ₹ 7,021 crore during 1996-97 representing a growth of 10.2 per cent over the premium income of 1996-97.

The net premium income of the general insurance industry in India during 1997-98 was ₹ 6, 725 crore as against ₹ 6,041 crore during 1996- 97 representing a growth of 11.3 per cent over the net premium income of 1996-97. The gross profit of the industry during 1997-98 were ₹ 1,623 crore as against ₹ 1,084 crore in 1996-97 recording a growth of 49.7 per cent over the previous year.

The net profits of the industry during 1997-98 were ₹ 1,255 crore as against ₹ 719 crore in 1996-97 representing a growth of 74.5 per cent over the previous year. Hut Insurance Scheme for Poor Families in Rural Areas provides fire insurance cover for huts and belongings of landless labourers, small farmers, artisans and other poor families in rural areas.

Under the Scheme, compensation is provided for an amount not exceeding ₹ 1,000 for a hut and ₹ 500 for belongings in the hut destroyed by fire. The Central Government is bearing the entire premium in respect of the scheme. During the year 1997-98, 40,554 claims involving an amount of ₹ 4. 85 crore were settled.

Mediclaim Insurance Policy has recently been revised. The revised policy does away with the sub-limits under the various sub-heads and offers just one sum-insured ranging from ₹ 15,000 to ₹ 3,00,000. The cover provides for reimbursement of medical expenses incurred by an individual towards hospitalisation/domicillary hospitalisation for any illness, injury or disease contracted or sustained during the period of insurance. Premium is calculated on the basis of age of the proposer and the sum insured opted forJan Arogya Bima Policy which is primarily meant for the larger segmentof the population who cannot afford the high cost of medical treatment, was introduced with effect from 12 August 1996.

The limit of cover per person is ₹ 5,000 per annum. The premium payable is very low depending on the age of the person covered ranging from ₹ 70 to ₹ 140 per person per year and ₹ 50 per dependent child below 25 years. The cover provides for reimbursement of medical expenses incurred by an individual towards hospitalisation/domicillary hospitali-sation for any illness, injury or disease contracted or sustained during the period of insurance.

The existing Overseas Mediclaim Policy offering emergency medical expenses cover to overseas travellers has been extended to include In-flight Personal Accident cover up to US $ 10,000 and Loss of Passport cover upto US $ 150 from 1 April 1997. The extended cover will be available without payment of additional premium under Business and Holiday cover and under the Corporate Frequent Travellers cover. A more comprehensive policy with additional benefits has also been devised.

A new policy called Videsh Yatra Mitra covering supplementary benefits besides providing indemnity for medical expenses during the period of overseas travel, has been introduced by the general insurance industry with effect from 1 January 1998. Two types of policies—one offering limit of benefits upto US $ 2,50,000 for worldwide travel but excluding USA and Canada and the other offering limit of benefits up to US$ 5,00,000 for worldwide travel including USA and Canada are available under the Scheme.

In addition to medical coverage, the policy also provides coverage for:

- Personal Accident up to US $ 25, 000;
- Loss of Personal Baggage up to US $ 1,000;
- Delayed Baggage up to US $ 100 and
- Personal Liability up to US $ 2,00,000.

The premium under the policy is only 14 per cent more than that under the existing Overseas Mediclaim Policy (OMD), while the medical benefits will be increased five times in addition to supplementary benefits.

Bhagyashree Child Welfare Policy covering girl child in the age group of 0 to 18 years whose parents' age does not exceed 60 years, was introduced with effect from 19 October 1998. In case of each of the girl child or both parents, an amount of ₹ 25,000 would be deposited in the name of the girl child with a financial institution. Fixed annual disburse-ments to the girl child up to the age of 18 years would be made from the amount to her credit, and the balance amount to her credit would be disbursed on attaining the age of 18 years. Raj Rajeshwari Mahila Kalyan Yojana offering security to women in the age group of 10 to 75 years irrespective of their occupation was introduced with effect from 19 October 1998. For a premium of ₹ 15 per annum, the policy provides a cover of ₹ 25,000 for permanent total disablement of the insured woman. The policy also provides a cover of ₹ 25,000 for the death of her husband. For the death of an unmarried woman, the policy provides a cover of ₹ 25,000 which will be payable to her nominee/legal heir.

Crop Insurance Scheme was introduced from 1985 Kharif season. The scheme is implemented in 15 States and two UTs. The scheme is administered by GIC on behalf of Central government. The premium and claims are shared by the Central and State governments in the ratio of 2:1 respectively. There are 11 Crop Insurance Cells at State capitals and UTs under GIC. These cells maintain close liaison with the State governments and monitor the implementation of the scheme.

The susbsidiaries of GIC have introduced Jald Rahat Yojana with an objective to expedite payment of compensation to road accident victims. Under the scheme a claimant is not required to go to Motor Accident Claims Tribunal for claiming compensation and can directly approach concerned insurance company. Non-fatal injury claims involving accident victims of 18 years and above are taken up. The scheme is in operation in Ahmadabad, Mumbai, Bangalore, Calcutta, Delhi, Kochi, Chennai and Pune.

DISINVESTMENT IN PUBLIC SECTOR ENTERPRISES

For the year 1998-99 a target of ₹ 5,000 crore was set for realisation through disinvestment of government's equity in public sector enterprises. the disinvestment programme of 1998-99 included offerings from Container Corporation of India (CONCOR), Gas Authority of India Limited (GAIL), Videsh Sanchar Nigam Limited (VSNL) and Indian Oil Corporation (IOC). The CONCOR offering was completed during November 1998 in the domestic market in which FIIs also participated. By divesting 90 lakh shares, the Government has realised about ₹ 222 crore.

The Government holding in company stands at about 63 per cent. In case of VSNL, the GDR/domestic offering of GAIL was completed in the first week of February 1999 and an amount of ₹ 785 crore approx. was realised. The domestic offering of GAIL was completed in the first week of February 1999 and an amount of ₹ 182 crore was realised. The disinvestment in IOC was deferred due to adverse market conditions. To have better synergies among the Oil Sector PSUs, ONGC, IOC and GAIL cross purchased each others shares among themselves realising about ₹ 4,200 crore for the Government. The total amount realised from the disinvestment during the year 1998-99 was ₹ 6,000 crore against the target of ₹ 5,000 crore..

LIFE INSURANCE IN INDIA

As a global sweet spot, India attracts the attention of every major insurer. The country started in 20th place in the global insurance league table when the market opened to private players in 2000, and it moved up to 11th place in 2010.

Since 2000, a total of 22 life insurance companies have set up operations in India. Most major multinational insurers are represented through joint ventures (the only option for foreigners), and all but two new players are licensed as joint ventures. Total foreign direct investment in insurance companies stands at close to ₹ 51 billion (about US$1.1 billion). While the state-owned Life Insurance Corporation (LIC) still holds a significant majority of market share, other companies have established footholds.

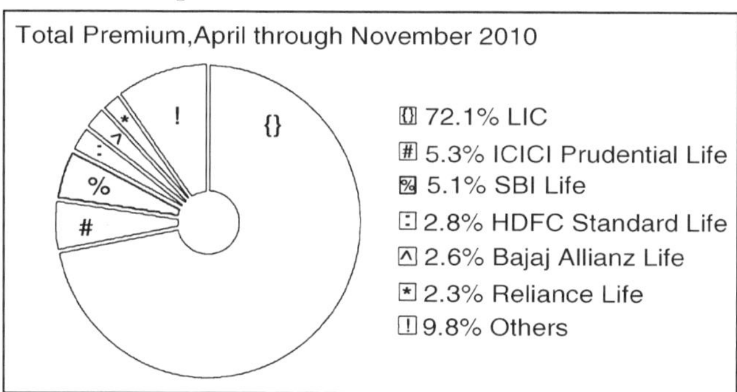

Fig. Market Share of Leading Life Insurers

FAVOURABLE ECONOMIC PROFILE

India is recognized globally for its trillion-dollar economy, consistent high growth of more than 8% per annum, its vibrant democracy and institutions, and cheap labour with good English skills. A recent study by McKinsey predicts that India's economy will grow fivefold in the next 20 years.

The country's favourable demographic profile is of special interest to insurers: 56% of Indians were under age 15 or over age 64 in 2010. Research by Morgan Stanley shows that India's working-age population will increase by 136 million by 2020. (China's working-age population, by comparison, will grow by 23 million.) Indian households save more than those in other emerging markets such as China and Brazil. Household savings were 25% of India's gross domestic savings in 2008, compared with 5% in Brazil and 15% in China. The figures for Britain and the U. S. are 2% and 1%, respectively.

India's life insurance penetration, defined as the ratio of premium underwritten to the GDP, was 4.6% last year, or US$47 premium per capita, and non-life business was just 0.6%. The large young population, combined with the current low rate of life insurance penetration and high rate of personal savings, points to the upside potential for the Indian insurance market.

INVESTMENT PLANS A KEY DRIVER IN INSURANCE SALES

This propensity to save has led to a surge in investment-linked life insurance policies. Almost the entire insurance premium generated by private insurers in India is from investment plans, with pure term insurance least preferred by buyers (and least actively marketed). Customers prefer to channel insurance savings into unit-linked investment plans (ULIPs), which are regarded as more transparent and give policyholders some say in the investment strategy. The strong performance of Indian stock indices has aided this growth. The Indian stock market gave returns of 22% in 2010, a significant drop from the dizzying 90% gain in 2009, but still impressive.

The total business premium generated by insurers from ULIP sales for the fiscal year ending 2010 is ₹ 115 billion (US$25.6 billion), or about 45% of total business, according to a recent report by the regulator. Private life companies generate more than 90% of business from single and regular premium ULIPs.

Insurance savings are backed by attractive tax benefits. Life insurance premiums, along with a few other long-term saving instruments up to ₹ 100,000 (about US$2,200), qualify for a tax deduction. Maturity proceeds and death benefits from life policies are tax-free.

GROWTH OF DISTRIBUTION CHANNELS

A major contributor to the growth story is the distribution network. Indian regulations allow distribution by insurance companies throughout India, unlike in China, which opened its market province by province. There are close to three million licensed life insurance agents, split almost equally between the state-owned LIC and the private players. Agents generate 80% of LIC's new business and about half for private companies. There are also about 3,000 corporate insurance agents, mostly banks, brokers and firms, engaged in personal loans.

Bancassurance is now emerging as a key distribution channel through a network of more than 70,000 branches of banks. Last year, banks generated about 20% of new business for private life companies. Banks are the primary sales channel for a few insurers such as HDFC Standard Life and SBI Life, and they contribute about 40% of their new business. A few recent joint ventures, such as that of HSBC, Dai-ichi Life and the U.K.'s Legal and General, are exclusively bancassurance models that employ no individual agents. A potential move by the regulator to allow banks to represent more than one insurer is expected to provide a fillip to the bancassurance channel.

WHAT MULTINATIONALS HAVE LEARNED IN INDIA

India has attracted a large number of multinational insurers in a short span of time. What have major players learned in the first decade of operations? There are five important sessions.

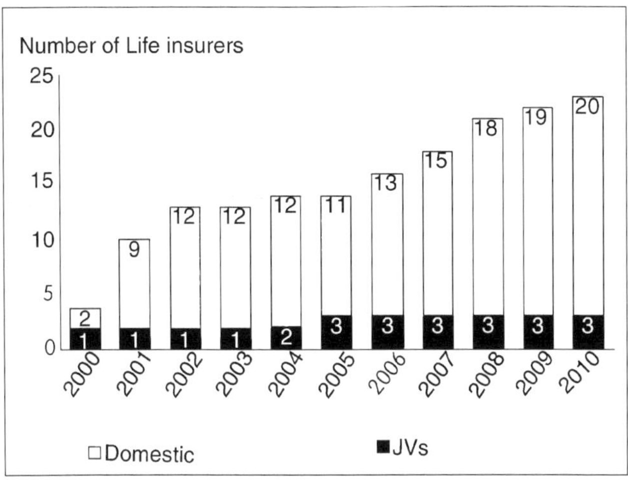

Fig. Domestic Life Company vs. Foreign Joint Ventures

IMPORTANCE OF STRONG LOCAL PARTNER AND BRAND

Private insurers have learned that the strength of their domestic partners and their market franchises is vital to sustainable growth. Insurance buyers rely more on the market standing and distribution network of local sponsors than the global image of their foreign counterparts. At the same time, a few joint ventures have experienced growth constraints because local partners have not been ready to pump in capital as needed to support business volumes and solvency needs.

As a result, well-capitalized banks are emerging as preferred partners in insurance ventures. Only sound and profitable banks get the necessary approval from the central bank to take a stake in Indian insurance businesses. In fact, entrants such as HSBC and Dai-ichi Life have offered high premiums to banks in order to forge partnerships.

Now several ongoing ventures are also trying to lure banks, including state banks, by offering them a slice of equity in exchange for their funding and distribution capabilities.

Reports indicate that leading multinational insurers, such as AXA, Aviva and Prudential (U.S.), each of which has had joint ventures in India for five or more years, are seeking commercial banks as additional shareholders. In a transaction last year, New York Life's joint venture, which has been in operation for a decade, offered attractive terms to lure a private bank.

FLEXIBLE PRODUCT STRATEGIES

Life companies in India have learned that product strategies need to be under constant review to respond to changing risk appetites and customer preferences. The variety of customer segments in India requires a large array of products: saving policies in various forms, term insurance plans with or without refund of premiums and individual products, not to mention plans for affinity and other groups, wealth management solutions, rural and micro-insurance plans, pension and annuity schemes, health insurance and so on.

As a result, product teams are under pressure to assess the market and come up with new plans, often on short notice, to satisfy distribution partners and as a response to the market environment.

ULIPs are a prime example of the need to really understand the marketplace. A few companies underestimated customer interest in ULIPs when they were introduced in 2003 and kept to their more traditional plans, thereby missing a slice of the pie.

On the other hand, companies that relied solely on ULIPs suffered in the global financial crisis when customers took a flight to safety, and again more recently in the wake of regulatory measures that sought to curb the excessive growth of ULIPs at the cost of traditional insurance plans.

DISTRIBUTION EFFICIENCY

A key session for insurers in India is in distribution, which is witnessing the emergence of new channels such as bancassurance. While agencies remain the backbone of distribution, mass recruitment led to quality and sales skill issues, and widespread complaints of misrepresentation of insurance plans.

Most agents consider insurance sales a secondary pursuit for additional income, and they often rely on their immediate contacts to make sales. This has led to high agent turnover and a high percentage of policy lapses, which has affected insurers' long-term profitability.

According to the regulator, the lapse rate on ULIP policies was 26% in 2006, and according to Towers Watson's estimates, that has climbed higher in recent years. The regulator has also voiced concerns about the status of orphan policies at many companies.

The low quality of sales and high incidence of policy discontinuance are also evident in bank distribution. A 2008 Towers Watson study that benchmarked bancassurance distribution in India, showed that distribution practices at bank branches are inefficient and are centered on sales push. Customer service is often mediocre. Indian banks have more than 400 million retail customers, and only about 1% of them have been cross-sold insurance. The potential is huge, and insurers are now waking up to the need for well-orchestrated implementation plans.

LARGE VOLUMES AND SMALL TICKETS

When the market opened, most private insurers underestimated the Indian market's potential volume and policy sizes. The volume of new business boomed.

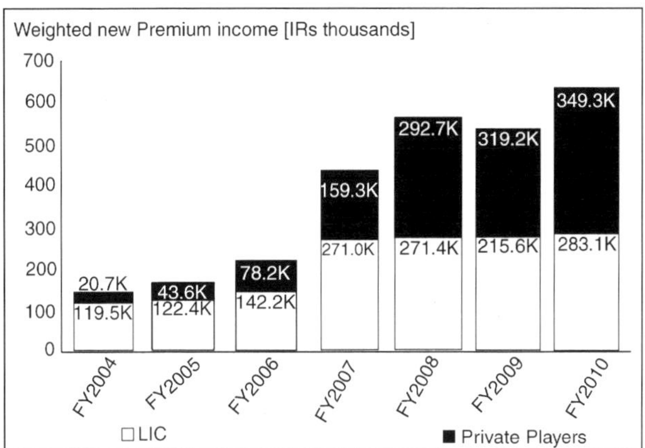

Fig. New Business Premium of Insurers

In 2010, private insurers issued a total of 14.5 million policies, and the state-owned LIC issued close to 40 million. This translates to an average first-year premium of about ₹ 20,000 (about US$440) per policy. But because policyholders can pay their premium semiannually or quarterly, transaction sizes are much lower than the annual premium. Managing the resulting huge transaction numbers and service levels has presented a challenge to insurers.

Insurers active in the rural and micro-insurance businesses have also learned to cater to customers who want small policies with annual premiums of ₹ 500 (about US$11) or even lower, and they have developed mechanisms to collect and account for small amounts. As a result, several technology innovations have emerged. For example, the New York Life joint venture launched Max Vijay, a microinsurance product that is essentially a prepackaged kit sold through corner shops in small towns and villages, and managed through an outsourced arrangement with IBM.

FOCUS ON COST MANAGEMENT

Despite robust growth, good cost management is a key issue for private players. Indian regulations prescribe caps on costs, including management expenses. Most private players have breached this limit, citing the additional costs of start-up. While the operating cost ratio for private insurers came down to about 21% last year—a decline of 5% from the previous year—a recent set of new regulatory measures drastically lowering policy surrender charges and capping fund management fees has required insurers to relentlessly pursue costreduction initiatives.

After a brief, hectic period of expansion, many companies are now rationalizing their branch offices in an effort to control costs. Private insurers have more than 8,800 branches—about three times more than LIC. The bulk of them (about 70%) are in small towns and semi-urban locations that offer robust business growth.

While local branch offices have helped insurers enhance their brand image and offer better customer service, there is a need for alternative strategies. Companies that have bank partners are now actively seeking to ride on the infrastructure and other facilities that banks offer at even their most remote locations.

STOCK LISTING

A regulatory change allowing foreign partners to raise their stake from the current ceiling of 26% to 49% has been long awaited, but the enabling legislation is mired in political debate, and there are indications that it might take more time for a broad consensus allowing a higher level of foreign ownership to emerge.

Indian policymakers have generally favoured stock listing for enterprises in every segment for the transparency and the wider accountability that it brings. In keeping with that philosophy, the insurance regulator recently announced that companies in operation for five years or longer would be eligible for listing. A recent report showed that of 22 private life insurers, seven have shown a profit in the last fiscal year, up from four companies in the previous two years. This is surely a sign of the increasingly steady profitability of private insurers.

While the regulator is finalizing policies for valuation, disclosure and other norms as part of the public offer exercise, a few joint venture companies have signaled their intention to seek retail participation in the near future. However, it remains unclear how much of their stake the various partners would be willing to give up in order to become listed. Indian laws regard ownership as a stake of 51% and above. Any foreign partner would be unlikely to accept any dilution of its stake below the current 26%—the minimum percentage needed to retain key veto powers. The level of dilution acceptable to local partners and the emerging shareholder relationships post-IPO would be key factors to watch in the period ahead.

These developments clearly show that the Indian insurance industry is poised for a big leap in performance and opportunities, notwithstanding the challenges and the strategic issues that the private players—and their foreign partners—face as part of this momentous growth.

THE AGENCY CONTRACT

In India, the relationship between Agent and Principal is primarily contractual in nature and is governed by the terms of contract entered into between them ("Agency Contract"). The law of agency derives its statutory base from Chapter X of the Indian Contract Act, 1872 ("Act"), which provides the framework of rules and regulations that govern formation and performance of any contract including the Agency Contract. Section 182 of the Act defines 'Agent' as 'person employed to do any act for another or to represent another in dealings with third person'.

Any person, who is of the age of majority according to the law to which he is subject, and who is of sound mind, can employ an Agent. As between Principal and third person a person may become an Agent, so as to be responsible to his Principal according to the provisions contained in the Act. No consideration is necessary to create an agency.

The authority of an Agent may be express or implied. An authority is said to be express when it is given by words, spoken or written. An authority is said to be implied when it is to be inferred from the circumstances of the case and things spoken or written or in the ordinary course of dealing may account for the circumstances of the case.

An Agent having an authority to do an act has authority to do every lawful thing, which is necessary in order to do such act. The Agent in doing that act must neither do anything that is illegal, not beyond the limits of his own authority, nor beyond the powers of his Principal.

An Agent has authority in an emergency to do all such acts for the purpose of protecting his Principal from loss as would be done by a person of ordinary prudence, in his own case under similar circumstance. Several types of commercial agents have been recognized under Indian law, which includes inter alia brokers, auctioneers, del credere agents, persons entrusted with money for obtaining sales and insurance agents.

INDEMNITIES AND/OR COMPENSATION

The right to claim indemnity arises primarily in the event of termination of the agency. An agency is terminated by the Principal revoking his authority; or by the Agent renouncing the business of the agency; or by the business of the agency being completed; or by either the Principal or Agent dying or becoming of unsound mind; or by the Principal being adjudicated an insolvent under the provisions of any act for the time being in force for the relief of insolvent debtors. Where the Agent has himself an interest in the property which forms the subject matter of the agency, the agency cannot be terminated to the prejudice of such interest.

The right to indemnity and/or the right to compensation to the Agent in the event of termination of the Agency Contract is subject primarily to the terms and conditions of the Agency Contract entered into between Principal and Agent. Since the Agent represents the Principal, the Agent has the right to be indemnified for all the lawful acts done by the Agent in the course of the agency. The Act contains specific provisions under Section 222 and 223, for the payment of indemnity or compensation in the event of revocation of the Agency Contract by the Principal prior to its term.

Unless the Agency Contract provides for the payment of full indemnity, the indemnity payable to the Agent is generally equitable. There is no limitation on the amount of indemnity to which an Agent may be entitled to and it is the Court, which determines the amount of indemnity that may be paid.

The Courts in India, from time to time have held that an Agent can claim indemnity against the Principal, if the Agent is able to prove that he has actually incurred a loss or that loss is eminent due to the wrongful termination of the Agency Contract. For an Agent to claim indemnity it is essential that the act done by him must be lawful. It is not sufficient that his acts are innocent or done in good faith. Further, it is important that the action in respect of which the Agent is claiming indemnity must have been performed in accordance with the authority conferred upon the Agent. There is no right to indemnity unless the Agent has acted within his express, implied or usual authority.

Subject to the terms of Agency Contract the Agent may, in addition to indemnity, claim compensation by way of damages, which may either be general or special. General damages are those, which result from 'direct and proximate' consequences from breach of contract.

Normally, what can be awarded is compensation for loss or damage, which can be directly or proximately attributed to the breach of contract. One way of assessing damages is the difference between the contract price and the market price on date of breach of contract, plus reasonable expenses incurred by him on account of the breach plus cost of suit in court of law. Special damages or consequential damages arise due to existence of special circumstances. Such damages can be awarded only in cases where the special circumstances were foreseeable by the party committing the breach or were specifically known to the party.

CONDITIONS OF INDEMNITY AND/OR COMPENSATION

Subject to the terms of the Agency Contract, the Act provides for the following situations where an Agent has to be indemnified/compensated by the Principal.

CONDITIONS FOR CLAIMING INDEMNITY

- *Section 222 of the Act Provides*: "The employer of an Agent is bound to indemnify him against the consequences of all lawful acts done by such Agent in exercise of the authority conferred upon him"; and
- *Section 223 of the Act Provides*: "Where one person employs another to do an act, and the Agent does the act in good faith, the employer is liable to indemnify the Agent against the cones quences of the act, though it causes an injury to the rights of third persons".

Section 222 of the Act provides that an employer is bound to indemnify an Agent against all the consequences of all lawful acts done by such Agent in the exercise of the authority conferred upon him. By virtue of this part, under the Indian Law there is an implied contract between the Principal and the Agent whereby the Principal has to indemnify the Agent against the losses and consequences of all lawful acts done by such Agent in exercise of the authority conferred upon him. For instance, where an Agent who is authorized to make contracts for the supply of goods, is authorized or is not forbidden to make those contracts in his own name, he becomes entitled to an indemnity against any personal liability in respect of any contract for the purchase of goods the moment he enters into such contract. His right of action in respect of this indemnity is not postponed to his satisfaction of the liabilities against which he claims indemnity.

It is important for the Agent to prove that the Agent has actually incurred a loss or that the loss is eminent. Further, in order to claim indemnity under this part it is essential that the act committed by the Agent must be lawful. Indian courts have held that an Agent is entitled to indemnity even in respect of void, but not illegal contracts. It has also been held by the Indian Courts that the Principal has to indemnify the Agent even in respect of the payments, which the latter is compelled to make even though he is not legally liable to pay the same.

Section 223 of the Act provides that an Agent has to be indemnified against consequences of unlawful acts, which are not criminal, done by him in good faith and without the knowledge that such act is unlawful. This provision entitles an Agent to claim indemnity in respect of the acts done in good faith though they cause injury to the rights of third persons.

The right to indemnity entitles an Agent to recover his commission remuneration and all his expenses that he has incurred on the Principal's behalf. It has been held by Supreme Court of India that the right of an Agent to obtain indemnity from his Principal is a matter entirely collateral to the main contract made by the Agent on behalf of the Principal, and is not affected by anything, which renders the main contract unenforceable.

Where the authority of the Agent has been properly revoked, he is entitled to recover the remuneration or commission already earned. Where an Agent acts within the scope of his authority he is entitled to full indemnity. Where an Agent purchases goods on behalf of his Principal and renders himself liable for the price of goods, the Agent has the same rights with regard to the disposal of the goods as he would have had, if the relation between him and the Principal had been that of the seller and buyer. If, therefore, the Principal improperly refuses to accept, the Agent is entitled to re-sell the goods and hold Principal liable for any deficiency arising from the sale. The deficiency is the measure of loss in respect of which the Agent is entitled to be indemnified and reimbursed.

CONDITIONS FOR CLAIMING DAMAGES/COMPENSATION

The general law of damages in India is contained in Section 73, 74 and 75 of the Act. The Act provides that in the event of breach of a contract the non-defaulting party is entitled to receive compensation for any loss or damage caused to such non-defaulting party thereby. Such compensation is payable when the loss has arisen in the usual course of things from such breach, or which the parties knew, when they made the contract, to be likely to result from such breach of it. The party in breach must make compensation in respect of direct consequences flowing from the breach and not in respect of loss or damage indirectly or remotely caused.

When an obligation resembling those created by contract has been incurred and has not been discharged, any person injured by the failure to discharge is entitled to receive the same compensation from the party in default, as if such person had contracted to discharge it and broken his contract.

In estimating the loss or damage arising from the breach of contract, the means that existed of remedying the inconvenience caused by the non-performance of the contract must be taken into account.

Where the contract provides for the payment of a specified amount or a penalty, by the defaulting party to the non-defaulting party in the event of breach, the non-defaulting party is entitled, whether or not actual damage or loss is proved to have been caused thereby, to receive from the defaulting party reasonable compensation not exceeding the amount so specified in the contract. Under the Act a person who rightfully rescinds a contract is entitled to compensation for any damage, which he has sustained through the non-fulfillment of the contract.

The law pertaining to damages and compensation in the event of termination of Agency Contract is set out in Section 205, 206 and 225 of the Act:

- *Section 205 of the Act Provides as Follows*: "Where there is an express or implied contract that the agency should be continued for any period of time, the Principal must make compensation to the Agent, or the Agent to the Principal, as the case may be, for any previous revocation or renunciation of the agency with out sufficient cause".
- *Section 206 of the Act Provides as Follows*: "Reasonable notice must be given of such revocation or renun ciation; otherwise the damage thereby resulting to the Principal or the Agent, as the case may be, must be made good to the one by the other".
- *Section 225 Provides as Follows*: "The Principal must make compensation to his Agent in respect of the injury caused to such Agent by the Principal's neglect or want of skill. "

Under the Act, liability to pay compensation arises when the Agency Contract is terminated without sufficient cause or where the Principal fails to give a reasonable notice before the revocation of the Agency Contract or where any injury caused to such Agent due to Principal's neglect or want of skill.

If the term of the agency is fixed in the Agency Contract, it is determined on the expiration of the term. The agency may be terminated before the expiry of the term in accordance with an express reservation in the contract or for a reasonable cause. If the Agency Contract is terminated by the Principal prior to its term without sufficient cause, the Principal is liable and must make compensation to the Agent for the previous revocation of the agency.

The Indian Courts have held that the following interalia will constitute 'sufficient cause' for the termination of agency:

- Loss of reputation by the Agent;
- Incapacity of the Agent, whether physical or mental;
- Misconduct on the part of Agent, if sufficient to justify dismissal; and
- Taking bribes.

The Act provides that where there is no express or implied contract that the agency should continue for any fixed period, reasonable notice must be given of the revocation or renunciation of the agency. In the event the Principal fails to give a reasonable notice to the Agent before the revocation of the agency, the Principal is liable to pay damages to the Agent for the loss incurred by the Agent due to such termination. Reasonableness varies from circumstances of each case.

In all indefinite mercantile or commercial contracts, the question whether the relationship of the Principal and Agent can be terminated by a reasonable notice or only by mutual consent is one of construction subject to the rules of law. There is no general rule of permanence. An agency may be terminated by various ways.

If the termination of agency is inequitable or works an unjust hardship on the Agent, the law requires a reasonable notice to be given. An absolute power of cancellation of contract cannot be validly reserved in favour of one of the parties. Such a clause in the contract is absolutely illegal and irregular. Under Section 225 of the Act, the Principal is liable to compensate the Agent in respect of any injury caused to such Agent due to Principal's neglect or want of skill.

In order to entitle the Agent to compensation he must prove that:

- Some injury was caused to him; and
- Such injury was caused by the Principal's neglect or want of skill.

The Agent cannot recover compensation, if the Principal proves that the Agent could have avoided the consequence of Principal's negligence by reasonable means. Further, the Agent cannot recover compensation, if the injury has resulted from the nature and circumstances of his employment, or if the injury is a natural and necessary consequence of his employment.

In addition to damages and indemnity, the Act gives additional right of lien to the Agent over the Principal's property. The Act provides that in the absence of any contract to the contrary an Agent is entitled to retain goods, papers and other property, whether movable or immovable, of the Principal received by him, until the amount due to himself for commission, disbursements and services in respect of the same has been paid or accounted for to him.

The Agent's lien does not confer unrestricted authority on the Agent to deal with the Principal's property, this right is limited in nature and the Agent can retain the property till his dues are paid by the Principal. This right can be availed of as a defence if the Principal brings and action for the recovery of the property in possession of the Agent. But this provision does not confer any authority on the Agent to sell or otherwise dispose of the property without the consent of the Principal in order to satisfy his lien. Besides the aforesaid, there are no specific provisions under the Act, which entitle an Agent to claim indemnity against or compensation from the Principal and it is open to the parties to formulate the terms and conditions for claiming indemnity under the contract.

Indian Limitation Act governs the law pertaining to the period within which the Agent should file a suit for claiming compensation/indemnity. According to the Limitation Act, 1963 when an Agent sues the Principal for money spent by him on behalf of the Principal and recoverable under Section 222 and 223 of the Act, the suit should be filed within a period of three years from the date of payment and not when the agency terminates. Suit for claiming compensation and indemnity should be filed within a period of three years from the date the right to sue has first arisen *i.e.* when the cause of action first arises. When the right to sue first arises largely depends on the facts and circum-stances of each case.

CALCULATION OF INDEMNITY AND/OR COMPENSATION

Unless the Agency Contract specifically provides for the payment of liquidated damages/compensation in the event of determination of the Agency Contract, in computing the compensation/indemnity payable to the aggrieved Agent the Courts in India apply the rules for assessing damages/compensation for other contracts. There is no fixed rule for determining the measure of damages, but must depend on the circumstances of each case. There is no specific provision under the Indian Contract Act or any other law regarding the calculation of indemnity and/or compensation. For the computation of compensation payable to the Agent the Court may take into consideration the amount the Agent would have earned, if the contract would not have terminated.

INDEMNITY AND/OR COMPENSATION FOR DISTRIBUTORS AND FRANCHISEE

Indemnity or compensation payable to distributors and franchisee is governed by the terms of the relevant contract and the Act. There is no specific law in India, which governs the payment of indemnity/compensation to the distributors and franchisee and it is open to the parties to determine the conditions for payment and the amount of compensation. Where the contract is silent the indemnity and compensation is determined in accordance with the Act.

2

Customer Servicing

INTRODUCTION

The mature insurance industry—comprised of accident and health insurance, property and casualty insurance, and life insurance and annuities—is faced with slow growth and consolidation.

Price competition is accelerating as customers turn to Internet data aggregators to shop for the best deal on many types of insurance. In addition, while the insurance business and the needs of policy holders and distributors are rapidly changing, many insurance companies can't keep up because they are unable to differentiate their business, reach customers likely to respond to new sales opportunities or make the most of their valued staff.

Insurers that define and implement solutions to these challenges are those that will successfully compete and thrive into the future.

This document examines the strategic role of the contact center in the insurance industry, and how it can deliver the increased revenues and cost savings that will drive profitability and shareholder value.

It also introduces ten essential strategies you can use to realise this potential by improving the customer experience, leveraging cross-sell and up-sell opportunities and promoting agent productivity and satisfaction:

- Facilitate Integrated and Consistent Cross-Channel Interactions
- Offer an Inviting "Customer Front Door"
- Get Customers Off the Phone and Onto the Web
- Handle Calls More Intelligently
- Give Agents the Information They Need to Do Their Jobs
- Initiate Proactive Contact
- Make More Effective Use of Customer Data and Segmentation
- Optimize Business Process Execution
- Create a Winning Team Effort with Contact Center Virtualization
- Boost Agent Productivity through Interaction Blending

THE KEY CHALLENGES FACING THE INSURANCE INDUSTRY

INDUSTRY MATURATION AND PRICE COMPETITION IMPEDE GROWTH

Data from Highline and the National Association of Insurance Commissioners show total U. S. insurance premiums totaled $955. 6 billion in 2005, down 0. 1% from $956. 9 billion in 2004. In fact, according to the National Association of Insurance Commissioners, growth in the mature life/ health and property/casualty markets has been slow for the past decade, except for the year 2000 when life insurance benefited as a result of the shift from public to private pension provisions.

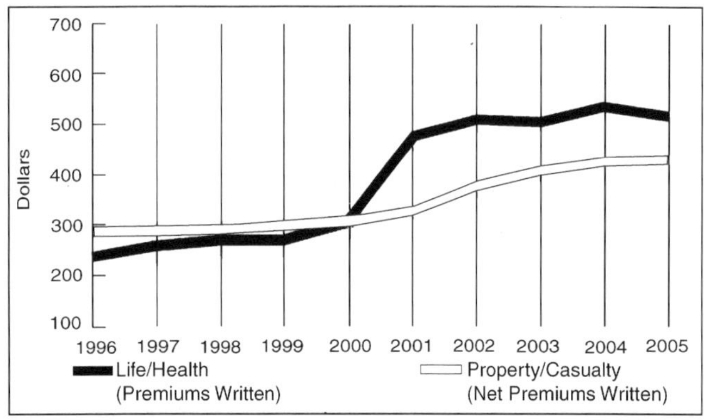

Fig. A Decade of Slow Growth in Life/Health and Property/Casualty Insurance

In light of slow industry growth, larger insurance companies have pursued merger and acquisitions to grow market share and to achieve economies of scale. The Insurance Information Institute reports that the transaction value of insurance-related mergers and acquisitions totaled $32.7 billion in 2005, up from $14.2 billion in 2004.

While there are still 5,000 companies providing insurance coverage, even after all of the merger and acquisition activity, just 50 of them have captured more than 60% market share, and this concentration is even higher in certain product segments.

The Capgemini World Insurance Report published in 2007 reveals that 31% of non-life insurance customers have changed providers in the last five years. This customer churn is often driven by consumers who aggressively shop for the best price, particularly for non-life insurance products.

In fact, downward pressure on profit margins will continue apace as more and more consumers surf the Internet to compare prices, assisted by the growing popularity of data aggregators that present insurance products from carriers as undifferentiated commodities sorted by price.

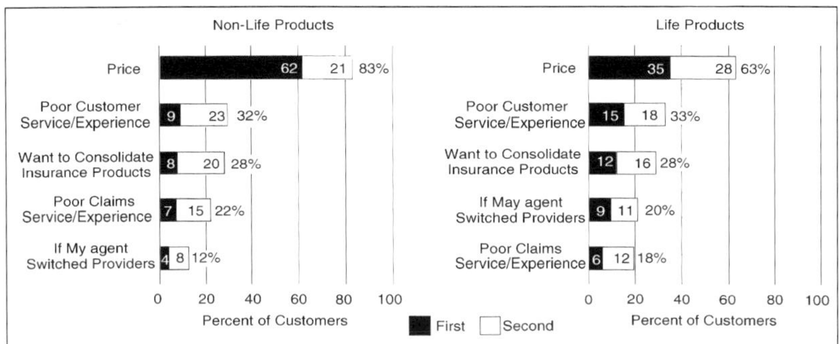

Fig. Reasons for Customer Turnover in Insurance

But, just because price matters the most doesn't mean that service matters little. A study by the Claes Fornell International Group, an employee and customer satisfaction consultant, showed that nearly 61% of insurance customers who have had a bad contact center experience will consider switching companies, and 26% said they will definitely switch companies because of a bad call center experience.

And, the 2007 Genesys USA Consumer Survey further highlights the high stakes of customer service. In this survey, 48% of U.S. consumers said that customer service has the biggest impact on their loyalty to a company, and 44% said that a poor call center experience was the sole reason they stopped doing business with a company.

Although customer service is clearly very important for winning new customers and retaining existing ones, insurance companies struggle to achieve acceptable customer satisfaction levels in their call centers. In fact, according to Claes Fornell, only call centers for personal computers rank lower than insurance companies in customer satisfaction.

Industry	Satisfaction with Call Center*	Overall Industry Satisfaction**
Aggregate of all Industries	71	75
Catalog Retailers	80	74+
Banking	77	77
Cell Phone Services	69	70
Cable and Satellite Television	68	62
Insurance	68	75++
Personal Computers	64	77

* As Measured by the Call Center Customer Satisfaction Index
** As Measured by the American Customer Satisfaction Index (ACSI), using the Same Methodology
\+ Score Represents ACSI for Retail Industry Overall, not Just Catalog Retailers
++ Includes Health, P&C, and Life Insurance

Fig. Satisfaction with Insurance Call Centers is Low Compared to other Industries

Not only are insurance companies failing to provide adequate overall contact center customer satisfaction, many carriers are having trouble meeting the needs of specific constituents—most notably agents and brokers who are among the most important sources of new business. For example, an insurance industry survey on customer service differentiation conducted by FileNet, an IBM company, shows that while more than half of insurance carriers identified current policy holders as the primary audience for their customer service efforts, only 20% identified agents and brokers.

According to a McKinsey and Company survey, ease of doing business and personalized service are the most important factors influencing agents when choosing which carriers to work with.

The McKinsey and Company analysis also shows that the insurance industry's one-size-fits-all model for servicing agents isn't working. Larger agencies may demand service level agreements and require dedicated service teams, while midsize agencies may need local service, and smaller agencies (who are expensive to service) may need centralized call centers and self-service tools.

INSURANCE COMPANIES ARE DISSATISFIED WITH THE RESULTS OF THEIR CROSS-SELLING/UP-SELLING EFFORTS

In response to slow industry growth, many insurance companies are trying to grow organically by cross-selling and up-selling more products. Opportunities abound as mergers and acquisitions have broadened offerings across accident and health insurance, property and casualty insurance, life insurance and annuities.

The Gramm-Leach-Billey Act in the United States has opened the doors for banks and insurance companies to combine their businesses to create economies of scale and enter new markets.

And legislation, such as the passage of the Pension Protection Act in 2006, has removed constraints for bundling life, annuities and long-term care products. A study by Axis Consulting revealed that 99% of insurance advisors feel that it's important, or even critical, to cross-sell effectively, however only 46% consider themselves successful at it.

Lack of customer interaction is one of many factors that limit selling opportunities in the insurance industry. According to Capgemini, an astonishing 71% of customers never or rarely (only once per year) interact with their principal distributor, which is in stark contrast to customers in the banking industry, who interact with their banks more than 200 times a year.

Consumers are increasingly bypassing distributors and using the Web to research products and prices. Celent, an international financial services strategy consulting firm, estimates that 70% of auto insurance purchases in 2007 will be at least Web influenced, 30% will be Web initiated and 10% will be fully purchased online.

Celent also estimates that over 20% of health insurance purchases in 2007 will be Web initiated, and over 50% will be Web influenced. Even in the more complex life insurance industry, Web initiated purchases are expected to be 10% and Web influenced sales are expected to be more than 40% in 2007.

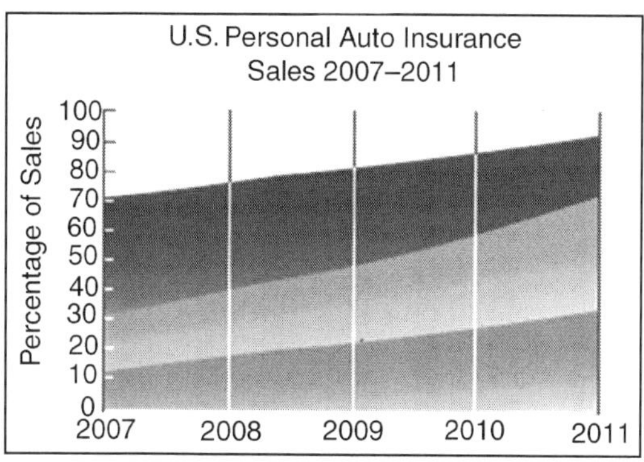

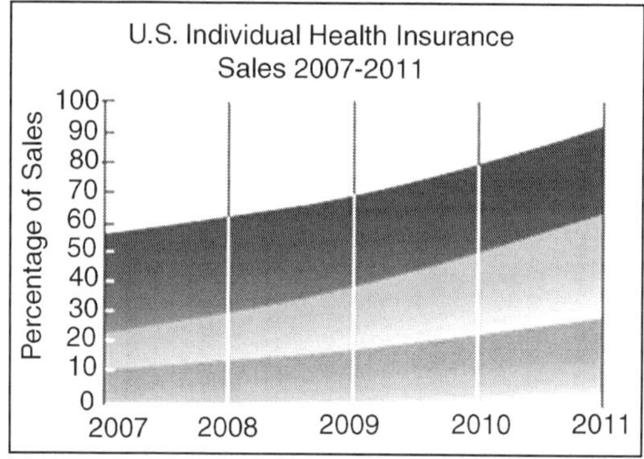

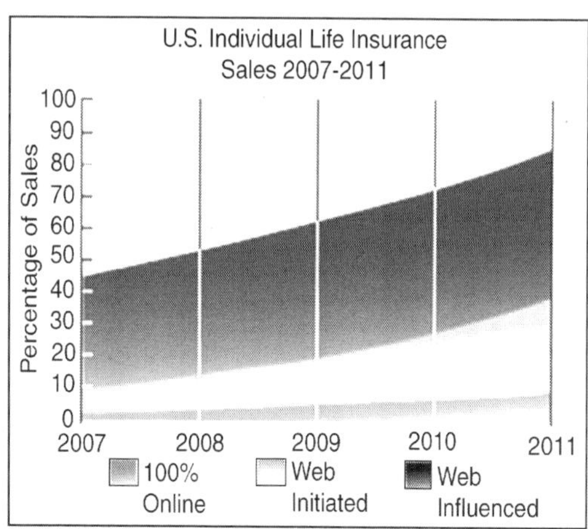

Fig. Web Influenced, Web Initiated and Online Purchase of Insurance Products Poised for Growth

While consumers often use the Internet for comparison shopping, very few actually complete a sale online, a fact that's generally due to the way most insurance company Websites are designed. Consumers usually prefer to seek advice before purchasing any type of insurance, but many Websites don't facilitate agent interaction. The result is that insurance companies lose sales because they're not able to engage the customer during the crucial key points in the decision making process. Further, many insurance companies face a massive challenge in aligning their back-end policy writing engines to their Web-based consumer facing applications. When insurance consumers complete their Web research and contact the agent to make a purchase, lack of multi-channel integration means that agents have no knowledge of the customer's prior interactions on the Web, making it more difficult to develop personalized sales strategies.

Insurance sales occur mainly by product silos, further limiting cross-sell and up-sell opportunities and making it difficult to differentiate products. But, to capture the full lifetime value of the customer, insurance companies should anticipate the needs of the customer as they move through life stages and strive to understand which channels their customers feel most comfortable interacting with.

Insurance companies will need to pay attention to demographic trends to identify and target promising opportunities, such as baby boomers who will soon retire, Generation X and Generation Y consumers who are technically inclined and ethnic groups who value products and services tailored to their needs.

KEEPING COSTS DOWN IS DIFFICULT

Insurance companies are trying to keep costs low without negatively impacting customer service. This tough task includes employing techniques that minimize contact center costs, such as decreasing call volume and handling times, and reducing workforce and overhead expenses.

Call Volume is High

In their efforts to reduce call volume, insurance companies are making progress transitioning customers to the Web, but adoption is still not what it should be. Claes Fornell International Group reports that 67% of those who use a method other than the call center, try the Website first. But, this is lower than in other industries where 80-90% of customers try the Website before using the call center. The customer service differentiation survey conducted by FileNet revealed that more than half of insurance companies were only able to handle less than 10% of their enquiries online.

Handling Times are Too Long

According to Claes Fornell International data, insurance call centers have lower satisfaction rates than most other industries because of their below-average ability to resolve customer issues. The key to decreasing handling times is to ensure that the information the customer service representative needs to handle calls is always readily available.

In many insurance call centers, however, this isn't the case and agents have to manually access dozens of screens, one at a time, causing the call to take longer than it should and sometimes leading to inadequate resolution. Because of the complexity of claim and membership enquiries, calls frequently need to be routed to appropriately skilled specialists. This process means that it can take days, or even weeks, before the customer gets the right answer.

Workforce Costs Continue to Increase

Because skill requirements for agents in the insurance industry are high, it has been difficult to reduce workforce costs without negatively impacting service quality. For instance, health insurance agents must handle a mixture of inbound claim and membership enquiries from members and providers, such as complex questions about claim status, billing, membership and benefits, as well as offer policy assistance to agents and brokers. And, due to the intricacy of insurance offerings and the increase in new product lines, product specialists are often required to handle calls.

This has added a new layer of complexity, as contact center agents must not only be trained to understand the new offerings, but also to effectively communicate them to customers and distributors. In the future, the skills issue in insurance will only get worse as more and more baby boomers retire. Already, according to ContactBabel, insurance contact centers have an annual attrition rate of 42%.

Overuse of licensed agents also adds to workforce costs. Insurance companies trying to reduce the use of expensive licensed agents in the contact center have trouble doing so for several reasons. First, the rules concerning who needs a license and for what reasons are constantly changing. Second, licensing is required on a state-by-state basis, so maintaining the list of who has which license, and determining whether the license is valid, is cumbersome at best.

Overhead Costs are Too High

Processing contact center requests is complex, often requiring information to flow between systems, between people and between the company and third parties. And, typically, the workload of agents is a mix of approximately 60% telephone-based assignments and 40% offline support involving paper-based processes. The offline work is often difficult and expensive to manage and, from both a routing and a workforce management perspective, is rarely integrated with telephone activities. The result is two separate silos of work that make poor use of agent resources.

With increased merger and acquisition activities in the insurance industry today, the consolidation of contact centers represents an obvious candidate for cost savings, as does the increased use of outsourcing. However, insurance customers value personalized service and prefer to work with a dedicated agent who will take care of all their enquiries. As a result, many insurance companies may find that outright contact center consolidation will frustrate and alienate their customers, and that alternative strategies such as contact center virtualization should be undertaken to reduce overhead costs.

THE STRATEGIC ROLE OF THE CONTACT CENTER IN INSURANCE

As recently as just a few years ago, the contact center in the insurance industry was simply seen as a way of dealing with customer requests. These operations were usually run as a so-called 'cost center, ' and a clear objective for manage-ment was to make sure the contact center was run on a lean budget while still providing acceptable levels of customer service. Today, however, contact centers are seen as a far more strategic asset.

Fundamental customer service goals that should be delivered by today's contact center include cross-selling and up-selling more products and services, and running more cost efficient operations by increasing agent productivity. Further, contact centers are now considered a key instrument in changing the public's perception of a company, creating a great customer experience and executing on the business goals of the company as a whole.

How can your contact center accomplish these service objectives? Depending on contact center maturity and business requirements, here are ten possible contact center strategies to make your goals a reality.

STRATEGY 1: FACILITATE INTEGRATED AND CONSISTENT CROSS-CHANNEL INTERACTIONS

The first step in ensuring an exceptional customer experience is to offer multi-channel contact center interactions comprised of phone, fax, e-mail, SMS text messaging, and perhaps even Web chat, so that prospects and customers can conduct business with you exactly when and how they like.

Offering superior channel interaction will encourage consumers to use insurance company Websites instead of, or in addition to, aggregator sites—which will give insurance companies a greater chance to differentiate their products and services, deliver more personalized services, improve cross-sell and up-sell rates and lower operating costs.

Providing customers with a seamless experience across all channels ensures that interactions are as consistent and efficient as possible, which will help to build a solid relation-ship with the customer. For relationship selling, agents require a unified view of interactions across all channels to effectively promote and sell insurance products.

In the early promotional stage, this means ensuring that insurance companies don't repeat the same offers to customers at different touch points, such as the call center and the Web. As the customer responds to the promotion, agents can pick up where the customer left off at each stage in the sales process, regardless of which channel the customer was using.

For example, if a customer had gone online to request a bindable quote, the call center would be aware of this and take steps to close the deal with her.

STRATEGY 2: OFFER AN INVITING "CUSTOMER FRONT DOOR"

When customers use the call center channel, the Interactive Voice Response (IVR) system provides the customer's first impression of the company. It also serves as a guide to the insurance company's services, and determines how well the company can decrease the volume of calls that agents must handle or reduce handling times. Traditional IVR menus have frustrated customers with long and confusing menu trees.

Open dialog call steering is emerging as an innovative alternative to traditional IVR menus. By asking what the customer wants and recognizing key words in natural speech, and by integrating with business rules and routing strategies, open dialog call steering applications take intelligent action to ensure the most efficient resolution of the call.

An example:

- *IVR*: "Thank you for contacting Premier Property and Casualty Insurance. How can we help you?"
- *Samantha*: "I would like to check the status of my insurance claim."

If Samantha's dedicated insurance representative is available, the Customer Front Door application could send Samantha's call to that person who might be able to use the opportunity to explore her needs for additional insurance. Or, the application can execute a self-service application for immediately processing Samantha's claim status enquiry.

STRATEGY 3: GET CUSTOMERS OFF THE PHONE AND ONTO THE WEB

Using Web self-service, members, providers, agents and brokers can interact with the company whenever they want, not just during weekday contact center service hours. Not only does Web self-service enhance customer service, it also helps to migrate calls away from expensive call center agents. Call center agents can dedicate their time to handling more complex enquiries and concentrating on selling activities, rather than responding to routine calls that can be easily automated.

The opportunities for self-service in insurance abound for all customer audiences. Members can view policy coverage, pay bills, make changes to policies, submit claims and check the status of claims progress. In the health insurance business, providers can use HIPPA compliant online tools to verify benefits or coverage, automate claims processing, review claims and correct errors. Agents and brokers can more easily obtain online quotes, proposals and plan designs for customers with different profiles and needs. And, they can more easily keep track of their own customer accounts rather than having to consult with a call center representative. Integrating self-service with agent assistance allows the customer to interact with an insurance company in a convenient way while still receiving the same personalized advisory service offered by call centers. As customers increasingly engage in online research and transactions, they can be offered agent assistance to make their interactions go more smoothly.

For instance, Samantha goes to an insurance Website and decides to request a quick quote. As she reads the quote, an online chat window pops up inviting her to speak with an insurance specialist. Samantha accepts and is able to immediately ask the outstanding questions she has after reviewing the online materials and quote.

STRATEGY 4: HANDLE CALLS MORE INTELLIGENTLY

When taking calls, the number one priority for insurance companies is to make sure they provide acceptable customer service. Skills-based routing, virtual hold and business priority routing are three key approaches for meeting service requirements as efficiently as possible while also making the most of opportunities to drive new revenues.

An IVR system not only identifies customers, but also why they are calling. With this knowledge, skills-based routing determines where the call should be directed—either to a self-service application, or to a customer service agent most qualified to efficiently handle the call based on license certification, selling skills, language skills, product knowledge or the ability to handle a specific type of claim, benefits, billing or sales enquiry.

During times of peak volume, virtual hold technology allows customers to receive a callback at a convenient time rather than wait on hold. This technique complies with requirements for call response times and improves customer satisfaction levels without adding costs for additional resources.

Often, response times are easily met during periods of low call volume and agents have free time to focus on other activities, such as calling clients to review their current coverage and additional needs. Business priority routing uses business rules to prioritize calls based on customer value, customer segments, available channel resources, hold times and other factors.

For instance, when Samantha, a health insurance customer, calls during a period of low demand, she is passed straight through to a contact center agent rather than routed to the self-service application.

The call center agent handling her request then proceeds to explain the company's life insurance products to Samantha and how she can save money by buying both her health and life insurance policies from the same provider. It turns out that Samantha had already been considering life insurance, and after discovering the discount she will receive from her insurance provider, she signs on. Using business priority routing, insurance companies can also match service priorities with the needs of different types of carriers. Calls from larger agencies can be directed to dedicated service teams as soon as they are received, while calls from smaller agencies can be directed to self-service when possible.

STRATEGY 5: GIVE AGENTS THE INFORMATION THEY NEED TO DO THEIR JOBS

The integration of back-office system information with everyday contact center activities helps agents resolve calls more quickly and effectively. As soon as the agent takes the call, relevant customer information is displayed within a single screen so that agents don't need to manually navigate through systems to find the information they are looking for.

Workflow management allows the service representative to efficiently take all necessary steps to resolve customer issues, reducing the time it takes to get customers the answers they are looking for. As back-office integration with the call center and workflow management decreases average handling times and reduces unnecessary repeat contacts to resolve issues, customer satisfaction becomes higher while the contact center workload and costs are lowered.

STRATEGY 6: INITIATE PROACTIVE CONTACT

Because customers don't interact with the contact center on a frequent basis, insurance companies should consider initiating proactive contact to stay in touch with the customer. Insurance companies find that policy renewals increase with frequent communications leading up to the renewal event, and that the number of products sold per customer also increases.

Whenever an agent or broker opens or renews a large account, using proactive contact to send a thank you message can let these important distributors know that you appreciate their business. A global survey of 4, 300 consumers conducted by Genesys found that 87% of respondents indicated having a more positive opinion of a supplier after receiving a courtesy call to thank them for their business or to ask about their satisfaction.

Proactive contact management is also a useful form of automated telemarketing to scale the contact center for increased cross-selling and up-selling activities. Insurance companies can further use proactive contact to notify their customers of new products and services or special promotions.

STRATEGY 7: MAKE MORE EFFECTIVE USE OF CUSTOMER DATA AND SEGMENTATION

Given slow growth in a mature market, some insurance companies are abandoning their product-centric approaches to selling. Instead, they are maximizing the lifetime value of customers through cross-selling and up-selling. In this new paradigm, using customer data and segmentation to anticipate the future needs of individual customers becomes more import than mass marketing. Going one step further, high-value policy holders and distributors may interact, when possible, with a life-time advisor who is intimately familiar with the client's history and needs. Or, demographic matching is a way to assign the customer to an agent who has a common demographic profile. The result is that customers get to interact with agents who will more readily relate to the customer because they share certain commonalities, such as native language, age range, degree of technical competence, and so on.

Front-office integration in the contact center helps insurance companies move away from their siloed views of customer data. To make relationship selling a success, front office integration gives agents a 360-degree view of the customer, which helps in focusing on lifetime customer profitability. Agents have access to the right information across all touch points to enable effective interaction with the customer.

In this way, customers may receive advisory assistance and/or customised offers based on their current behaviour, recent interactions across all channels, existing insurance-wide product portfolio, claims records and detailed knowledge of the customer's demographics, life stage and propensity to buy.

For example, suppose Samantha, a Generation X customer who has no insurance products in her portfolio to help her plan for her retirement, calls to enquire about the status of a health insurance claim. The call is routed to a call center agent who is in the same age bracket as Samantha and who is a retirement planning specialist.

After updating Samantha about her claim status, the agent tells her about the importance of early planning for retirement and describes deferred annuity and life insurance products that will allow her to build taxdeferred cash values. Samantha is pleased that the contact center agent has taken the time to understand her personal situation and agrees to purchase these products.

STRATEGY 8: OPTIMIZE BUSINESS PROCESS EXECUTION

Insurance interactions usually involve multi-step business processes that may include multiple contacts with customers, service providers and other third parties. As the communi-cations hub for the company, the contact center can be harnessed to automate and expedite end-to-end business processes supporting these communications. By directly integrating a business workflow engine, the contact center becomes an active participant in driving business efficiency.

For instance, an automotive insurance provider can reduce the time and effort to sign up new customers, settle claims or collect payments by automating the various external interactions and notifications required to complete these processes. Contact center agents can play an even broader role in these and other processes through integrated workflow that enables the routing of back-office tasks as work items to available agents for processing.

STRATEGY 9: CREATE A WINNING TEAM EFFORT WITH CONTACT CENTER VIRTUALIZATION

Many insurance companies are moving towards a virtual contact center to allow geographically dispersed agents to operate as a single, winning team. Regardless of location, agents can be called upon, as available; to ensure appropriate response levels and to provide access to needed expertise.

A virtual contact center is vital for load balancing during times of peak demand, and is essential in the insurance industry where the appropriate resource for each call is not only highly variable, but is often unavailable in a centralized call center. A virtual contact center unifies the skills of licensed agents, home-based agents, outsourced agents, mid-and back-office specialists, field agents and other experts, regardless of their location.

When an agent takes a call and assesses that answering the customer query will require specialized skills, rather than frustrating the customer by only providing incomplete information, the agent can quickly locate available experts and seamlessly route the call to someone who has both the details of the initial conversation and the appropriate knowledge to satisfactorily complete the interaction. In this way, the customer isn't forced to repeat details of the previous conversation, and the company gains the benefit of a reduction in costs through operating multiple locations as one center.

Here is an illustration: Samantha has just telephoned the call center to ask about her homeowner's claim. The contact center agent needs help from an adjuster in order to properly answer Samantha's questions. The agent taking the initial call gathers the pertinent information, and then passes it to an adjuster in the back office for further action. Because of this seamless interaction, Samantha perceives the contact center experience more positively than she would have if she'd been forced to make multiple calls to various specialists to help her with her claim.

STRATEGY 10: BOOST AGENT PRODUCTIVITY THROUGH INTERACTION BLENDING

Insurance companies benefit from optimizing their agents' time as much as possible. Call blending allows agents to handle both inbound service calls and outbound sales calls as call volume and skills permit, while task blending allows agents to offer their assistance at different interaction channels. For instance, contact center agents can be switched to answering e-mails or engaging in text chats with customers. Not only does this maximize agent productivity, but interaction blending also breaks up the potential monotony of the position.

3

Environment of Insurance Marketing

RISK, INFORMATION AND INSURANCE

DIFFERENT ATTITUDES TOWARDS RISK AND THE TRADITIONAL FUNCTIONING OF INSURANCE AND REINSURANCE MECHANISMS

Economic actors have different attitudes towards risks. It depends on several factors, including the nature of the risk, the probability of loss, the potential magnitude of the loss and the ability to absorb its economic consequences.

Assuming rationality and perfect information, economic actors are able to calculate the actual value of a given risk by discounting the magnitude of the loss by the probability of its occurrence. Once the risk is properly identified and evaluated, however, risk management decisions still need to be taken.

In this perspective, economic actors may be:

- *Risk Averse*: If they are willing to pay even more than the actual value of the risk in order to transfer its harmful consequences to someone else;
- *Risk Preferring*: If they prefer to retain the risk of loss, rather than transferring it by paying upfront an amount equal to its actual value.
- *Risk Neutral*: If they are indifferent with respect to the alternative between retaining the risk and transferring it to someone else by paying upfront an amount equal to its actual value.

Risk aversion, therefore, generates demand for insurance. Insurance companies, in turn, are willing to undertake the risk in exchange for an amount of money relatively close to its actual value, because the law of large numbers makes them able to manage such risks effectively, by making predictable, with reasonable accuracy, the claims they will pay from year to year.

This mathematical law, the larger the number of exposures considered, the more closely the losses reported will match the underlying probability of loss. This means that insurance companies need to pool together a rather large number of homogeneous but independent risks in order to become risk neutral.

The traditional insurance mechanism can be divided into four phases:

1. Risk Assessment (The evaluation of risk, which is usually performed through statistical and probabilistic analyses)
2. Risk Transfer (The shifting of its harmful consequen-ces by way of the insurance contract)
3. Risk Pooling (The placement of the risk in a pool of homogeneous but independent risks allows the insurer to spread the risk and to benefit from the law of large numbers)
4. Risk Allocation (The pricing of the risk though premium setting)

As the magnitude of expected losses increases, the insurers' financial ability to absorb them can be severely jeopardized. In other words, over and above certain levels of financial exposure, insurers themselves tend to be risk averse. In this context, coinsurance and reinsurance are viable options for primary carriers who are willing to cede part of the risk they undertook, in exchange for the payment of a fraction of the premiums they collected.

Traditional reinsurance agreements may be of different types, among which:

- Quota share (proportional) treaties (by which the reinsurer undertakes a quota of the risk transferred to the primary carrier)
- Excess of loss (stop loss) treaties (by which the reinsurer undertakes the upper layer of the risk, after a certain attachment point).

RISK PREDICTABILITY, GENERALIZED UNCERTAINTY AND INFORMATIONAL ASYMMETRIES

Insurance is able to perform its functions correctly under specific conditions of risk and uncertainty. All agree that, in order to be insurable, the risk must be predictable, at least by means of past experience and statistical calculations.

Severe problems are posed by:

- *Generalized Uncertainty:* Which may undermine the insurer's ability to properly evaluate and assess the risk exante
- *Informational Asymmetries*: In favour of the prospec-tive insured, generating distortions and agency problems:
  - Adverse selection
  - Moral Hazard

This report shows, inter alia, how traditional insurance and reinsurance mechanisms can face difficulties in covering:

- The environmental liability risk and
- The natural catastrophe risk.

Environmental liability risk is tightly connected with the underlying legal and regulatory framework, whose features may generate uncertainty, or otherwise limit risk insurability. Factual uncertainty concerning the nature of the risk and its consequences are also problematic. Finally, obstacles are posed by relevant information asymmetries.

The traditional insurance mechanism may also not be appropriate to cope with natural catastrophe risk, since risk predictability, the ability to spread the risk spatially and the financial capacity of the market are severely limited.

In both cases, furthermore, the magnitude of expected losses and the information problems affecting risk predictability and assessment require joint efforts by several insurers and reinsurers. It is worth noting that the highlighted need for information sharing practices and market concentration–in order to increase capacity–suggests a careful approach to antitrust regulations and competition policies in this area.

ENVIRONMENTAL LIABILITY RISK AND INSURANCE

ENVIRONMENTAL POLLUTION AS A NEGATIVE EXTERNALITY

The use, impairment and endangerment of natural resources–such as air, water, land, flora and fauna-are commonly considered in the law and economics literature as external costs of production generated by the industry. The environment is a public good and, therefore, pollution can be conceived as a negative externality which affects the society as a whole; if the costs of production are not fully internalized, an industrial activity may receive incentives even if it has inefficient outcomes, given the fact that part of its costs are socially borne. Nowadays, environmental protection is a worldwide growing concern: natural resources are becoming really scarce on our planet and-in this perspective-all the nations are affected by inefficient uses of them.

DIFFERENT LEGAL APPROACHES TO THE EXTERNALITY PROBLEM: REGULATION V. LIABILITY

The goal of imposing full internalization of pollution externalities is, therefore, very important and, theoretically, it can be achieved through different legal devices. A way of dealing with this problem is characterized by the strict centralized enforcement of a sophisticated net of regulation; those command-control rules, setting standards and sanctions, operate ex ante and reflect the results of a costs-benefits analysis already performed by the authorities.

A second possible solution is the ex post imposition of the external costs on the actors through a mechanism of liability rules, enforced by courts; in this perspective, the polluter can pursue his own activity but he is forced to pay for the damages that he causes to the environment, thereby internalizing the cost of pollution.

Of course, both these alternative approaches have already been widely analysed and criticized: the former mainly because of its own intrinsic rigidity and the latter in light of the relevance of litigation costs and of the so-called 'judgment proof' problem. It has been said that possibly a combination of the two is the most efficient solution.

This report tries to go a step forward, by focusing upon the impact of modern environmental insurance on both the liability system and the regulatory framework. In particular, the advantages and the limits of the ex post mechanism of environmental liability and the role of professional ecological insurance in preventing the most common failures of this device are considered and discussed.

ENVIRONMENTAL LIABILITY: COMPENSATION AND DETERRENCE

It is often said that environmental liability regimes should be aimed at achieving efficient levels of compensation and deterrence. In other words, applying economic theory to environmental policies, the introduction of a civil liability regime in response to the ecological emergency can be explained as an attempt to pursue two important and interrelated policy goals:

1. Compensation for environmental harm (or restoration of the impaired resources) and
2. Deterrence of inefficient activities (thereby preventing pollution that is not cost justified).

The Choice between Negligence and Strict Liability

In determining the features of a liability rule, the first choice is between strict liability and a negligence standard. Negligence is of course an effective mechanism of risk spreading, but it has been shown that strict liability is more efficient in circumstances where the potential tortfeasor is in a better position to evaluate the costs and benefits of a particular level of activity than either the potential victims or the court (finder of fact).

The negligence standard, in fact, provides incentives to the parties only with respect to:

- The level of care (the diligence in performing a given activity) but not with respect to
- The level of activity (the intensity and frequency of a given behaviour or activity).

Both these variables, however, affect the probability of an accident. When the injured party has substantially no control over the risk of materialization of the loss (unilateral accidents), there is no need to give her incentives to invest in precautions and it is sufficient to take into account the behaviour of the potential tortfeasor.

A strict liability standard, imposing a full internalization of the negative externalities, forces the potential tortfeasor to consider both the level of care and the level of activity and, therefore, it generates incentives to behave efficiently.

Environmental pollution events, in the vast majority of cases, are unilateral accidents. Hence, to protect the environment through an efficient level of deterrence, strict liability proves to be more appropriate from a law and economics point of view.

As regards the compensation perspective, strict liability has many advantages compared to a negligence standard, at least in the industrial pollution setting. In the typical pollution case, the proof of negligence can be perceived by the injured parties as a probatio diabolica-an obstacle often too difficult to overcome-given the difficulties in accessing relevant information and the technical character of the notions involved.

A strict liability rule, instead, is conceivable as a form of insurance whose beneficiaries are the injured parties. Moreover, deprived of any punitive character, this form of liability is more easily transferable on the commercial insurance marketplace. In this sense, environmental insurance would work as a form of reinsurance.

Direct v. Indirect Protection of the Environment

A second set of options, which characterizes the process of introducing an environmental liability rule, has been pointed out by scholars engaged in the comparative study of environmental laws.

On one hand, we have the possibility to conceive a general notion of environment (or natural resources) and to grant it direct protection as a good itself. In case of a polluting event, the legal system will therefore hold the tortfeasor liable for compensation of any kind of damage caused to natural resources, in addition to and apart from any property damage, bodily injury or economic loss indirectly suffered by individuals as a consequence of pollution. A public authority (generally, the State) will then be entitled to receive compensation on behalf of the citizens. This peculiar choice has been made in the United States, in Italy, in Switzerland and in Portugal.

On the other hand, nevertheless, stands the option to introduce tougher liability rules for the violation of other fundamental rights, such as health or property, whenever those violations take place in occasion of a polluting event; in doing so, the environment receives indirect protection, because the polluting activity works as a signal of endangerment of natural resources. This view is embodied in the German Umwelthaftungsgesetz of 1991.

Imposing the obligation to compensate for natural resources damages and cleanup costs-compared to the indirect protection scheme-has the clear advantage to force the tortfeasor to fully internalize the negative externalities of her activity, but introduces new problems, the most important of which is related to the evaluation and quantification of the harm, still unresolved.

In particular, the issue of damages is extremely controver-sial with respect to the value of natural resources that cannot be fully restored or replaced after the polluting event. In order to overcome this problem, it could be better to hold responsible parties liable for the cost of clean up of impaired resources, once clean up standards have been determined by the authority with a sufficient level of predictability.

With respect to this last issue, it is extremely important to point out that in several legal systems, instead of civil liability, there are other administrative and/or criminal rules imposing obligations to cleanup contaminated sites. In case of pollution, the owner and/or operator of the site or facility, in other words, is forced by the public authority to adopt immediately security and preventive measures and then to decontaminate the site, under the threat of fines, or even imprisonment.

In any event, from an insurability perspective, it is very important to distinguish between liability (being it civil, administrative or criminal) for cleanup of soil or water pollution and the obligation to pay natural resources damages (NRDs).

Allocation and Apportionment of Concurrent Liabilities

Another dilemma arises in the very usual situation in which more polluters are involved in the same environmental accident: should the liability be imposed on an individual basis or should all the polluters be held joint and severally liable for the clean-up costs? If the compensation profile is considered alone, joint and several liability clearly offers great advantages to the injured parties.

The deterrence goal, however, requires that each polluter pays for the consequences of her own activity: if liability is not individual, the mechanism of incentives will not work, given the difficulties for the potential polluter to perform a costs-benefits analysis. Moreover, if insurability issues are taken into consideration, a strict joint and several standard should be avoided, because it impairs the ability of risk-carriers to evaluate and assess the risks posed by prospective customers.

Defences: Pro and Contra

- Force majeure
- Regulatory compliance
- Development risk
- Contributory negligence

ENVIRONMENTAL LIABILITY RISK AND INSURANCE: FACTUAL UNCERTAINTY

Environmental risk, however, presents many difficulties to the insurance industry, specially when the focus is on the so-called gradual pollution phenomena, which are characterized by:

- Factual uncertainty and
- Long terms effects (long tail liabilities).

Insurance is able to perform its functions correctly under specific conditions of uncertainty. Environmental risk is a peculiar one, given that it includes components of both factual and legal uncertainty. This is true particularly when we consider the so called gradual pollution, that kind of pollution which develops slowly and secretly over a long period of time and whose damaging effects show only in the long run. In this context, there are problems of asymmetrical information as well as of generalized uncertainty.

Given the complexity of modern production technologies, problems of adverse selection could be widely present in environmental insurance settings, whenever the classification of every specific risk undertaken is not accurately performed by the insurer.

Moral hazard phenomena are also seriously involved in this context: it is easy to understand how the industry could erroneously perceive the insurance coverage and the insurance premium as a license to pollute. To tackle these further problems, risk-carriers have to introduce monitoring and bonding devices.

Gradual pollution events, moreover, present relevant aspects of generalized factual uncertainty: in most cases it is very difficult to determine when pollution began and how long it lasted; synergetic pollution is a quite common phenomenon and it is far from easy to identify single contributions; long terms effects of pollution raise problems related to the adequacy of traditional trigger-of-coverage clauses as well as of policy limits.

The factual uncertainty regards also the potentially damaging effects of new technologies and substances; in other words, the relevance of the so called development risk plays a great role in this context. These peculiar features of environmental risk are common to every legal system and they can explain why, at present, this risk is almost everywhere excluded from general liability insurance and gradual pollution coverage is provided only under very specific policies.

ENVIRONMENTAL LIABILITY RISK AND INSURANCE: LEGAL UNCERTAINTY

What differentiates the situation is the level of legal uncertainty.

This variable represents the level of generalized uncertainty introduced by the legal system itself and basically depends on:

- The way in which legal rules (*i.e.* the environmental liability regime) are designed and shaped by the authority;
- The way in which those legal rules and propositions are interpreted and applied by legal actors (agencies, judges, scholars etc.) in a given institutional framework.

Environmental risk is, for the insurance industry, a risk of liability and the choices made by law and policy makers greatly affect risk insurability. The domain of risk insurability is limited. If generalized uncertainty-being it factual, or legal, or both-become excessive, then insurance will become a mere gamble: the unpredictability of losses, in fact, will prevent the prospective risk-carrier from performing effectively her statistical calculus of probabilities.

In such a situation, insurers may change their attitude towards risk, moving from risk neutrality to risk aversion. This, of course, would undermine the very basis of the whole insurance mechanism.

The level of legal uncertainty may be detected from two different perspectives:

1. On one hand we have to consider specific features of the environmental liability regime adopted in a given legal system and
2. On the other we have to test the intrinsic coherence of each legal formant as well as the coherence among different formative parts of that system.

Features of the Liability Regime

As regards the first component of the level of legal uncertainty, the choice of a strict liability standard–made by a legal system in light of its efficient outcomes–would not constitute a problem in terms of insurability; to the contrary, more problems would be caused by a negligence standard which involves a punitive profile that is not easily reconcilable with the transfer of liability to the insurer.

In the allocation of liability phase, a joint and several standard creates excessive uncertainty for the insurer because she would have to compute not only the risk created by the prospective insured, but also the risks generated by all the other actors whose conduct may eventually combine with the one of the insured in the causation a polluting event.

The insurer, moreover, would bear the risk of insolvency of these other subjects, without being able to monitor or control them. Such problem would notably increase the cost of insurance. Hence, an individual standard seems much better once insurability issues are taken into consideration. If a direct protection scheme is chosen, legal uncertainty is negatively affected by the controversial and sometimes obscure criteria used by the courts in order to evaluate natural resource damages.

The value of impaired resources is very difficult to determine and there is no agreement on the subject. The only damage measure that at present seems to be reasonable and predictable is the cost of cleaning up impaired amenities. In the process of implementation of an environmental liability regime, the outlined concerns should be taken into account. As long as the damages awarded in pollution cases are almost completely unpredictable ex ante, in fact, the insurance industry will not be able to assess environmental risks properly and, therefore, will not be willing to offer reasonably priced coverage.

On Legal Formants and Incoherence: A Complex Analysis

To detect the second variable which affects the level of legal uncertainty, it is necessary to look at the way in which a given legal system actually works.

The notion of legal formants is fundamental to this layered analysis. In every legal system, what is written in a statute may sometimes differ remarkably from the judgments of the courts on the same legal issue.

The rule formally announced by the court in its opinion may turn out to be incompatible with the actual outcome of the case. In Italy, for example, a negligence standard is officially adopted by legislation, but courts tend to enforce a strict liability regime. Retroactive liability is not imposed by Law 349/86 (the Italian statute on environmental liability), but again, some recent decisions of the Italian Corte di cassazione impose civil liability for environmental harm retroactively.

The only decision on the issue of quantification does not provide any guidance for the implementation of those criteria set forth in art. 18 comma VI of Law 349/86. In the United States, the provision of CERCLA regarding damages to natural resources has been seldom enforced by courts. Case law on environmental liability insurance issues, moreover, is quite confused and contradictory. Those evidences of incoherence among legal formants greatly affect the level of legal uncertainty, introducing elements of destabilization that eventually undermine the effectiveness of any insurance mechanism.

MODERN ENVIRONMENTAL LIABILITY INSURANCE APPROACHES

Integrated Risk Management Approach through Differentiation

In response to the outlined problematic factual features of environmental risk, the insurance industry has developed new techniques to cope with this peculiar phenomenon.

The traditional insurance mechanism works on a four phases basis (risk assessment, risk transferring, risk pooling, risk allocation) and the insurer remains basically external to the situation assessed in the first step, merely accepting or refusing to undertake a given risk. In modern environmental insurance, instead, professional risk-carriers have the knowledge and technical abilities needed to actively intervene on the risk features during a new phase (risk remodeling), which takes place before the transfer of risk.

Pollution coverage is currently provided only on an site-specific basis; in fact, the modern philosophy of ecological insurance requires an extremely careful evaluation and classification of the risk to be transferred. As for this, a comprehensive inspection of the industrial installation is performed in limine by a team of qualified engineers belonging to the insurance company.

As soon as the risk is properly assessed-if the minimal insurability (safety) requirements are met-the risk carrier will cooperate (in a new phase) with the prospective insured in order to reduce the risk and to enhance loss prevention strategies. Such feature plays a very important role: prevention of environmental harm should be a primary goal of every ecological policy. Even if insurance coverage gives effect to the compensation function of environmental liabilities, it could easily be the case that impaired natural resources are unique and not replaceable or repairable; loss prevention, therefore, acquires great importance. After this 'remodeling' phase, in which cooperation between insurer and insured is fundamental, pollution coverage is tailored on the insured needs and it is provided by the risk carrier on a long term basis.

A long term commitment is needed by both parties; pollution coverage is provided to the insured with the peculiar time limitations of:

- Claims made or
- Manifestation/discovery

Formulas and a stable relationship is essential to justify the reciprocal investments in cooperation. In this way, the insurer will participate with her expertise and technical knowledge in the development of each customer's risk-management strategy. During the entire period in which the contractual relationship is in force, the risk carrier will closely monitor the insured, generating additional incentives; investments in precautions and in safety devices will be rewarded by the insurer with a reduction in the annual premium and/or with a broader coverage, thereby enacting and implementing a flexible mechanism of surrogate regulation.

The point just made, therefore, lines up with the broader perspective that considers the opportunity to conceive liability insurers, in various instances, as efficient regulators of the practice of their customers. Furthermore, in addition to loss prevention strategies and financial coverage, the insurers started recently to offer integrated services, the most important of which is crisis management.

Different Products for Different Needs

From an insurance point of view, a correct approach to the pollution risk entails the need for a few technical distinctions:

- First party v. third party coverage
- Known v. unknown pollution
- On site v. off site contamination

Insurers are moving away from using traditional policies and conventional tools for assessing environmental exposures because they may provide inadequate cover. In the recent years, the international environmental insurance sector has developed several types of new products aimed at meeting different needs, taking into account that often businesses must assume the costs of cleaning up their own polluted sites, as well as others that may have been contaminated by their activities.

The most important are:

- Environmental liability policy (EIL) (third party coverage)
- Coverage for on site cleanup liability (first party coverage)

- Cleanup cost cap (this type of policy covers excess remediation costs due to unknown or undiscovered contamination, poor remedial technology performance, regulatory changes and natural disasters. It is generally designed to address the risk and uncertainty associated with beginning or continuing an environmental remediation project)
- Contractors pollution legal liability
- Transportation coverage
- Environmental coverage for landfills (integrated insurance/financial products)

Moreover, some carriers offer the possibility to combine different coverages in a single tailor made insurance policy.

Increased Market Capacity through Pollution Insurance Poolsk

In some European countries insurance companies have created Pools to deal with the peculiar problems posed by environmental liability risk:

- *Italy*: Pool RC inquinamento
- *France*: Assurpol
- *The Netherlands*: Nederlandse milieupool
- *Spain*: Pool español de riesgos medioambientales

Alternative Risk Transfer (ART)/Alternative Risk Financing (ARF) Methods

An alternative to insurance is offered by:

- Captive insurance companies
- Finite risk products
- Loss portfolio transfers (buyouts)

Statement of Environmental Commitment of the Insurance Industry

It is worth noting that participants in the insurance sector began to play an eminent proactive role in the environmental arena, voicing their concerns and interests in public and committing themselves to the Principles of Sustainable Development affirmed in the 1992 Rio Declaration on Environment and Development.

Under the auspices of the United Nations Environmental Programme, a Statement of Environmental Commitment was signed in a ceremony at the UN offices in Geneva by 17 leading insurance companies on November 23, 1995. At present, 88 insurance companies (+ 5 associated members) from 27 countries joined the initiative by signing the Statement and the number of participants is constantly increasing.

In this significant document the general principles of sustainable development are fully recognized and translated into a commitment towards environmental protection by means of insurance practice, risk management strategies and loss prevention.

ENVIRONMENTAL RISK AND INSURANCE: A PROBLEM OF INCENTIVES

In light of this modern and innovative attitude adopted by the industry, insurance seems to be an appropriate legal and economic tool available to correct most of the failures of both the decentralized liability mechanism and the regulatory approach to the ecological emergency. Modern environmental insurance would in fact solve (at least partially) the judgment proof problem that affects the liability approach and it would also introduce and enforce a full set of technical safety standards characterized by a sufficient level of precision and flexibility. It may also contribute in lowering transaction costs.

At present, however, it can be empirically observed that environmental insurance is not widespread at all. Gradual pollution coverage is still perceived as too costly by the industry and most firms do not decide to insure against these environmental risks spontaneously.

The cost of environmental insurance policies is affected by the complexity of the new techniques outlined, by the factual features of the risk itself and by the level of legal uncertainty. An explanation of the difficulties experienced by most insurers in marketing Environmental liability policies (EIL) and other environmental coverages can be found in the fact that gradual pollution risk is a so-called low probability/high consequences risk and, generally, such risks are not rationally faced by economic actors: they can be easily underestimated or even ignored.

Moreover, even from a pure rational choice theory point of view, the limited liability structure of corporations introduces significant distortions, altering the correct incentives mechanism. Given the magnitude of losses in the environmental field, in fact, it will often be the case that the amount of potential ecological damage is much greater than the measure of potential liability of the polluter.

Another phenomenon that widely occurs is the following: after the plant has passed the severe insurability inspection performed by the risk-carrier's engineers, the prospective insured refuses to purchase coverage because she feels that her activity is safe enough. Of course, the fact that a plant is insurable does not mean that it is completely safe and that an accident will never occur.

The satisfactory results of the inspection, instead, indicate only that the risk created by that particular plant has all those characteristics of predictability that allow a professional risk carrier to undertake it. In any event, many firms have clearly stated that they will not buy pollution coverage unless they are obliged to do so.

COMPULSORY ENVIRONMENTAL LIABILITY INSURANCE

In light of these considerations, a system of mandatory pollution insurance-at least for those activities that are particularly dangerous for the environment-would seem a desirable solution. Even this conclusion, nevertheless, turns out to be rather problematic. A system of compulsory insurance can be bilateral or unilateral. In the former case, the firm has the obligation to buy coverage in order to be allowed to operate and the insurance industry has the obligation to provide coverage at pre-determined conditions to each and every applicant. Bilateral mandatory pollution insurance, however, is incompatible with the very nature of modern environmental insurance techniques.

Environmental policies are tailor-made and site-specific and not every plant necessarily has all those characteristics that make it insurable. Standard conditions set by legislature and applicable to every insured, moreover, would drag pollution insurance back to the traditional insurance scheme, which has proved to be highly inappropriate in this context. As long as unilateral mandatory insurance is concerned, purchase of pollution coverage is still a condition to operate for the firms, but insurers do not have any obligation and they may, therefore, refuse coverage to anyone at their own discretion.

In this latter case, the incentive mechanism embedded in modern environmental insurance would be able to work properly, but the insurance industry would be placed in the uncomfortable and inappropriate position of environmental policeman. In fact, the insurer would be entrusted with the power to decide which firms can continue their activity and which should instead withdraw from the market. This is a policy choice that the authority has to make.

FINANCIAL SECURITY: POSSIBLE ALTERNATIVES TO LIABILITY INSURANCE

- Self insurance through tax deductible reserves
- First party insurance
- *Ex ante* deposits
- Guarantee provided by financial institutions
- Risk sharing agreements:
  - P&I Clubs (Protection and Indemnity Mutual)/Oil Pollution Funds
- Compensation funds
  - Limitation fund
  - Advancement fund
  - Guarantee fund
  - Restoration fund

FINANCING PAST POLLUTION: THE ISSUE OF RETROACTIVE LIABILITY AND THE LIMITS OF LIABILITY

Retroactive liability and insurance are, in principle, incompatible. Limited applications: cleanup cost cap coverage (brownfield sites).

Limits of liability:

- Past pollution
- Chronic pollution
- Diffuse pollution

Suitable alternative → Restoration fund

A PROPOSED INSTITUTIONAL MODEL

In summary, in an efficient institutional model the authority would introduce an environmental liability mechanism for clean up costs or restoration of impaired resources enforced on a strict, individual and non retroactive basis. It would also regulate dangerous activities, setting standards of operation at the minimum level of insurability and requiring proof of adequate financial guarantee.

Hence, having encouraged the operators of dangerous activities to seek pollution coverage, the legal system could rely on the new techniques developed by modern environmental risk-carriers and on the incentives created by long term insurance relationships. Several types of environmental damages will be excluded from the liability regime (diffuse and chronic pollution, past pollution, etc.). As for the residual environmental damages, the efficient institutional system could rely on a complementary method of compensation based on a no-fault Compensation Fund.

A COMPARATIVE ANALYSIS OF DIFFERENT LEGAL AND REGULATORY FRAMEWORKS

The purpose of this part is not to explore the details of the selected systems, rather to outline their most relevant provisions with respect to environmental liability and insurance, in order to compare them with the proposed institutional model.

- The U. S. System
- The German System
- The Italian System

The proposal for a "Directive of the European Parliament and of the Council on environmental liability with regard to the prevention and remedying of environmental damage" presented by the Commission of the European Communities on January 23, 2002

COMPARATIVE REMARKS AND POLICY CONCLUSIONS

The comparative analysis shows how different legal framework affect environmental risk insurability.

Modern environmental insurance may well provide the tools to bridge the gap between liability and regulation:

- Ecological insurance, in fact, gives effect to the compensation function of the environmental liability regime, providing the victims with a reliable source of funds when the accident occurs;

- Moreover, with a view to reducing the risk of a polluting event, the insurer may act as a surrogate regulator, trying align the interests of the insured with environmental safety concerns;
- Furthermore, by imposing the ex ante internalization of environmental costs, ecological insurance gives appropriate incentives to prevent the persistence of inefficient activities.

In order to encourage the growth of a pollution insurance market, law and policy makers should put their best efforts in circumscribing, limiting and defining with a sufficient level of predictability the risk of environmental liabilities.

This reports suggests an institutional model of interaction among regulation, liability, funds and insurance that conveys the results of a comparative law and economics analysis.

NATURAL CATASTROPHE RISK AND INSURANCE

THE PROBLEM

Large losses created, among others, by hurricane Andrew in Florida in 1992, the Northridge earthquake in California in 1994, the Kobe earthquake in Japan in 1995, the Kocaeli earthquake in Turkey in 1999, windstorms Lothar and Martin in Europe in 1999, the Bhuj, Gujarat earthquake in India on January 26, 2001 and tropical storm Allison in the USA in 2001 put large strains on the capacities of the reinsurance markets and, consequently, the availability of catastrophe insurance coverages has decreased substantially.

MARKET FAILURES IN NATURAL CATASTROPHE INSURANCE

Natural catastrophe risk is a low probability and high consequences risk. *This poses several problems to the traditional functioning of insurance:*

- Bounded rationality of individuals
- Low level of risk predictability
- Geographical risk spreading problem (cumulative risk in the primary market)
- Limited market capacity:
  - Magnitude of losses (aggregate claims)
  - Inter-temporal spreading problem (mismatch between size of annual premiums and size of the expected loss)
- Adverse selection

The outlined problems and failures of the private market for catastrophe insurance call for an evaluation of alternative risk management solutions.

THE IMPORTANCE OF PUBLIC-PRIVATE PARTNERSHIP FOR DISASTER MANAGEMENT

Since the private insurance sector encounters several difficulties in handling catastrophe risks which do not fully meet the prerequisites of insurability, some sort of intervention of the public sector is advisable. Besides, the trend worldwide is generally towards co-operation between governments and the private sector in the management of disaster risks.

The public authority can play a fundamental role by:

- Providing the requisite legal framework
- Subsidizing the cost of administering the disaster management scheme
- Subsidizing the cost of insurance to the beneficiaries
- Being a reinsurer of last resort

The private insurance sector, in turn, has the requisite expertise for:

- Expedite loss assessment
- Effective surrogate regulation

The creation of government-subsidized insurance schemes is the most common example of partnership.

A COMPARATIVE ANALYSIS OF DIFFERENT LEGAL AND REGULATORY FRAMEWORKS

Complex governmental risk management strategies have been implemented in several legal systems.

Some of the most relevant institutional arrangements involving a publicprivate partnership are discussed in this section:

- *France*: National Disaster Compensation Scheme CAT NAT/Caisse Centrale de Réassurance CNR (In France, a disaster compensation scheme has been established by law in 1982. It provides for a compulsory disaster extension on all property damage policies. Coverage under the catastrophe extension is triggered when the state of natural disaster is declared by inter-ministerial decree. The Caisse Centrale de Réassurance (CCR), a state-owned company, entered into an agreement with the Authorities that allows it to offer reinsurance cover with a Government guarantee in the field of natural disasters. This staterun cover does not, however, give CCR a monopoly in natural disaster reinsurance. In fact any insurer may seek cover for itself from the reinsurer of its choice, and may even take the risk of not underwriting reinsurance. Nevertheless, CCR remains the only company within its sector of activity which offers a whole range of reinsurance solutions with unlimited cover. This is an advantage for insurers, since it gives them absolute security in the event of a major loss, be it a large-scale event such as a flood occurring every hundred years or a geological problem such as subsidence, which causes all kinds of damage. CCR thus provides a guarantee of solvency and security for insureds within the natural disaster compensation scheme.)
- *Spain*: Consorcio de Compensación de Seguros (The Consorcio is a stateowned company, which is included in the category of public

business entity, and it is a separate legal entity that has full powers to act. The Consorcio has its own assets and liabilities, separate from those of the State, and its activity is governed by private law. This means that the new company, when doing insurance business, apart from being governed by the terms of its own Legal Statute, is subject, like any other private insurance company, to the legal rules laid down in the Private Insurance Ordering and Supervision Act and its enacting regulations, and to the Insurance Contract Act.)

- *USA*: National Flood Insurance Programme (NFIP) (In 1968, the US Congress created the National Flood Insurance Programme in response to the rising cost of taxpayer funded disaster relief for flood victims and the increasing amount of damage caused by floods. The NFIP makes federally-backed flood insurance available in communities that agree to adopt and enforce floodplain management ordinances to reduce future flood damage)
- *Califonia*: California Earthquake Authority (CEA) (Established in 1996 to relieve pressure on private insurers, the California Earthquake Authority is a privately financed, state-run insurance programme that sells a "mini-policy" with a larger deductible and more limited coverage of external structures than conventional earthquake insurance policies. There State offers no guarantee: therefore, if losses from an earthquake drain the established fund, the CEA may run out of business and claims will be paid out on a pro-rated basis.)
- *Florida*: Florida Hurricane Catastrophe Fund (FHCF) (In 1993, the State of Florida established the Florida hurricane catastrophe fund to allow insurers to transfer a portion of their catastrophic risk. The Fund reimburses a fraction of insurers' losses caused by sever hurricanes and it is funded by premiums paid by insurers that write policies on personal and commercial residential properties. An important provision limits the Fund's obligation to pay losses to the sum of its assets and borrowing capacity.)
- *Hawaii*: Hawaii Hurricane Relief Fund (HHRF) (In 1993, Hawaii created a voluntary homeowner's catastrophe fund in order to provide hurricane insurance for customers of insurers which would no longer voluntary offer such coverage. The Fund discontinued its operation by the end of 2000, in light of improved private market conditions.)
- *New Zealand*: Earthquake Commission (EQC) (The Earthquake Commission is a Crown Entity, wholly owned by the government of New Zealand and controlled by a board of commissioners. Crown Entities are not Government departments or state-owned enterprises but nevertheless belong to the Government and are subject to public

sector finance and reporting rules. EQC administers the Natural Disaster Fund. The Government guarantees that this fund will meet all its obligations.)

- *Japan*: Japanese Earthquake Reinsurance (JER) (In accordance with the promulgation of the law concerning earthquake insurance and following the launch of sales of dwelling earthquake insurance to be written in conjunction with dwelling and shop-owners comprehensive insurance policies, Japan Earthquake Reinsurance (JER) was established by the 20 domestic non-life insurance companies in 1966. The law stipulates that the government underlies the funds of the company. Thus, there is no problem with the company's solvency.)
- *Turkey*: Turkish Catastrophe Insurance Pool (TCIP). (Following 1999 earthquake disasters occurred in the Marmara Region and Duzce, earthquake insurance has been made compulsory primarily for dwellings, through a Earthquake Insurance Programme. Earthquake insurance premiums are ceded to the Turkish Catastrophe Insurance Pool, which is managed by the Natural Disasters Insurance Council, DASK in the Turkish abbreviation.)

RISK SHARING THROUGH CAPITAL MARKETS

With a view to increasing market capacity and to lower reinsurance costs, the landscape of risk transfer alternatives has evolved significantly in recent years. Governments, primary carriers as well as global reinsurers now have the option of turning to the capital markets for supplemental catastrophe protection. Catastrophe securities are a recent development in investing: by floating such bonds for specific risks over limited time periods in defined geographic regions, insurers and reinsurers reduce risk by transferring it to investors.

Investors, in turn, have viewed the introduction of the insurance-linked security as an opportunity for the development of a new market, with the added attraction that so-called cat bonds are largely uncorrelated with other financial instruments. Investors (usually hedge funds or other major institutional financiers) get a high rate of return, in exchange for the possibility of losing much of their principal or interest, or both, in the event of disasters. Cat bonds have the potential to greatly increase the amount of capital available for catastrophic risk, as well as alter the pricing of risk.

Physical Trigger vs. Loss Trigger

Catastrophe bonds entail almost no credit risk, since the money are in escrow or in a trust fund, invested in liquid securities and, therefore, readily available. However, the use of physical trigger cat bonds entails a different risk, named basis risk. In contrast to traditional reinsurance, in fact, this kind of coverage may not be a perfect hedge for the insured portfolio. It is necessary to compare the reinsurance credit risk with the indexed cat bonds basis risk.

HEDGING VERSUS FINANCING INSTRUMENTS IN THE MANAGEMENT OF DISASTER RISKS

In developing countries the insurance market might be less attractive to international reinsurers, due to rather low profitability.

Since some developing countries are catastrophe prone areas, it is important to discuss the alternative to catastrophe reinsurance in the management of disaster related costs.

- Risk hedging instruments (pre disaster)
  - Cat bonds versus traditional reinsurance:
    a. Basis risk v. credit risk
    b. Immediate payoffs from cat bonds v. delayed payment from reinsurance indemnity
    c. Cost of implementing each measure
    d. Cost of each instrument
- Risk financing instruments (pre/post disaster)
  - Catastrophe Reserve Fund (pre)
  - Catastrophe Tax (post)
  - Government Debt instruments (post)
  - International Loans (post)
  - Budget Diversion (post)

Disaster risk spreading through governmental programmes can be negatively affected by:

- Ineffective tax collection system
- Inefficiencies and corruption in the governmental agencies

REGULATION AND CATASTROPHE INSURANCE

Regulatory policies greatly affect the development of markets for disaster risk coverages and, consequently, the availability of effective catastrophe insurance.

This section of the chapter discusses the effects of:

- Regulatory constraints
- Market entry/exit rules
- Rules on the admissibility of ART
- Financial and fiscal issues
- Regulation of claims practices
- Antitrust and competition policies

Integrated risk management strategies: catastrophe bonds and insurance can be coupled with incentives and other regulatory mechanisms to reduce disaster losses. An effective disaster risk management strategy requires the proactive involvement of all the stakeholders.

- Key Stakeholders:
  - Homeowners and businesses at risk
  - Government
  - Insurers/Reinsurers
  - Investors in cat bonds
- Principles of Catastrophe Risks Management:
  - Integrated approach
  - Scientific risk estimates
    a. Risk predictability
    b. Expected loss estimates
  - Structural mitigation and vulnerability reduction
  - Incentives to minimize adverse selection/moral hazard
  - Expedite settlements

Well-enforced regulatory measures, such as building codes, can complement insurance and other financial instruments by forcing the adoption of cost-effective risk mitigation measures (RMMs). Incentives are needed since property owners often underestimate the risks from disasters (low frequency/ high severity risks). In addition, effective mitigation measures may produce positive externalities by reducing other costs arising out of a disaster.

4

The Regulation of the Individual Health Insurance Market

INTRODUCTION

Although the majority of Americans with health insurance obtain their coverage through group health plans offered through their employers, many individuals obtain their coverage through the nongroup insurance market. Currently almost 18 million persons, or almost seven per cent of the United States nonelderly (under age 65) population, obtain coverage through individual plans purchased directly from insurance issuers.

Several initiatives at the state and federal level, as well as policy proposals involving health system reforms, have proposed utilizing the individual health insurance market as a means of expanding access to affordable health insurance policies. While health insurance purchased in the individual market has the advantages of being portable (not tied to a person's employment) and potentially being a better match to a person's preferences for health coverage than policies purchased through group plans, it does have aspects of significant concern.

Among these concerns is how laws and regulations surrounding the individual health insurance market affect its ability to meet various population needs. It is necessary to understand these issues to determine how market reforms would interact with these policies. Insurers marketing health plans in the individual market use approaches different from those used in the group insurance market to examine insurance applicants. One such approach is that of medical underwriting to identify applicants just as to their health status.

Some applicants may be categorized as likely to cost the insurer more in claims than a healthier person, resulting in insurers charging them higher premiums or restricting or denying coverage. Other differences between the group and individual market involve the application of different state versus federal regulations in the marketing of products, and other accountability requirements of entities selling individual policies. In reviewing how insurance is regulated, it is important to keep in mind an understanding of what insurance is and why it is regulated.

This has been expressed rather succinctly in an intro-duction to a recent chapter on insurance regulation:

- *Health Insurance Serves Several Public Policy Goals:* It enables consumers to spread the risk of health care expenses and provides them access to medical services that they might otherwise not be able to obtain. Because of the importance of health insurance to the general public welfare, states have been regulating private health insurance companies and products since the late 19th century. State insurance regulation has sought to promote several policy objectives, such as ensuring the financial solvency of insurance companies, promoting the spread of risk, protecting consumers against fraud and ensuring that consumers are paid the benefits that they are promised.

Health reform initiatives can choose to work within these constraints or change the rules to facilitate the success of health policy options.

BACKGROUND

The business of insurance, including health insurance, has traditionally been regulated at the state level. States license entities that offer health insurance coverage and have established laws that control their structure, finances, and obligations to the people that they insure. However, a number of federal laws also have an impact on private insurance coverage, most notably the Employee Retirement Income Security Act (ERISA) of 1974 and the Health Insurance Portability and Accountability Act (HIPAA) of 1996.

In 1945, preceding ERISA and HIPAA, the McCarran Ferguson Act restored the primary role of states in regulating the business of insurance. Passage of McCarran-Ferguson was prompted by state and industry concern over a U. S. Supreme Court decision rendered in 1944 (U. S. v. South-Eastern Underwriters Assn. , 322 U. S. 533 (1944)) which held that insurers that conducted a substantial part of their business across state lines were engaged in interstate commerce and thereby subject to federal antitrust laws.

McCarran-Ferguson provided that the "business of insurance, and every person engaged therein, shall be subject to the laws of the several States..." The act specified that federal law that does not specifically regulate the business of insurance will not preempt a state law enacted for that purpose. States regulate individual insurance products differently from group insurance products. Additionally, the regulation of small group business policies may be subject to some regulations that do not apply to larger groups.

This chapter will concentrate on individual health insurance regulations, with reference to the group market where necessary to differentiate practices and/or processes. The chapter will discuss some of the major areas of state regulation, trends in the number of states with various regulations, and some of the effects of these regulations on health insurance coverage, costs and access.

MAJOR REGULATIONS

Every state has adopted certain basic standards for health insurance that apply to all types of health insurance products. These standards protect consumers by requiring insurers to be financially solvent and capable of paying claims, pay claims promptly, and adhere to certain market conduct requirements. Regulation begins with the licensing of entities that sell insurance within the state. Licensing involves reviews of finances, management, and business practices to ensure an entity can provide coverage promised to policyholders. States also license agents and brokers who sell insurance within the state.

Examples of several financial standards include periodic financial reporting and minimum capital requirements, or amount of net worth that an insuring organization must have in order to operate. This minimum must be available to pay for claims submitted by policyholders. States also examine investment practices and may perform on-site financial examinations. As another measure of financial protection for policyholders, states have established guaranty funds which are non-profit organizations set up to pay claims of insurers that become insolvent. These non-profit organizations are created by statute and financed by imposing assessments on insurers in the market.

Market conduct requirements relate to claims and underwriting practices, advertising, marketing, rescissions of coverage, and payment of claims. These allow states to address unfair trade and claims practices, such as failure to pay claims fairly or promptly, and perform market conduct examinations to make sure insurers are complying with state regulations such as describing products accurately, avoiding deceptive advertising, and using sound actuarial principles to price products. Insurers must adhere to requirements of prompt claim payment and claims appeals processes.

They must also have policy forms (*i.e.* the documents that establish the contractual relationship between the insurer and purchaser) reviewed and/ or approved by the state to conform to standards of definition and content. Most often, states review forms issued to individuals and small groups, presuming larger groups are more knowledgeable and need less state oversight. Other aspects of regulating the business of insurance vary by state and by type of coverage. Although most states have instituted patient protection laws like access to emergency services and specialists, these standards vary by state. An example of state variation exists with external review laws; while most states have external review laws, different standards exist as to the types of disputes eligible for review, the amount of applicable fees, filing time frames, etc.

Other types of health insurance regulations that can vary by state can be grouped into several major areas including access to health insurance, rating, and covered benefits. The following paragraphs describe these regulations as they apply to the individual insurance market.

ACCESS

States have sought to improve access to insurance policies through several regulatory approaches. Absent state individual insurance regulation, insurers in the individual insurance market adopt practices that seek to minimize risk to avoid losses, including denial of coverage for applicants who have health conditions or a history of health problems.

Because most health care expenses are concentrated in a relatively small per centage of individuals, even a small number of high cost individuals can substantially impact overall insurance results (benefit costs, administration, profitability, etc.) in a particular group of individuals with the same insurance policy. As a result, an estimated 10 per cent of individual insurance applicants are denied coverage for some medical reason(s).

Standards relating to access address when, and on what terms, health insurers must accept an applicant for coverage. While most states require insurers to provide coverage to small employers, few apply these requirements to the individual insurance market. State regulations addressing access involve requirements for guaranteed issue and/or guaranteed renewability of health insurance policies. Federal law also includes requirements for access under HIPAA.

Guaranteed Issue

Guaranteed issue laws prohibit insurers from denying coverage to applicants based on their health status. While all health policies sold in the small group market (generally employers of 2 to 50 employees) must be sold on a guaranteed issue basis, only a handful of states require insurers to sell coverage on this basis in the individual health insurance market.

Some states require limited guaranteed access based on HIPAA eligibility and some require open enrollment periods during which insurers may not deny coverage due to a medical condition. Because these requirements vary by state, this results in consumers in some states having more protections than consumers in other states.

Another means of access to health coverage is through high-risk pools. Approximately two-thirds of states have implemented high-risk pools as a safety net for the "medically uninsurable" population. These are people who have been denied health insurance coverage because of a pre-existing health condition, or who can only access private coverage that is restricted or has extremely high rates.

Risk pools are not created expressly to serve the indigent or poor who cannot afford health insurance. The indigent can access coverage through state medical assistance, Medicaid or similar programmes. Risk pools are designed to serve people who would not otherwise have the right to purchase health insurance protection. However, some state risk pools do have a subsidy for lower income, medically uninsurable people.

Though differing by state, risk pools operate as a state-created non-profit association overseen by a board of directors made up of industry, consumer and state insurance department representatives. The board contracts with an established insurance company to collect premiums and pay claims and administer the programme on a day-to-day basis. Insurance benefits vary, but risk pools typically offer benefits that are comparable to basic private market plans. Generally, there are no exclusions. However, risk pools do have waiting periods for coverage of pre-existing conditions. Risk pool insurance generally costs more than regular individual insurance, but the premiums are capped by law in each state. The caps range from as low as 125 per cent of the average for comparable private coverage, up to 200 per cent of the average or more.

Risk pools are not a panacea for coverage of the uninsured because of their higher premiums and typical funding concerns. All state risk pools inherently lose money and need to be subsidized at roughly 40 per cent of overall operating costs. Subsidy arrangements include assessments levied on insurance carriers, HMO's and other insurance providers; appropriations from state general tax revenue; special funding sources, such as a tobacco tax, or a hospital or health care provider surcharge; or a combination of these. Because of these funding concerns, access in some states is limited by waiting lists. There are currently less than 200, 000 people enrolled in high-risk pools.

Guaranteed Renewability

Guaranteed renewability laws prohibit insurers from canceling or not renewing coverage based on medical claims or diagnosis of an illness. This is a protection afforded to policyholders once coverage is obtained. Following the passage of HIPAA, all group and individual health insurance policies must be guaranteed renewable. While guaranteed renewability is at the option of the policyholder, the insurer may increase premiums based on the claims experience of the group of individuals with the same policy. Insurers are generally prohibited from singling out policyholders for premium increases, called re-underwriting, because they got sick after buying coverage. However, insurers are not prohibited from canceling all their policies and leaving the market, though there is a time penalty on market re-entry.

Other protections for access to individual private health insurance coverage implemented by states include guaranteed access for special populations such as continued coverage for dependent handicapped adults who were covered by their parents' policies as minors and automatic coverage of newborns for 30 days under their parents' policy provided the policy covers dependents.

RATING PRACTICES

With some variation, there are two distinct approaches to rating methods, or the process by which insurers calculate policy premiums, allowed by states.

Insurers in a handful of states must offer policies to all applicants (guaranteed issue) and are limited to rates that are similar regardless of health status. This is called adjusted community rating. For these states, rates will generally vary by age and gender but not with health conditions. In states that do not require community rating, individual health insurance policies are underwritten, meaning that past health conditions of individuals are examined and rates are set just as to the health risk of the applicant. A number of other factors are also considered in determining the rates charged.

Factors Utilized in Rating Practices in the Absence of State Regulation

Medical underwriting (examining health status) is the process that insurers use to evaluate an application for insurance. An insurance application is an offer, by the applicant to the insurer, to enter into an insurance contract. In states that allow medical underwriting, the insurer may evaluate an applicant's health status and then accept that offer, decline it, or make a counteroffer with different benefits, a different premium, or both. Insurers use information reported by the individual, as well as medical records.

Based on this examination, there are generally three possible outcomes:

1. An applicant answers a variety of health status questions and is underwritten as a "standard risk" and receives an offer of insurance at standard rates that are generally lower than those for an employee or dependent in the group market. This occurs because the person is found to be healthy at time of policy issue, rather than being of "average health" typical of an employee or dependent of an employee that is covered by a group plan offered through their employer.
2. An applicant with some past or current health conditions might be offered a policy at higher rates than average (called a "rate up" offer) or with coverage of certain specified conditions excluded for a period of time (called a "pre-ex" offer, for a pre-existing condition). Some applicants may be offered a policy with an elimination rider which specifies that coverage is provided except for the particular condition(s) that existed prior to the issuance of the policy.
3. Some applicants with more serious health conditions will be denied coverage since the insurer would not be able to charge a sufficient premium in an underwritten market to pay for the average claims for these individuals.

Prior health care claims are examined to determine if premiums need to be adjusted to sufficiently cover expected claims in the future. Insurers are generally prohibited from singling out policyholders for premium increases, but will look at the experience of the class of individuals with the same policy when considering rate changes. Age can be used in determining premiums with insurers usually charging older people higher premiums than younger people. Premiums also generally rise as the group of policyholders gets older.

Gender is a factor in some policies with insurers often setting higher premiums for women of childbearing age than they do for men. However, for older individuals, insurers may charge more for men than women. Particular types of business or industry present higher or lower risk to the individuals working within them. Insurers often charge people in higher-risk occupations, such as the construction trades, higher premiums than they charge to people in lower-risk occupations, such as office workers.

Geographical location is taken into consideration because higher premiums are charged for residents and workers in locations where health care expenses are typically higher. Family composition is more important than the number of persons in the family when determining health insurance policy premiums. Insurers often set lower premiums for a parent with a child than they do for a couple. Similarly, they may set different premiums for other kinds of families.

Lifestyle or participation in wellness activities has become more important in recent times as interest in cost containment has increased. Insurers have long charged higher premiums to smokers than nonsmokers, but have recently also begun to charge higher premiums for obese enrollees and lower rates to people who participate in health plan "wellness programmes. "

State Rate Reforms

A handful of states have enacted rating reforms for the individual health insurance market, prohibiting or restricting insurers from charging higher premiums based on health status or the risk of having future medical claims. These rating restrictions are generally of two types: rate bands and community/adjusted community rating. Rate bands limit how much insurers can vary premiums for each policyholder based on the health and claims of the policyholder. These limits force insurers to spread some of the risk more broadly across all policyholders. The extent to which premiums can vary depends on the size of the rate band and the factors that insurers can consider when setting premiums.

The rate band sets an upper and lower limit around an "average" premium. For example, if an average individual premium is $200 a month and a state allows an insurer to vary premiums by plus or minus 50 per cent from the average premium, this allows a three-fold variation in premium from $100 (50 per cent of the average) to $300 (150 per cent of the average). Some states that use rate bands also allow variation based on factors other than health status, such as age and geographic location.

States that use rate bands also often limit price increases for individuals who renew their policies. In such a state, an individual whose health has deteriorated will not suddenly be charged significantly higher premiums. This limit is based on the health status and past claims experience of the individual and may be in addition to any increase that would otherwise apply to all policyholders due to increases in the cost of medical care.

Community rating, sometimes called pure community rating, requires insurers to charge the same premiums for everyone with the same policy. Insurers are not allowed to vary rates based on the health status or claims of the person. In theory, the price reflects the value of the benefits and not the risk factors of the people who purchase the policy. The community rate may be different for different insurers based on the claims experience (and other factors such as adminis-trative costs) of people enrolled with that insurer.

At the time of renewal, premiums are based on the claims experience of all people with the policy, so that people who had claims for health expenditures are not charged higher rates than others with the same policy who may not have submitted any claims. Variation is allowed depending on the family composition of the person(s) applying for the policy. Adjusted or modified community rating likewise prohibits insurers from varying premiums based on health status. All persons in the same community are charged the same premiums, but premiums can vary by geography. Additional variation may be allowed for age, but adjustments for gender are usually not allowed.

The amount of variability among states in the extent of regulation surrounding insurers' premium rates reflects states' attempts to balance the challenges of greater access to private health coverage with the policies' affordability. Additionally, states change rating practices over time in response to changing markets and political circumstances.

COVERED BENEFITS

While almost all health insurance policies cover the usual medical expenses associated with hospital, surgical and out-patient care received from licensed facilities and medical personnel, other requirements for coverage can be implemen-ted through state regulations. One way to spread the cost of a medical condition or treatment among a broad population, making it less expensive for the group of people who need such coverage, is through a benefit mandate. It is also a way to encourage people to seek certain care that otherwise may not be received.

Mandates are laws that require health insurers to offer or include coverage for certain benefits or services. These required benefits may include coverage for certain providers such as chiropractors and social workers, certain benefits such as well child care and acupuncture, and certain populations such as adopted and non-custodial children. The number and type of mandates varies considerably across states. States may apply these mandates to certain markets, differentiating between group and individual policies, and between types of plans such as health maintenance organizations (HMOs) versus other health insurance policy types.

It is sometimes difficult to determine whether a mandate in a particular state applies to only the group health insurance market or to individually purchased policies as well because some states allow health insurance coverage issued to "groups of one" (*i.e.*, one person is considered a group) to be classified as a small group. While mandates make health insurance more comprehensive, they also make it more expensive because mandates require insurers to pay for care consumers previously funded out of their own pockets. However, in the absence of mandates, adding optional benefits to a policy may distort premiums if only those people who need the benefit select the coverage.

Policymakers make tradeoffs, balancing higher premiums with the need to help finance certain illnesses. Many times mandates are implemented due to the strength of a particular advocacy group representing a particular constituency (advocates for coverage of diabetic self management and disposable testing materials) or because an instance of a denial of benefits caused some harm to a constituent patient (non-coverage of cancer medications). However, because mandates increase the cost of health insurance, states have begun to consider costs before passing new legislation with some states requiring a cost impact study before mandates would be approved.

An analysis of the number of mandates that have been enacted over the past decades is shown below. This chart indicates that there were over 1400 mandates in effect in the year 2000. A more recent report on mandates compiled by the Council for Affordable Health Insurance (CAHI) indicates that as of early 2008 that number had risen to almost 2000.

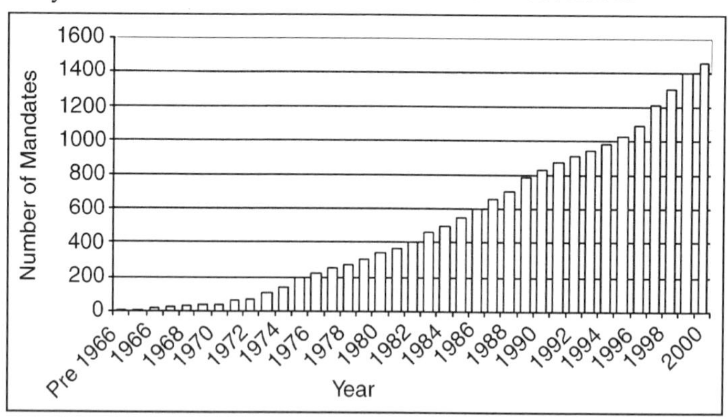

Fig. State Mandates Enacted from Pre–1965 to 2000

A grid developed by CAHI which shows the number and types of mandates by state for 2008. As this grid demonstrates, some of the more frequently state-mandated services are breast reconstruction, diabetic supplies, and mental health parity (even before federal legislation was considered). Frequently, mandated providers include chiropractors, optometrists, and psychologists, with coverage of adopted, handicapped, and newborn children among categories of frequently covered persons.

OTHER STATE INSURANCE REGULATIONS

States have issued other types of regulations to ensure access to the individual private health insurance market. Among the more common are pre-existing condition limitations and medical loss ratios.

Pre-existing conditions are those conditions for which a policyholder was diagnosed, sought advice, sought treatment, or received care during a specific period of time prior to an application for insurance. Some insurers use pre-existing condition limitations to manage insurance costs by limiting or eliminating coverage of these conditions for some defined period of time after the initial purchase of a policy. Most states have implemented limitations on how far an insurer can go back to find prior claims for conditions (the look-back period) and how much time can elapse before coverage of these conditions begins (the exclusionary period).

A medical loss ratio is the percentage of dollars paid out as benefits to policyholders in relation to the premiums collected for the policies. For example, a state may require that an insurer spend at least 75 per cent of the premiums they collect on medical claims. Loss ratios can be calculated for a particular policy form or design, a line of business, or a health insurer's overall business. Only a handful of states require all insurers in the individual market to spend at least 75 per cent of every premium dollar on medical care. Some states establish minimum loss ratios and reserve the right to review or approve the rates submitted by state-licensed insuring organizations. Insurers must estimate what they will spend on medical claims over the course of a year and set their premiums accordingly.

Because premiums must be set at the start of a policy year, actual claims may be more or less than anticipated. If an insurer has underestimated or overestimated the amount of claims, it may adjust the policy premiums in the following year to make up for the discrepancy. In some states, if claims are lower than expected and medical claim expenses do not meet the loss ratio, the insurer must refund the excess premium to policyholders at the end of the year.

VARIATION IN REGULATIONS WITHIN STATES

The previous parts of this report describe some of the types of regulations that states can implement in their governance of the individual insurance market. However, within each of the major areas of regulation there is wide variation in the requirements that have been implemented.

For example, within a rating structure that may be imposed on health insurance premiums, there are state actions that range from no rating requirements to pure community rating with various levels of rate bands in between. Similarly, states have a range of requirements for regulating pre-existing condition limitations from no restrictions to very tight time frames of a six-month look back and six-month exclusionary period. Though individual market reforms are the focus of this report, the chart displays both individual and small group policy regulations. A majority of states (27) have no requirement for guaranteed issue (GI) of individual insurance policies and no rating structure for variation in premiums. Where states have implemented some form of GI (11 states), this is often accompanied by some rating requirement, usually pure or modified community rating.

Several states (12) use the HIPAA requirements to grant access to the individual insurance policies, but this applies to persons with prior group insurance coverage and there are usually no rate restrictions on the amount of premiums insurers can charge for these policies, depending on the health status of the applicant. Most states (37) allow policy elimination riders (policy provisions that eliminate coverage for particular conditions).

Almost all states have some limitation on the pre-existing condition look-back/exclusionary periods. While some states indicate they have none, this usually applies to persons exercising their group to individual portability rights under HIPAA (persons whose pre-existing limitations are eliminated because of previous coverage). The most common look-back period was either a twelve month (14 states) or six month (13 states) period. The most common exclusionary period was 12 months (22 states) followed by 24 months (10 states).

IMPACT OF STATE REGULATION

States, in their actions, can and do make very different decisions about how to regulate the individual health insurance market. These actions reflect different values, political climates, and expectations. They also are designed to achieve specific policy goals, such as expanding access, with most states having considered laws and/or regulations of guaranteed issue, guaranteed renewability, and rate reforms. However, achieving these goals often requires trade-offs.

For example, establishing rating rules that allow high-risk, older individuals to get low-cost health insurance without exclusions can make health insurance affordable for this population, but increases the price that younger, healthier persons would otherwise pay in this market. When the pool of insured persons does not include the participation of younger individuals, their absence heightens the need for increasing premiums as health care use and costs rise among the existing pool of older persons.

A chapter by the Heritage Foundation examined several studies on insurance regulation and presented an analysis of state health plan premiums, comparing premiums to the number of mandates and the existence of several types of reforms in the states. The author concluded that while some of the variation in health insurance premiums could be due to regional differences in underlying health care costs, overall "state level regulations of heath insurance are correlated with higher premiums." In terms of the impact state regulation has had on the market for individual health insurance, the research examined indicates that while access to coverage generally increases, affordability is still a major problem.

A study by the Commonwealth Fund examined insurance markets in seven states with varying degrees of market reforms. Among its key findings was the determination that stricter regulation made an important difference by creating "individual health insurance markets where comprehensive coverage is available to all," but with premiums more affordable for higher-risk people at the expense of less-affordable coverage for younger and healthier people. It also found that older and less healthy people faced a range of problems in less regulated states including higher rejection rates for applicants. Of five states in the study with relatively strict regulations, only three still maintain all of those in place at the time of the study; the other two states subsequently rolled back many of their reforms.

A similar study of eight states by Milliman, that included several of the same states as the Turnbull and Kane analysis, found consistent results of decreasing individual insurance enrollment and increased premiums. An additional finding in the Milliman study, which concentrated on guaranteed issue and community rating reforms, was that a deteriorated market resulted after reforms were enacted, with insurance companies choosing to stop selling individual insurance.

A column of information that attempts to quantify the cost impact on premiums for each of the mandates listed. CAHI estimates that mandated benefits increase the cost of basic health coverage from less than 20 per cent to more than 50 per cent depending on the state and its mandates. Several other studies conclude that the effect of regulation is small. While persons with higher expected expenses due to chronic health conditions living in unregulated states paid higher health policy premiums and were somewhat less likely to obtain coverage, the variation between premiums and risk is far from proportional.

This is because in looking at regulated versus unregulated states, using guaranteed issue and community rating as measures of regulation, that there was considerable pooling of risk in unregulated states. They concluded that the effect of regulation was to produce a "slight increase in the proportion uninsured, as increases in low risk uninsured more than offset decreases in high risk uninsured."

These studies are not inconsistent. Pauly and Herring do agree that requirements such as community rating and guaranteed issue do cause higher premiums for some insured and lower premiums for others, and lead to an increase in the total number of uninsured. However, they observe a higher degree of risk pooling in unregulated states that would otherwise be believed. Additionally, other studies looked at requirements beyond community rating and guaranteed issue to include coverage mandates that affected the amount of premiums paid by policyholders.

SUMMARY

The nongroup (individual) health insurance market provides access to coverage for persons who cannot obtain health insurance coverage through their employer or do not qualify for public programmes. For some persons it provides a temporary source of coverage while between jobs or for early retirees who are not yet eligible for Medicare.

The population covered through the individual market is relatively small, and this market provides relative ease of access to affordable coverage for persons who are comparatively young and/or in reasonably good health. For older, less healthy persons there can be some barriers to health coverage in the nongroup market. Applicants for coverage usually must go through an underwriting process, which may result in higher premiums than they might pay for coverage in the group insurance market, lack of coverage for specific conditions, or rejection for coverage entirely. States, as the primary regulators of insurance companies and insurance products, try to improve access to health insurance through the passage of various types of laws and regulations. In the absence of federal reform activities, some states have implemented their own reforms with greater or lesser degrees of success.

Some states such as Maine, Massachusetts, and Vermont, have implemented compre-hensive reforms to emphasize shared responsibilities for obtaining health coverage, while at the same time easing access to affordable plans. Other states have taken more incremental approaches such as Washington and Illinois, to cover all children, while states such as Connecticut, Idaho, Indiana, and others have expanded coverage to young adults by changing the definition of "dependent" and extending coverage for those older than 18. Actions such as implementing guaranteed issue, community rating laws, various mandated requirements, and reforms, have differing effects on the cost and availability of health coverage for insurance applicants of differing characteristics. Policymakers must be cognizant of how these laws and regulations surrounding the individual health insurance market affect their ability to meet various population needs as they attempt to reform the health insurance market.

5

Competition in Health Insurance

THE INDIAN HEALTHCARE INDUSTRY

The Healthcare Sector in India comprises of hospitals and allied sectors such as; diagnostics and pathology, medical equipments and supplies, medical tourism and private medical insurance. According to Yes Bank and Assocham Report, from the current estimated size of US $35 billion it is projected to grow at 23% p.a. to touch US$77 billion.

During the period 2000-09, the sector has registered a growth of 9. 3%, comparable to the sectoral growth rate of other developing nations such as China, Mexico and Brazil. The growth of the sector will be driven by healthcare facilities in private and public sectors, medical diagnostic centres and pathlabs and the medical insurance sector. The share of private expenditure as to the total expenditure on health has grown from about 60% to almost 80% over the last decade. The current share of public expenditure on health is 20%.

With a view to raise government expenditure on health as a proportion of GDP from 0. 9% to a target of 2-3% by 2012 and the government launched the National Rural Health Mission in 2005. At present the central government and the state governments cumulatively contribute 0. 34% and 0.56% of GDP respectively to healthcare and related services.

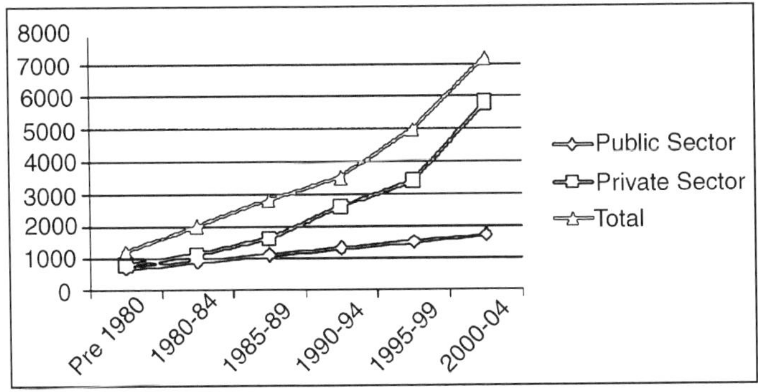

Fig. Growth of Public and Private Facilities, India

There are an increasing number of private players changing the nations' health delivery landscape beyond recognition. New hospitals are mushrooming even in Tier II and Tier III Cities and leading healthcare entrepreneurs with deep pockets are expanding their empires, often overseas.

At the root is the new age patient who is ready to undertake the best possible treatment that money can buy. State of art technology, wonder drugs and five star facilities are now the hospital mantra. It is booming industry both in terms of revenue and employment. Currently the industry employs over 4 million people making one of the largest service industries in the economy.

The key issues driving growth in the healthcare industry have been identified as follows:

- *Population Growth*: This is the prime driver of growth in the healthcare sector. With the population currently at 1. 1 billion and increasing at the rate of 2% p.a. , it is estimated that by 2050 the population will reach 1.6 billion. This massive population is due in part to a decrease in infant mortality, a general increase in life expectancy, greater affluence among people and better hygiene. This way a growing elderly population will soon place an enormous burden on India's healthcare infrastructure.
- *Expanding Middle Class*: Parallel to India's thriving economy is rapid urbanization and creation of an expanding middle class with more disposable income to spend on healthcare. With women entering workforce, purchasing power and thus affordability has increased and people can buy western medicines.
- *Rise of Disease*: Two kinds of diseases are largely prominent among people these days-one is communicable diseases and the other chronic degenerative diseases. While infectious/communicable diseases such as polio, hepatitis, tuberculosis, pneumonia were thought to have been brought under control via the extensive government programmes however now they seem to have resurfaced or have developed a rather stubborn resistance to drugs. Another problem that seems to be on the rise these days is AIDS. Among the urban population there have been a significant number of health problems which may be called lifestyle diseases. Unhealthy diets, sedentary work and affluent lifestyle has given rise to hypertension, cancer, diabetes, obesity etc. Lifestyle disorders are expected to grow in the future at a faster rate than infectious diseases in India and to result in an increase in cost per treatment.
- *Medical Tourism*: With specialty and super specialty hospitals equipped with the latest equipment and the best surgical procedures at relatively inexpensive charges on the rise has made India a hub

for people from the west to get treatment here-giving birth to a concept called Medical Tourism. With the healthcare costs increasing in many developed nations and the time for waiting for a procedure also increasing, especially in Britain, it is expected that the medical tourism industry will grow.

THE PUBLIC HEALTHCARE IN INDIA

The public health infrastructure of India has grown since independence, but it is yet to match the basic healthcare facilities in many other countries. While in 1947 the number of hospital beds was 3.2 per 10,000, the present number of 9 per 10,000 is commendable, but still far behind those of other developing countries. The healthcare system consists of primary, secondary and tertiary healthcare centres, and the focus of public healthcare has been on Primary healthcare as well as centres providing healthcare services and education.

Health is a state responsibility, however the central government does contribute in a substantial manner through grants and centrally sponsored health programmes/schemes. Various public health schemes taken out by the central government include the Rashtriya Swasthya Bima Yojana which provides health insurance to poor families who are unable to afford medical care or hospitalization or cannot afford private medical insurance. As a part of the public healthcare scheme, there are a number of hospitals who offer free services to the poor who are unable to pay for their treatment.

Drawbacks of the public health system:

- There is a fragmented approach since the conceptuali-zation and planning of the all the programmes is centralized and the specific needs of the local area are not taken into account.
- Accessibility, utilization and acceptability of the programmes is low because the infrastructure set up by the government is based on population norms rather than habitation.
- There is a gap between the demand and supply of human resources thereby causing people to waste time waiting in queues for treatment or consultation.
- Though there is implementation of infrastructure but the quality of service offered is not consistent.

PRIVATE HEALTHCARE IN INDIA

Compared to nations such as EU and Japan where major spending in healthcare sector comes from the government India is an exception here insofar that it has one of the highest private spending on healthcare. With a significant proportion of the Indian population still below the poverty line public facilities are largely to cater to this segment however in the urban and sub-urban areas private healthcare facilities are preferred. With rising income levels and exposure to international standards/quality has raised the demand for quality private healthcare facilities. The private health sector consists of the 'not-for-profit' and the 'for-profit' health sectors. The not-for-profit health sector includes various health services provided by Non Government Organisations, charitable institutions, missions, trusts, etc. Health care in the for-profit health sector consists of various types of practitioners and institutions. The licensed practitioners range from general practitioners (GPs) to the super specialists, various types of consultants, nurses and paramedics, licentiates, and rural medical practitioners (RMPs).

The out-of pocket spending on healthcare by Indians is one of the highest, constituting 94% of the total spending in the private health industry. Out of pocket is the direct outlay of households, including gratuities and payments in kind, made to health practitioners and suppliers of pharmaceuticals and other goods and services, intended is to contribute to the restoration or to the enhancement of the health status of individuals or population groups. An average household contributes 4–6% of its household income to healthcare with close to 80% going to the private sector.

The advantage to the private sector comes from little government interference and unlike many developed nations, the healthcare policies do not work on a reimbursement model. The widespread demand for quality healthcare has resulted world class quality of such facilities at cost competitive rates. Although health insurance is still in its infancy and has not percolated to all sections of the society but it has been predicted that with more complicated services being offered and increased demand for better quality, the insurance sector will boost the private healthcare market.

On the basis of infrastructural requirements and the types of services offered hospitals can be broadly classified into the following categories: Primary Healthcare (PHC) These institutions are generally clinics with one or more general practitioners. Though these are not equipped for ICUs and surgeries they are the most important contact point for healthcare in rural India and has limited private players.

Nursing Homes can have one or more doctors and at least 20 beds. There are various types of nursing homes such as ophthalmic, orthopeadic, cardiac, dental clinics, Ear Nose Throat (ENT) clinics and maternity homes. Secondary Care Hospitals are bigger hospitals with typically 100-300 beds with surgical wards and ICU facilities. They can be further classified as general hospitals and specialty hospitals. While general hospitals offer inpatient facilities along with radiology, emergency care, general surgery and a few departments such as obstetrics, paediatrics, gyneacology etc. and dedicate 10% of their beds to ICU use.

On the other hand specialty care hospitals, apart from general hospital departments also offer at least one specialty care such as cardiology, neurology, dermatology etc. Moreover these hospitals dedicate 25% of their beds to ICU usage. There are secondary care hospitals in certain cities but none have pan

India presence. Examples include-Manipal Specialty Hospital, Bangalore. Tertiary Care Hospitals have around 300 beds and doctors offering top of the line facilities in specific specialties. Examples include Sankara Nethralaya (Chennai), Escorts Heart Institute and Research Centre (New Delhi), National Institute of Mental Health and Neuro Sciences (NIMHANS)etc. While these are single specialty hospitals there are multi specialty tertiary hospitals as well which offer a number of specialty services under one roof. Some prominent examples are the Manipal Hospital, Bangalore and Max Hospital, Noida.

Quaternary Care Hospitals are tertiary care hospitals offering super specialty surgical procedures including advanced cardiac, joint replacement, neurological etc. Osmania General Hospital (Hyderabad) and Apollo Children's Hospital (Chennai) are examples.

PUBLIC PRIVATE PARTNERSHIP (PPP)

Recognizing the increasing demand for better quality of healthcare, the government has devised a strategy for health development through public private partnerships. With the objective to improve the health of the population PPPs are seen in the context of viewing the medical sector as a national asset with health promotion as a goal of health providers public as well as private.

The utilization of hospital services in public and private sectors varies greatly from one state to another. The private sector has provided useful contribution in improving the healthcare provision besides the role of the public sector in of the states of Kerela and Tamil Nadu. The private sector too is keen to enter into PPP since it's the easiest route for them to enter into the market as well as to expand in lesser time. Since private players are faced with infrastructural constraints thus entering into PPP serves their purpose through leveraging public assets.

Models for Partnership

- *Franchising*: In such a model the franchiser develops specialized skill, knowledge and strategies for franchisees who in return contribute resources of their own to set up a clinic and pay membership to the franchiser.
- *Contracting Out*: In this model the private providers receive a budget to provide certain services and manage a government health unit. The parties concerned agree on the quantity, quality and the duration of the agreement.
- *Contracting In*: The government hires an individual on a temporary basis to provide services such as maintenance of buildings, utilities, housekeeping, meals, medicine stores, diagnostic facilities, communications etc.

- *Build, Operate and Transfer (BOT)*: BOT requires financing of projects by the government, financial guarantees, subsidized land and assurance of reasonable returns on investment. These models are useful for establishing large hospitals.
- *Joint Venture Companies*: Companies launched with equity participation from the government and the private sector. This model has not succeeded in India due o the lack of understanding, trust, and appropriate governance.

Examples:

- The Rajiv Gandhi Super Specialty Hospital at Raichur, Karnataka is the result of a partnership between the Government of Karnataka with Apollo Hospitals Group with the financial support from the OPEC Fund for International Development. It has a mission to provide low cost specialty care to families below the poverty line. The Uttaranchal Mobile Hospital and Research Centre is a three way partnership among the Technology Information, Forecasting and Assessment Council (TIFAC), the Government of Uttaranchal and the Birla Institute of Scientific Research (BISR) with a motive to provide health care and diagnostic facilities to poor and rural people at their doorstep in difficult and hilly terrains. However there still remain a number of challenges faced by PPPs. A major reason for this lies in the gap between the priorities between the government and the private sector. Moreover operational and structural issues also act as a deterrent for the private players to enter a PPP such as lack of enabling infrastructure, project management, shared decision making, lack of appropriate governance and accountability for delayed payments by the Government.

Allied Health Services

Diagnostics and Pathology

Parallel to the healthcare industry growth, the Indian diagnostics and pathology testing market is set for steady growth. The market is valued at close to INR 6000Cr in 2008 and is growing at 20% per annum. The industry is highly fragmented and encompasses over 40000 laboratories, very few of which are accredited.

These include:

- Pathological laboratory chains (corporate laboratories)
- Regional laboratories
- Hospital run diagnostic facilities

While there is a high demand for clinical pathological tests however the rampant supply leads to intense competition with respect to pricing, which directly has an impact on profitability. The advent of new techniques has stimulated the need for more accurate and wider test parameters and laboratories are trying to differentiate themselves by offering specialized services. Key players include SRL Ranbaxy, Dr. Lal Path Labs, Apollo Clinics and Piramal Diagnostics.

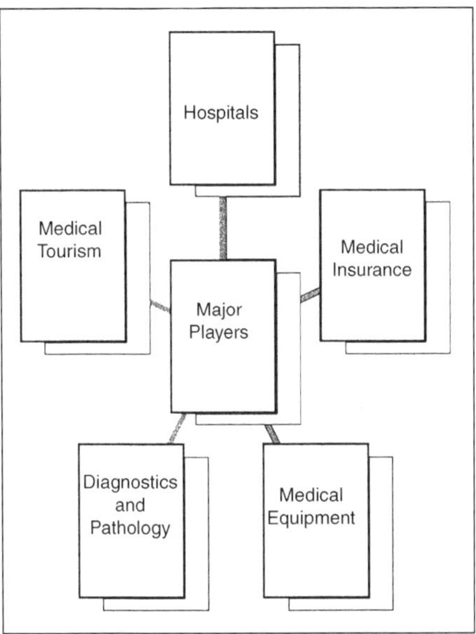

Medical Equipments

The Indian market for medical equipment and supplies estimated at US$2. 7 billion has been ranked among the world's top in 2o in 2009. Out of the total market size of India, more than 85% equipment is imported from other countries. The Indian companies with strong domestic presence in this sector include Medived innovations, Opto Circuits, Trivitron Healthcare etc. These companies manufacture niche products with international accreditations; they are mostly export oriented rather than supplying the Indian market.

Medical Insurance

The recent liberalization of the Indian healthcare sector has led to the emergence of a much needed health insurance industry. Post 1991, with the passing of the Insurance Regulatory Development Authority Bill (IRDA) the insurance sector was opened to private and foreign participation, thereby paving the way for the entry of private health insurance companies. The Bill also facilitated the establishment of an authority to protect the interests of the insurance holders by regulating, promoting and ensuring orderly growth of the insurance industry.

In India, the penetration of insurance remains very low, with only about 10% of the population having some sort of health insurance coverage in 2007-08. However in the private sector the no. of insured account for only 3. 5% of the population. Major insurance companies offering health insurance schemes in the private sector include Bajaj Alliance, ICICI, Royal Sundaram, Cholamandalam.

Public Sector companies including New India, United India, National Insurance and Oriental Insurance have a combined market share of 62%, of which New India Assurance has the largest market share of 24%. ICICI Lombard has the second largest market share of 17%. Over the years however the rising costs of healthcare and the prospering middle class has supported a significant increase in the average household consumption in healthcare. This has stimulated a greater awareness of the benefits associated with insurance coverage.

Medical Tourism

This is a developing concept where people from all over the world come to India for their medical and relaxation needs. India is becoming a hub for medical treatment owing to its low costs and superior quality of services. The most common treatments include knee transplant, heart surgery, cosmetic surgery and dental care. Studies have in fact indicated that with an increasing number of foreign patients coming in, India could make ₹ 100 million through medical tourism by 2012.

Pharmaceutical Industry

As one of the leading industries in India, the Indian Pharmaceutical Industry represents 8% of the global total industry by volume and 13% by value. The "organized" sector of India's pharmaceutical industry consists of 250 to 300 companies, which account for 70% of products on the market, with the top 10 firms representing 30%. India's a leading producer of generic drugs and at the domestic level is self-reliant as it meets 95% of the country's pharmaceutical needs. Some of the leading brands in the retail pharmaceutical market are Cipla, Ranbaxy, GlaxoSmithKline, Nicholas Piramal, Sun Pharma, Zydus Cadila etc.

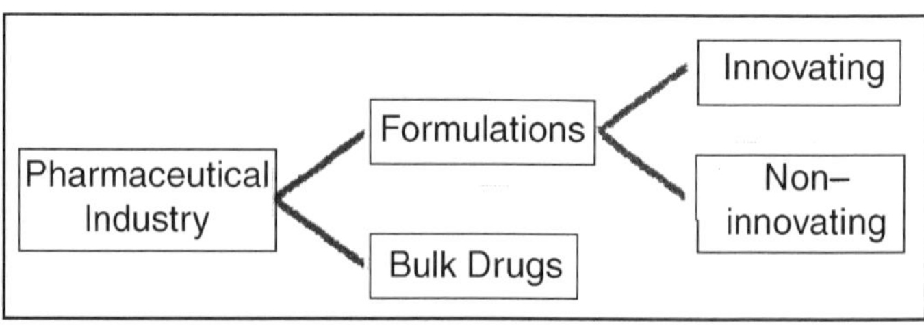

The pharmaceutical industry is roughly divided into formulations and bulk drugs. Firms specializing in pharmaceuticals may be further classified as innovating and noninnovating. Innovating firms are those which engage in research and development of new medicines and the firms which do not do so are called non-innovating firms.

India is among the top 5 producers of bulk drugs in the world and has a share of 20% in the pharmaceutical market. The Indian sector produces about 60000 formulations and 400 bulk drugs. The Indian market for over-the-counter medicines (OTCs) is worth about $940 million and is growing 20 per cent a year *i.e.* double the rate for prescription medicines and recent government initiatives have been towards widening the availability of OTCs to outlets other than pharmacies.

The Indian sector is highly technology as well as knowledge intensive and has wide ranging capabilities not only in drug manufacturing but research and development as well. However R&D is not a prominent feature in the domestic industry as the expenditure on R&D stands at 1. 9% whereas that of global counterparts at 10-16%.

But with the product patent regime now in place some major domestic pharmaceutical companies are making huge investments in R&D. Assocham, the new patent regime will lead to development of innovative new drugs, which will lead to increased profitability for MNCs and also force domestic players to focus on R&D.

THE PRESENT REGULATORY FRAMEWORK

THE PHARMACEUTICAL INDUSTRY

The pharmaceutical industry is regulated by the Drugs and Cosmetics Act 1940 (DCA), and the Drugs and Cosmetics Rules (DCR) made there under. This legislation applies to the whole of India and all products, whether imported or made in India. The office of the Drug Controller of India (DCI) has the primary responsibility of enforcing the law.

However, at the field level, enforcement is done by the individual State governments through their Food and Drug Administrations. Matters of product approval and standards, clinical trials, introduction of new drugs, and import licenses for new drugs are handled by the DCI. However, the approvals for setting up manufacturing facilities, and obtaining licenses to sell and stock drugs are provided by the State Governments.

All manufacturing of drugs in India requires a license. A license is required for each such location at which drugs are to be manufactured, and also for each drug to be manufactured. The license has to be renewed periodically.

MEDICAL EQUIPMENT

The Indian Medical Devices industry is still largely unregulated. Most importantly quality of medical equipment is still not under the radar of authorities. The authority principally responsible for regulating medical devices in India, is the Central Drugs Control Organization (CDSCO) under Ministry of Health and Family Welfare (MoHFW).

Foreign as well as Indian Companies must register with the CDSCO before the company's products can be introduced into the Indian market. Both the sellers as well as manufacturers have to register with the CDSCO and the Indian importer has to obtain a no objection certificate to import and sell in India. In 2008 the DCG(I) prepared a list of 160 medical devices which require registration.

MEDICAL EDUCATION

The Medical Council of India (MCI) is the regulatory authority for medical education. Its guidelines only government or trust hospitals can set up education facilities. They also have specifications as to the amount of land required, the number of classrooms, and on their size before the hospitals can actually be set up.

For instance, there is a restriction of a 500-bed care unit on hospitals for getting permission to set up training colleges. The healthcare education facility is required at a minimum have a 10- acre campus. However there arise a number of issues since such a framework creates a supply bottlenecks. The Nursing Council of India requires 50 beds minimum and large size campus but trains only 50 nurses while much smaller buildings with 10, 000 square feet for example in Singapore are training 500 nurses a year.

Likewise, the Nursing Council of India's regulations are also seen to be arcane. The Nursing Council does not allow private players to enter into nursing education unless they form trusts. Hospitals need to tie up with another organization in order to grant a PG diploma in hospital administration. Again, there are requirements on land and infrastructure, such as requiring a 500 seater auditorium, 25 acres of contiguous land, conditions which are difficult to fulfill in first tier cities.

MEDICAL INSURANCE

Less than 10% of India's population today is covered by health insurance, either voluntary or as part of the Employees State Insurance, Central Government Health Scheme or Community Insurance. The low share of insured patients is seen as one of the main reasons that healthcare services have not grown as much as they could in India. There is also an allied problem of low awareness about medical/health insurance. Thus, there is considerable scope for increased market penetration.

The growth of the medical insurance industry also depends on the presence of a capable regulator that will through various initiatives boost the penetration of private medical insurance products. For example the IRDA in 2007 eliminated tariffs on general insurance to encourage scientific rating and independent pricing for each line of business so that the premiums are based on actual risks and costs. Currently, the IRDA is focused on standardizing medical definitions to ensure consistent pricing and products and is providing incentives for standalone insurance companies to attract private players into the industry.

HOSPITALS/NURSING HOMES

The government does not have a proper framework to guide the setting up of hospitals and nursing homes. The government does not set benchmarks for service delivery or demand players to comply with basic norms, and also does not do any kind of local or zone based marked needs assessment before allowing new facilities to register. It was noted that without a uniform disclosure policy and sharing of information by hospitals, a mature healthcare delivery system cannot materialize. Government needs to insist on getting proper information from all establishments in order to ensure adherence to norms it lays down.

Independent regulatory bodies are required to ensure standards are maintained through frequent audits and disclosure of information. The lack of a regulatory framework for setting up establishments and monitoring their standards adversely affects quality, creates unwarranted competition for manpower, and also results in excess supply of medical facilities in some zones, making some players unviable.

The current private health sector is highly unregulated and there is a need for establishing an accreditation body because of:

- The increased competition in the health sector
- No advantage enjoyed by hospitals maintaining certain standards
- The realisation that standards needs to be improved and updated and
- The emergence of health insurance.

The body will ensure quality health care through:

- Assessing hospitals for compliance to set standards,
- Providing assistance to hospitals to upgrade their standards,
- Ensuring proper patient care, and
- Aiding to upgrade standards of hospitals through education, training and Consultation.

Accredited hospitals need to be monitored for standards, quality, price and consumer satisfaction.

DIAGNOSTICS AND PATHOLOGY

In India, this industry lacks a regulatory framework and hence has a low entry barrier with the only requirement being registration under the Shop and Establishment Act. The National Accreditation Board for Testing and Calibration Laboratories (NABL) is the sole accreditation body with the criteria assuring accuracy, reliability and conformity of the tests results. Since it is an autonomous body under the Ministry of Science and Technology with limited prowess thus the speed of accreditation is slow and a few laboratories are accredited by NABL or CAP.

MAJOR PLAYERS

APOLLO HOSPITALS ENTERPRISE LTD.

Apollo Hospitals Enterprise Ltd. was launched as a single hospital in Chennai in 1983 and today it has expanded its global reach with the opening of Apollo Bramwell hospital in Mauritius. Apollo Hospitals secured $50 million worth of loan from International Finance Corporation (IFC), a member of the World Bank Group, to set-up high quality hospitals in remote areas of India and is planning to add 2,000 beds within the next two years for an investment of Rs 1,500 crore to Rs 1,600 crore.

Currently it manages a network of 43 specialty hospitals and clinics with a bed capacity of 7543 across country and abroad. The Hospital chain has recently launched a healthcity in Hyderabad and intends on doing so pan India. It has also tied up with Indian Oil Corporation to set up pharmacies at its petrol stations.

FORTIS HEALTHCARE LTD.

Fortis Healthcare Limited, a leading healthcare delivery company in India was formed with the vision of "creating a world-class integrated healthcare delivery system in India, entailing the finest medical skills combined with compassionate patient care". Fortis Healthcare will acquire nearly 23.9% strategic stake in Singapore-based healthcare group, Parkway Holdings from TPG Capital (formerly Texas Pacific Group), in an offmarket deal, estimated to be around USD 685.3 million. The company's net sales and operating profit are expected to grow at CAGR of 28. 67% and 48. 07% from 2008 to 2011.

MAX HEALTHCARE

Max Healthcare operates 18 healthcare facilities in National Capital Region (NCR) of Delhi, has a bed capacity of around 865 beds and is expected to increase to 1, 500–1, 600 beds in the next few years. Has collaborated with Singapore General Hospital in the areas of medical practices, nursing, paramedical research and training. It plans to raise US$ 85. 36 million to expand its hospital.

NARAYANA HRUDALAYA

This super specialty hospital is the first of its kind offering cardiac care facilities and is located in Bangalore. It was set up by the Asia Heart Foundation with the ability to perform 25 cardiac surgeries a day. The hospital is based on a model that facilitates social inclusion by charging each patient based on his affordability.

TERTIARY HOSPITALS AND MEDICITIES

Large corporations such as the Reliance ADA Group and Aditya Birla Group have entered the industry to capitalize on the attractive growth that corporate hospital chains have been experiencing. The Kokilaben Dhirubhai Ambani Hospital and Medical Research Institute at Mumbai, a tertiary multispecialty hospital has been set up by the Reliance ADA Group. Lately, health cities aimed at catering to larger populations and the medical tourism industry by offering multiple specialties, alternative therapies, research and development centres, educational institutions and residential facilities; have been setup by corporate hospital groups. Dr. Naresh Trehan's Medicity, a large area catering to the medical and recuperative aspects for patients, is an example of health cities in India.

COMPETITION RELATED ISSUES IN THE HEALTHCARE SECTOR

In theory, competition ensures provision of best possible goods and services at the lowest possible prices. It is in the absence of effective competition that efficiency of markets is hampered. Different government policies may encourage or adversely affect competition, and hence consumer welfare, particularly in the context of the present globalising environment.

In addition, sector specific policies in various areas such as health, electricity, telecommunications, financial services etc. , also affect competition in the economy. The market for healthcare services is quite distinct in its functioning with asymmetries of information and market power prevailing in the industry.

The complexity of the market for health services arises because of three reasons:

1. Asymmetry of Information
2. *Complexity of Production*: Since each patient requires different treatment procedures and standardization of such procedures is not feasible.
3. *Local Market Power due to Economies of Scale and Costs of Travel*: In urban areas there are economies of scale since they cater to a larger segment of the population compared to the rural segment and hence have significant local market power.

It is such complexity of market for health services that makes it even more difficult yet essential to ensure free and fair competition and thus efficiency in the market. Competition issues in the healthcare sector can be looked upon by segregating them into issues at domestic level and those at international level.

DOMESTIC ISSUES

Entry Barriers to Private Players in the Medical Education Sector

Until very recently only government and charitable trusts could set up medical colleges. Private players were not permitted by the MCI to start such facilities. This created major supply bottlenecks since there were only about 13500 post graduate vacancies and many students had to go abroad to pursue their post graduation. Moreover the entire approach is infrastructure and volume based rather than value based and does not focus on quality and functional excellence since the MCI had land requirements and area specifications for the medical colleges.

Ironically, the Medical Council has not permitted corporate hospitals to set up training facilities, which would benefit them and the healthcare sector at large, it has permitted a plethora of substandard private medical colleges, many of which lack basic faculty, equipment, and infrastructure and are unable to provide relevant and quality training. It is only very recently in March 2010 that the MCI has permitted hospital chains such as Apollo Hospitals, Fortis Healthcare and Max Healthcare to start medical colleges in the light of acute shortage of seats for post graduate medical students.

Issues in the Medical Insurance Sector

An excellent growth rate and the promise of becoming an international destination for healthcare belie statistics citing that a very low percentage of the Indian population can access healthcare facilities. The poor and lower middle class strata of the society cannot afford corporate hospitals while the state of public hospitals is disappointing. Even among the middle class people only those with insurance go to corporate hospitals and the others go to government hospitals or small nursing homes.

In India, more than 50 per cent of the total health expenditure comes from the individual, as against state level contribution of below 30 per cent. Currently only about 0.2 per cent of the population are covered under voluntary medical insurance while 3% to 5% of Indians are covered under any form of health insurance. The Indian health insurance scenario is a mix of mandatory social health insurance (SHI), voluntary private health insurance and community-based health insurance (CBHI). The main provider of health insurance in the public sector is the governmentrun General Insurance Company (GIC), along with its four subsidiaries, The New India Assurance Company, Oriental Fire and Insurance Co., National Insurance Co., and The United India Insurance Co.

While over 75 per cent of private health insurance is concentrated with six leading players —ICICI Prudential, SBI life, Bajaj Allianz, Reliance Life, Birla Sun Life and HDFC Standard. The existing mandatory health insurance schemes in India—the Employees' State Insurance Scheme (ESIS) and the Central Government Health Scheme (CGHS)—were first started as pilot projects in 1948 and 1954, respectively in the context of achieving universal coverage via the SHI.

The reasons for the lack of penetration of health insurance among the masses:

- *Lack of Regulations or Control over Provider Behaviour*: The unregulated environment and a near total absence of any form of control over providers regarding quality, cost or data-sharing, makes it difficult for proper underwriting and actuarial premium setting. This puts the entire risk on the insurer as there could be the problems of moral hazard and induced demand. Most insurance companies are therefore wary about selling health insurance as they do not have the data, the expertise and the power to regulate the providers. Weak monitoring systems for checking fraud or manipulation by clients and providers, add to the problem.

- *Unaffordable Premiums and High Claim Ratios*: Increased use of services and high claim ratios only result in higher premiums. The insurance agencies due to lack of adequate information also tend to overestimate the risk and fix high premiums. Besides, the administrative costs are also high— over 30%, *i.e.* 15% commission to agent; 5. 5% administrative fee to TPA; own administrative cost 20%, etc. Patients also experience problems in getting their reimbursements including long delays to partial reimbursements.
- *Reluctance of Health Insurance Companies to Promote their Products and the Lack of Innovation*: Since health insurance is not exclusive as a product by itself therefore insurance companies do not take any initiative at promoting it. This is so because insurance companies cannot sell both life and non-life insurance products and hence finding non-life insurance such as theft, fire, health more profitable. Insurance companies tend to compete by adding a low incentive such as a premium health insurance to select clients thereby cross-subsidizing the resultant losses. With a view to get the non-life accounts, insurance companies tend to provide health insurance cover at unviable premiums. Thus, there is total lack of any effort to promote health insurance through campaigns regarding the benefits of health insurance and lack of innovation to make the policies suitable to the needs of the people.
- *Too many Exclusions and Administrative Procedures*: Apart from delays in settlement of claims, non-transparent procedures make it difficult for the insured to know about their entitlements, because of which the insurer is able to, on one stratagem or the other, reduce the claim amount, thus demotivating the insured and deepening mistrust. The benefit package also needs to be modified to suit the needs of the insured. Exclusions go against the logic of covering health risks, though, there can be a system where the existing conditions can be excluded for a time period—one or two years but not forever. Besides, the system entails equity implications.
- *Inadequate Supply of Services*: There is acute shortage of supply of services in rural areas such as there are very few hospitals where even basic surgeries are performed and barely one or two for specialist treatment. So an orthopedic or cardio consultancy one might have to make a trip to the nearest town/city.

- *Covariate Risks*: If the prevailing level of risks that could affect a majority of people is high more so in a nation like India where the incidence of communicable diseases is high, the insurance industry would become non-viable. There would be no gains from forming large pools and the premiums would be high as well again restricting the affordability of health insurance.

Another issue with the health insurance sector is the existence of a number of failures that characterize the insurance market. Firstly, it is the asymmetry in information that puts both the patient and the insurer at a disadvantage due to their inability to resist or challenge medical opinion regarding an existing condition or future treatment. Another is that in the absence of knowledge of prices the provider can actually overcharge.

Moreover a cashless insurance creates disincentives to control costs as the patient as well as the provider start perceiving it as a free good often resulting in excessive treatment by the producer for example he may increase the hospital stay of the patient or for that matter the patient may actually go to the hospital for a condition that could have been cured by a home remedy (moral hazard).

Thirdly, it is only the patients who know their health status. Since it is normally those in need of health care who tend to subscribe to health insurance, this puts the risk on insurance agencies to resort to extensive processes of risk selection, such as medical examination, before being given admittance as an enrollee and focusing on low risk groups, such as the young or healthy. Risk selection in individual-based policies however results in increasing the loading fee and consequently the cost of premium. For these reasons private insurance companies take only select consumers-young, rich and healthy while leaving the bad risks to the government.

Market Failure due to Information Asymmetry

The market failure arises in this case due to the fact that the consumers play no role in deciding the kind of goods and services to be purchased in this case medicines and healthcare facilities since they lack the knowledge to make such decisions and rely on the decision taken by their doctor or pharmacist.

This sort of market failure does not characterize the market for bulk drugs because the buyers of the same are pharmaceutical companies who are very aware consumers. The competition in the formulations sector is distinct. In any market producers compete to sell the best quality product at the lowest possible price however in the formulations sector this is not the case since the demand for medicines is highly price inelastic and hence the producers have no incentive to keep their prices low.

In most developed nations most individuals are covered by either public or private insurance and hence it is the government which bears most of the cost of the medicines. Thus the government in its role as a monopsonist will regulate prices and try to keep them reasonably low. However in the developing nations most patients are neither covered by public nor private health insurance. Companies in such nations do not compete via prices but rather through innovation.

In such cases where consumers are not the decision makers are often misguided by doctors and pharmacists into purchasing expensive medicines and sometimes even irrational combinations of medicines leading to medical complications. It is here where the efficiency of the market is lost with patients not being provided with the best possible treatment/medicines at the lowest possible prices. Alternatively, this market failure can be addressed in a similar situation of self referral, a doctor may refer a patient to a particular diagnostic centre in return for incentives say in the form of a commission even though it is expensive and the patient could have availed similar services at much lower charges elsewhere.

Low FDI in the Healthcare Sector

Post 1991- the healthcare industry has completely opened up to FDI in hospitals however actual statistics show that there is very little presence of FDI in the industry. Out of 90 FDI projects approved for hospitals and diagnostic centres between the years 2000-2006 only 21 were for the hospitals. In fact private equity funding turns out to be more prevalent than FDI in the sector. This shows that there are definitely issues curtailing long term FDI to be an attractive and beneficial investment. Possible factors at work are of both types domestic as well as external.

Domestic factors include:

- Massive upfront costs of setting up as a result of infrastructural constraints
- The Indian Medical Device industry largely relies on imports and capacity for local manufacturing is very low and thus the costs are huge.
- The medical education sector being inappropriately regulated is a major cause for shortages of medical professionals among other inadequacies of the medical education sector.
- Healthcare is still inaccessible for a large section of the Indian population largely due to the low penetration of private health insurance and absence of mandatory public health insurance.
- Absence of an adequate regulatory framework for maintaining quality and standards of services provided.

External factors such as the limitation in the developed countries on the number of private players who can invest abroad; lack of localized information about the market of the country where the investment is to be made influence the investors decision to invest.

INTERNATIONAL ISSUES

International Cartels

India has been a victim of an international cartel once which costs the nation a grossing US $ 3 million. This was the case of the bulk vitamins cartel. Other issues in this regard arise from export cartels as well as import cartels. Although most countries exempt export cartels from their antitrust laws so long as they don't distort the domestic market. Import cartels formed by domestic importers, or buyers and similar arrangements(such as boycotts of, or collective refusal to deal with, foreign competitors), may be a threat to maintaining competition in the market.

Cross Border Mergers in the Pharmaceutical Sector

Large pharmaceutical companies often in order to get a foothold in market of another country or to adopt a quick growth strategy enter into cross border mergers and acquisitions. India known for its generics, cost effectiveness and cost competitiveness is a favourite destination when it comes to mergers. Recently cross border mergers into India have been on a rise. The year 2009 saw the biggest merger in the generic market when Japan's 3rd largest drug maker Daiichi Sankyo took over India's Ranbaxy Laboratories.

Cross-border mergers place Indian companies on the global map. Being a significant part of the global pharmaceutical sector will help the Indian companies to take further steps in maintaining the global pharmaceutical standards which would be beneficial for them in all segments including exports, increased profitability, increase in the R&D laboratories, funding received by the companies, increased number of patented products, expansion of their market share etc. This in turn will be beneficial to the global pharmaceu-ticals as well since the cost effective techniques used by Indian companies and the huge market India provides to this sector can help enhance the research and creation of newer and improved drugs. However this is so long as such mergers do not hamper the efficiency and competitiveness of the domestic market.

High Import Duty on Pharmaceuticals

Barring a few life saving drugs that face an import duty of 5%, all other pharmaceuticals are levied at 10%. Such high rates of duty hamper import competition and thus reduce access to affordable medicine. It is thus suggested that lowering of import duty will help promote competition.

ANTI-COMPETITIVE PRACTICES IN THE PHARMACEUTICAL AND THE HEALTH DELIVERY SYSTEM

THE PHARMACEUTICAL INDUSTRY

The Indian Pharmaceutical industry is highly fragmented and there is no single market. It is divided into therapeutic segments *i.e.* vitamins, respiratory disorders, cardio ailments, anti-fungal etc. It is highly technology and knowledge intensive sector ad its capabilities are not limited to only drug manufacturing but research and development as well. The market is very different from others in that it is characterized by market failure particularly in the formulations sector.

The organized sector majorly responsible for the formulations comprises of some 250-300 players and accounts for about 70% of the total value of production. The top ten companies account for 30% of the total sales. Even though the individual market shares of companies is small this does not however imply that the market is characterized by intense competition. This again is primarily due to the fragmented nature of the market and that there are several relevant markets.

Apart from the distinct competition scenario, it is to be noted that a number of anticompetitive practices pervade the pharmaceutical industry worldwide, including in India.

Such practices may be categorised into primarily three classes:

1. Collusions
2. Mergers and Acquisitions (horizontal or vertical)
3. Abuse of Dominance (intellectual property rights related)

Though knowledge about most anti-competitive practices is not in plenty, as India did not have an effective competition regime, several mergers and acquisitions have taken place in recent years and many of them might have had serious implications for competition in the market.

Collusions

Collusions in the pharmaceutical sector can range from cartelization, cross licensing to bid-rigging. Though there haven't been as such cases of collusions in the Indian pharmaceutical sector but there for sure is scope and tendency for such a possibility. There was an international cartel of bulk vitamins present for quite some time and cost India about US$25mn, in the 1990s, as a result of overcharging. While the cartel was penalized in all rich country jurisdictions, but not in a single developing country. Cartelization through cross licensing may also be anti-competitive since by doing so competitors allocate territories among themselves and create entry barriers. In fact with India now having adopted the product patent regime it is more vulnerable to collusive practices more so because of the increasing presence of MNCs in the Indian industry.

Mergers and Acquisitions

At present the market for pharmaceuticals is highly fragmented and mergers and acquisitions could lead to consolidation of market shares. Such consolidation of market position can be done via brand acquisition, company acquisition or product rationalization. Recently Nicholas Piramal has taken the ownership of 17% of biosyntech that is a major pharmaceutical packing organization in Canada.

Matrix has acquired Docpharma, a major pharmaceutical company of Belgium. While, Sun Pharmaceutical Industries had announced its plans for acquisitions in the US and had earmarked $450 million for this purpose. However such acquisition becomes anti-competitive in nature when it leads to creation of a dominant position in the market in which they operate and if there is abuse of such a dominant position leading to higher prices and reduced output.

Abuse of Dominance

The ownership of an IPR grants the company exclusive rights to produce and sell their drugs in the market for a limited period of time. Such rights are particularly important for the pharmaceutical products since the manufacturing process is easy to replicate and can be copied with a fraction of the investment of that required for research and clinical testing. It is often believed that the patent law is an exception to the general rule in favour of competition but the argument for patent is that without granting a temporary monopoly, there would be no incentive for the firms to invest in research and development.

However patentees often such misuse these rights to the detriment of the consumer by selling the medicine at monopolistically profit maximizing price levels and thereby curbing access to affordable medicine. Till such time India had a patent regime protecting the process involved there was no threat of abuse of dominance. With India adopting product patient regime in 2005 such instances may become frequent as producers resort to monopolistic practices. Another strategy used in abuse of dominance is that of restricting the entry of generics in the market.

This can be very detrimental to the consumers as they'll lose access to affordable medicines. Often companies with patented products create artificial entry barriers for generic drug manufacturing companies by setting up their own range of generics so as to recover the losses that they would have to bear upon expiry of the patent. Other practices resorted to by patentees include refusal to license, resale price maintenance and patent pooling. In the health delivery system we shall limit ourselves to the anti-competitive practices widespread among doctors, pharmacist, hospitals and diagnostic labs.

DOCTORS

One of the most rampant unethical practices witnessed among doctors these days is irrational drug prescription. Doctors sometimes motivated by the kickbacks received from the pharmaceutical companies and sometimes simply do not make any effort to find cheaper alternatives and continue prescribing the expensive drug. This practice is seen often is because of the market failure that exists here with the patient who is not at the deciding end.

Since such a practice violates the basic competition policy *i.e.* provision of the best possible services at the lowest possible prices, thus it is anticompetitive. Moreover doctors often accept commissions for referrals which does not lead to rational decision making again impinging upon a basic tenet of competition policy. Therefore do not practice free and fair competition. Having said this does not take away from the fact that it is not always the case that there is a profit motive behind the doctor prescribing an expensive drug or referring their patients to a particular diagnostic centre.

At times it is also the case that they are aware that the prescribed drug is more effective or has fewer side effects than its cheaper counterpart. Similarly, the doctor may send his/her patient to a certain diagnostic lab due to the superior quality of services offered there.

PHARMACISTS

Most pharmacy owners in India are members of a trade association, All India Organisation of Chemists and Druggists (AIOCD). This association is nothing short of a cartel with almost 64. 25% of all pharmacists are members of AIOCD.

The AIOCD is known to launch boycotts against drug companies in order to grab higher profit margins. In fact price decontrol has led to greater trade margins for the pharmacists in fact this actually beats the purpose of decontrol of prices *i.e.* to allow the manufacturers o be able to spend more on R&D. In fact this manner while the pharmacists grab greater profits the retail price continues to be higher with the consumer being the ultimate sufferer.

Company	Brand	MRP	Purchase Price of Retailers
Ranbaxy	Stannist	26	1 80
Cadila Healthcare	Ceticad	26	1. 60
Cipla	Ceticip	27. 5	2. 00
Lupin	Lupisulide	24	1. 94
Wockhardt	Setride	25. 2	1. 70
Lyka Labs	Lycet	25	1. 44
Ranbaxy	Pyrestat-100	25	1. 50
Welcure Drugs	Omejel Caps	33	4. 50
Wockhardt	Merizole-20	39	6. 48

However high trade margins are not only due to the bargaining power of the pharmacists but also due to manufacturers strategy to capture greater market shares through providing incentives to doctors and pharmacists. Another instance of anti-competitive practices to be considered is the informal collusion of the pharmacists at the local level.

For example consider this, the Maximum Retail Price (MRP) that is set by the manufacturers under the guidelines of the National Pharmaceutical Pricing Authority (NPPA), is the ceiling on the retail price and need not be the actual selling price. However retailers do not compete and the MRP becomes the reference price for them to collude informally.

HOSPITALS

There is not much that is known about the practices of hospitals. Though there have been cases now and again about hospitals entering into agreements with drugs manufacturers to exploit consumers.

There was a case brought in front of the consumer forum in Andhra Pradesh In which a private hospital had entered into an agreement with a drug manufacturer to supply drugs to the hospitals at prices above the market price. Such hidden costs are anti-competitive in nature as the consumer pays more than warranted.

An anti-competitive practice that is particularly prevalent in the healthcare system is that of Tied Selling. Tied Selling refers to situations where the sale of one good is conditioned on the purchase of another good. Tied selling is sometimes a means of price discrimination. It may foreclose opportunities for other firms to sell related products or may increase barriers to entry for those who do not offer a full-line of products. Tied selling can occur if market players act in collusion and all the players force such tied selling.

Several surveys have revealed that consumers visiting private doctors or private hospitals witnessed tied selling of medicine as well as diagnostic tests. Doctors would instruct that their patients to buy the prescribed medicine from a particular shop or to get a test done from a particular laboratory. Though there is a chance the doctor advise their patients to take the test at a particular diagnostic centre due to greater reliability of its services however profit motive cannot be ruled out as a motive.

Often what is also done by doctors is suggesting more tests than necessary which may again be because of some arrangement for profit between the doctor and the diagnostic centre. This also violates the basic tenet of competition as it fails to provide the best possible service at the lowest possible price and hence is anti-competitive in nature.

In a survey conducted by CUTS International, only 15% of the respondents claimed that they had been asked to purchase medicine from a particular shop. On an average, those visiting private doctors or private hospitals, reported higher incidence of tied selling of medicines. When healthcare service providers were asked about tied selling of medicines, only 11% admitted that they had ever resorted to such practices while 35% of them believed that other doctors resorted to tied selling practices with a profit or commission consideration.

Consumers with higher income have relatively less problems with such practices since the price differentials may have lesser significance for richer people and easy availability may be a greater concern. However it is the poor who suffers here since he has to pay a price beyond his means and little resources to spare for finding alternative solutions.

COMPETITION LAW AND THE HEALTHCARE SECTOR

IS THE COMPETITION LAW APPLICABLE TO THE HEALTHCARE SECTOR

Healthcare sector is distinct from other sectors in that there exists an inherent asymmetry of information that renders it difficult for the sector to compete in the manner that other sectors do. For this reason it is often believed that the competition law may not be applicable to healthcare in the way it is applied in other sectors. However the ultimate purpose of any competition law is to protect the interest of the consumer and to ensure efficiency and competitiveness in the market. The competition law is applicable to healthcare players if they can be considered as undertakings. Since hospitals, health professionals, health insurers, pharmaceutical firms, pharmacists, etc. perform economic activities thus they can be considered to be undertakings and hence are subject to competition rules. Even in countries where there is little competition among the health care players due to excessive regulation, a hospital entering into an agreement with another hospital or pharmaceutical firm would have to comply with the competition law.

THE ROLE OF COMPETITION LAW IN ENSURING QUALITY PROVISION OF HEALTH SERVICES

The application of competition law improves the quality of care by protecting the patient against unfair and anticompetitive practices such as abuse of dominant position, distribution agreements, etc. At times practices that restrict competition may themselves be quality enhancing in that case competition law may make an exception. In the United States competition law has opened the door to alternative practitioners and forms of practice and enhanced quality by maximizing choice in the marketplace.

COMPETITION LAW IN INDIA AND THE HEALTHCARE SECTOR

The competition policy in India is laid out in the Competition Act, 2002. When the Competition Act replaced the MRTP Act, 1969, there was a shift in the focus from curbing monopolies to promoting competition. The Competition Act 2002 aims to prevent practices having an adverse affect on competition and abuse of dominance of enterprises either by entering into anti competitive agreements, or combinations.

The Act typically focuses on four areas:

1. Anti-Competitive Agreements
2. Abuse of dominance
3. Combination Regulation
4. Competition Advocacy

The first three areas give rise to competition concerns in the pharmaceutical and the health delivery system as seen earlier.

Anti-competitive Agreements

In Section 3 of the Competition Act deals with the prohibition of agreements, which have an adverse effect on competition. It states that no enterprise or association of enterprises or person or association of persons shall enter into any agreement in respect of production, supply, distribution, storage, acquisition or control of goods or provision of services, which causes or is likely to cause an appreciable adverse effect on competition within India.

The specific anti-competitive practices of the pharma-ceutical and health delivery system covered under Section 3 of the Act are collusive agreements including cartels, tied selling, exclusive supply agreements, exclusive distribution agreements, refusal to deal and resale price maintenance. The prohibition of cartel agreements (price fixing, output restricting, market sharing or bid rigging) between enterprises or persons is the strongest provision in the Act however the act shall not apply in case such an agreement increases efficiency in production, supply, distribution, storage, acquisition or control of goods and provision of services.

Having said this it must be noted that cartels may increase efficiency but alongside may also increase prices that may be detrimental to the consumers. However there is an exception in the law for IPR-related agreements. Section 3(5) states that under reasonable conditions that an IPR holder may apply to protect his rights may not be regarded as anti-competitive, although what is reasonable has not been defined well.

Abuse of Dominance

The Competition Act does not prohibit the mere possession of a dominant position but only the abuse of such dominance by the way of imposition of unfair or discriminatory conditions of purchase/sale or unfair/discriminatory pricing. Abuse of dominance may arise in the pharmaceutical industry in the case of abuse of monopoly status granted by patents. Thus in case pharmaceutical companies engage in overpricing patented products or are unreasonable with respect to licensing terms etc then the competition law may be resorted to for redressal.

It is important to note that increasing prices of drugs *per se* is not an anti-competitive practice however considering the peculiarity of the pharmaceutical industry wherein the consumer cannot choose the lowest price medicines it may actually be anti-competitive. This can be understood in the following manner- in case a drug is overpriced and there are generic substitutes available then there'll no impact on competition.

However if the pharmaceutical firm manages to convince a number of doctors of the superiority of their drug and doctors prescribed accordingly then the drug in question would attain a monopoly position. In this manner overpricing can actually have anti-competitive effects. The Indian Act has provisions for unfair or discriminatory pricing however excessive pricing is not mentioned expressly and hence it is considered to be a part of the former. This is an important provision considering the issue of accessibility to medicines under the recently adopted product patent regime.

Mergers and Acquisitions

Section 5 of the Competition Act deals with what is denoted by a combination of enterprises and persons, delineating the specific circumstances as per which the acquisition of one or more enterprise by one or more persons. The Act provides for merger review beyond a certain threshold level which would be defined as the turnover of the group to which the enterprise would belong after the completion of the acquisition or merger. Unlike most other countries merger notification in India is not compulsory and is only voluntary. Moreover since the threshold level for regulation is quite high, the Indian industry may become an easy target for MNCs for acquisition.

Cross Border Competition Issues

The Competition Act, 2002 has extra-territorial jurisdiction reach with respect to having an effect on competition in India.

- Anti-Competitive Agreements
- Abuse of Dominance
- Combinations

However the provision only empowers the commission to enquire into such an agreement, it does not mention anything about the option to pass an order in this regard.

CHALLENGES AHEAD

Notwithstanding the sector's rapid growth and potential, in many respects, India's healthcare sector falls well below international benchmarks for physical infrastructure and manpower, and even falls below the standards existing in comparable developing countries. The total number of doctors (all kinds included) per thousand persons stood at only 1.27 in 2006 and 0.5 physicians per thousand persons in India, compared to a world average of 1.5. The number of nurses per thousand persons stood at 0.9 in 2006 compared to a world average of 1.2.

Added to this deficiency is the mal-distribution between rural and urban areas and shortages of specialized personnel. These ratios are projected to remain below the existing world averages even in 2016. The current ratio of beds per thousand persons is a mere 1.03 (well below the WHO norms) compared to an average ratio of 4.3 for developing countries like China, Korea, and Thailand, and in the best of circumstances is projected to reach 1.85 per thousand persons by 2012. It is estimated that over a million beds have to be added to attain this 1. 85 ratio, which translates into a total investment of $78 billion (₹ 350,830 crores) in health infrastructure.

An additional 800,000 physicians are required over the next 10 years, which in turn translates into huge investments in training facilities and equipment. In order to reach even 50-75 per cent of the present levels of other developing countries, the sector will require an estimated investment of $20-30 billion. Thus, India's healthcare sector needs to scale up considerably in terms of the availability and quality of its physical infrastructure as well as human resources so as to meet the growing demand and to compare favourably with international standards.

INCREASE IN GOVERNMENT SPENDING

Level of public expenditure needs to be enhanced considerably. Moreover regional disparities existing in the provision of health services also need to be brought down. On a priority basis government should fill up vacant seats of medical professionals, improve quality of infrastructure and availability and accessibity to medicines.

ESTABLISHMENT OF AN INDUSTRY BODY

The healthcare sector is highly fragmented and thus there needs to be formed a common industry body comprising of the representatives from all the segments of the industry. The body can address the issues faced by the industry; provide frameworks for improvements in the level of services provided and achievement of higher industry standards.

INCREASE PPPS

There is surely a need to increase the number of PPPs alongside efforts should be made to strike a good balance between the objectives of the public and the private sector. This can be ensured by building a scalable and financially sustainable business model as well as providing equitable healthcare services. Besides these, the anti competitive practices cited in the above stages some of which even though not much prevalent in India in the present day context pose as a potential threat to the efficient provision of medical services to the common man. The tied selling of medicines and diagnostic tests often is detrimental to patient who is largely uninformed and thus easily falls prey to such practices.

Following are some issues that need to be addressed not only to tackle anti-competitive practices but also to foster competition in the sector and ensure quality healthcare services to the consumers.

- Absence of a regulatory framework to monitor rent seeking behaviour of doctors and pharmacists.
- With the product patent regime now in place, mergers and IPR related abuse of dominance will raise competition concerns in time to come and thus there is a need for preparedness to tackle such problems.

- Identification of anti-competitive practices in the sector that are not explicit. Since competition does not affect the healthcare sector the way it does other sectors there is a need to devise a mechanism to ensure identification of such issues.
- A provider information disclosure needs to be put into place so as to reduce the asymmetries of information for consumers and insurers. Ensuring that information about procedures and ailments reach consumers will help reduce the informational barrier to some extent. This can be done through media and internet.
- Regulatory barriers in the medical education sector need to be looked into to ensure adequate supply of well trained professionals.
- Reduction of the present high import duty in order to foster effective import competition and ensure accessible and affordable medicine to all.

6

The Experience and Problems of Insurance Marketing

INTRODUCTION

The insurance business has been growing relatively fast in the latter years in India. At the end of 2004 there were operating 28 insurance companies in India: 9 life insurance companies and 19 non-life insurance companies. The effective way of contemporary development and improvement of insurance activities is the active and ingenious application of marketing methods and activities. In the latter years, all Western insurance companies systematically, methodically and thoroughly has been using insurance marketing in order to stay up on the insurance market or to take the bigger part of it. The interest of insurance marketing began growing only since 1996 in India. Approximately in 1998 several big insurance companies established marketing departments.

Nevertheless, insurance marketing in India is still not systematic and methodical and is being applied only episodically, without any additional profound marketing research.

- *The Subject of the Research*: The marketing activities of the Indian insurance companies.
- *The Object of the Article*: To evaluate the condition of insurance marketing applying in Indian insurance companies.
- *The Main Objectives*: To analyse the marketing application experience in Indian insurance companies while overviewing the experience of Western companies; to reveal preconditions and trends of the insurance marketing application development in Indian insurance companies.
- *The Methods of the Research*: Observation, search for analogues and interpretations, theoretical analysis and characterization.

THE NECESSITY AND POSSIBILITIES OF INSURANCE MARKETING APPLICATION IN INDIAN INSURANCE COMPANIES

The necessity of applying insurance marketing in Indian insurance companies arose due to the development of market relations and because of the growth of private insurance business. The legal preconditions for the insurance business development in India were framed in 1990. The organizational problems of insurance marketing application are directly related to the Indian insurance market's condition and to its development tendencies. The latter may either induce or restrict the necessity of marketing application.

The private insurance business in India has been developing in difficult and contradictory conditions, constantly influenced by the consequences of the economic and social life stagnation. Today it is possible to state without any doubt that the Indian insurance market has already experienced the primary stage of its development. From the organizational point of view it is a whole of insurance services suppliers and consumers, connected by certain juridical and economic relationship. This market sells specific product–the insurance service that guarantees insurance security. Although the present day Indian insurance market is still in a way a market of a transition period, it already has comparatively complex system.

It consists of the following main elements:

- Economic contents influenced by the relations between market participants and their interests, related to rendering insurance services that would satisfy the needs of all clients;
- *Organizational Contents*: It is being defined by institutional, root, territorial and inner structures;
- Mechanism of regulation of insurance market's processes.

It is necessary to pay attention to the fact that even from the very beginning of the 21st century some development tendencies of the Indian insurance market that influence the necessity to apply insurance marketing in the activities of the insurers more actively and thoroughly have been noticeable. While the competition between the insurers on the Indian insurance market is getting more and more severe, the tendencies of their specialization become visible. The insurers try to involve into new segments of their customers and to occupy certain niche in their market. Furthermore, some structural changes take place in the insurance companies themselves–the organizational management system, founders, stock structure, etc.

Nevertheless, it is still too early to speak about the stability of the Indian insurance market, for not all the registered insurance companies are able to render qualified insurance services. Some of them approach the fold up, the other have already bankrupted. The majority of the Indian insurers are not able to insure big risks.

Without any doubt, the more rapid development of the Indian insurance market is not possible due to the comparatively small purchasing power of the people and the subjects of economy. So far, there are no reinsurance companies in India that would be occupied with reinsurance business. This influences negatively the development of the Indian insurance market. There is no separate reinsurance services market in India.

The approach towards insurance business is changing in India, especially the approach of the legislative and executive power. There are visible attempts to comprehend that insurance is able to influence economical processes and, therefore, it should receive bigger support from the executive. Insurance business, successful activities of which are only possible under the conditions of stable economy, could become the factor subject of such stabilization.

Meanwhile, the development and further expansion of the market intercourse relations influences the middle layer of the society and the businessmen-it helps them to understand their state and that no one could guarantee them stable state. Only due to their own endeavours and insurance, that would compensate all the possible losses, it is possible to retain the achieved level of personal life or business, or, in some cases, even improve it.

At present, foreign capital companies dictate the terms in the Indian insurance market, though, leaving some space for the so-called niche companies as well. There should be distinguished bank insurance companies, which receive their clients directly from banks. The so-called niche insurance companies that generally are oriented towards one kind of insurance still have possibilities to stay on the market. The changing environment helps to ascertain that small insurance companies are able to react timely to the changes of the market and submit quality objects of the insurance services.

Young and foreign capital related insurance companies have been operating in the Indian insurance market since 2000. 15 insurance companies were controlled directly by foreign shareholders in 2004. 67.8 per cent of all insurance companies authorized capital belonged to the direct foreign shareholders. Foreign capital insurance companies, while entering the market, submit cheaper insurance products; therefore other participants of the market are forced to reconsider their payments' tariffs.

The entrance of the western insurers into the Indian market should be considered positively. They use their long-lived business organization experience and have great potential to guarantee safety to the insured. The investments of the western insurers are much bigger than those of the Indian insurers. On the other hand, foreign investors have accumulated insurance marketing application experience. Since the competition on the Indian insurance market is getting more and more severe it is necessary for the Indian insurance companies to start applying marketing means in their insurance activities as well.

There are general preconditions for this. The heads of Indian insurance companies and other specialists study the experience of applying insurance marketing in western insurance companies. Qualification improvement courses and seminars on insurance marketing for employees are being organized. It is necessary to mention that some of Indian insurers not only comprehend that it is necessary to apply insurance marketing in their activities, but also try to implement some of its complex elements in their business organization system. Nevertheless, in many cases this process takes place spontaneously, for little attention is being paid to the marketing researches and marketing activities' planning. There are little discussions on insurance marketing in mass media, there are no theoretic and practical recommendations given.

On the other hand, the Indian insurance market is still a long way off its mature stage. Therefore, it is too early to speak about the complex and thorough application of insurance marketing means and activities. However, heads of the Indian insurance companies should without delay professionally prepare to apply marketing means and activities. Those insurers, who up to now did not pay enough attention to the sectional applying of marketing means, should reconsider their attitude before the competition becomes even harsher and other insurers start aggressive activities on the market.

For even partial application of marketing means will enable insurers to solve problems of the contemporary market more effectively and become more prepared for the period when the market condition will require rapid implementation of insurance marketing complex based on the concrete marketing researches and planning.

THE MAIN TENDENCIES AND IMPROVEMENT PRECONDITIONS OF INSURANCE MARKETING APPLICATION

When analysing further development of insurance marketing in the Indian insurance companies it would be purposeful to name the factors that stimulate and disturb to apply insurance marketing.

- The development perspectives of the insurance marketing application are determined by:
  - The fact, that bigger insurance companies pay more attention to the individual customers' market (families) and this requires more active marketing activities;
  - The entering into the Indian insurance market western insurance companies, which pay much attention and spend funds to the research of that market;
  - The strengthening competition that would require more attention to the insurance marketing as to the important lever in fight for every client;
  - The establishment of marketing departments in separate insurance companies and more energetic activities of the independent insurance marketing consultants.
- Factors impeding the application of insurance marketing are as follows:
  - Insufficient experience of insurers while expanding insurance business, non-existence of long-term development strategies of insurance companies and the fact that insurers orient mostly to short-term needs;

- The complex application of the contemporary insurance marketing means is too expensive–many smaller insurance companies can not afford it;
- While trying to apply more actively insurance marketing means it is necessary to change the whole organizational management structure of an insurance company, the channels of insurance products sales, technologies of communication with clients, and etc.

THE MISSION OF THE INSURER AS ONE OF THE PRACTICAL DIRECTION OF INSURANCE MARKETING APPLICATION

Application of some insurance marketing element is first of all connected to the conceptual strategic aspects of insurers' activities. These aspects could be briefly defined by the functional purpose of an insurance company, the main principle of a company's activities and its mission. While attempting to reach competition advantages and adapt to the changes of the insurance market it would be advisable for insurance companies to determine their mission in two aspects: the outer and the inner one. The inner mission shows the development of insurance company itself.

Practically, it is related to the concept of the insurance company's management and marketing. The outer mission of an insurance company determines clients anchoring while satisfying their insurance needs. The inner mission helps to solve practical problems, related to the formation of the fold. This mission also helps to prevent manifestations of regionalism and search for egoistic additional privileges, etc. The outer mission becomes the inner energy of an insurance company, its, vital force" and the effective lever of competition fight.

The formulated mission of an insurance company determines its objectives, quantitative and qualitative, short-term and long-term. The mission of an insurance company could be determined only after thorough analysis of the insurance market, the objective market of its clients, the possibilities of the company itself on the market when compared to the competitors.

The chosen mission makes it possible to prepare general marketing strategy of an insurance company. The reasoned and comprehensible general marketing strategy is necessary for any insurance company. Then the insurance company can prepare programme of its activities, to point out the strategic objectives in it, as well as means to fulfil these objectives.

When over-viewing the development of the Indian insurance market and insurance companies, it would be advisable to prefigure the main objectives and means related to the improvement of insurance companies in their programmes. While both referring to the worldwide practice of insurance marketing application and to the attempts of the Indian insurers to apply marketing in their activities it is possible to state that there are no obstacles to prepare the strategy programmes just as to the needs, interests and expectations of potential clients. On the other hand, the strategy development programmes should be prepared on the ground of the information received while analysing and forecasting the tendencies of insurance market development, and while comparing them to the inner possibilities, similarities and shortcomings of an insurance company.

It is very important to evaluate similarities and shortcomings of an insurance company when servicing its clients. The similarities should be highlighted to be able to use certain possibilities of clients' insurance market. Every shortcoming of an insurance company should be evaluated from the point of view of its importance, as well as the possibilities of its overcoming should be estimated in order to transform the shortcoming into a benefit as quickly as possible.

From the point of view of perspective the survival and further development of an insurance company depend on the possibility of the company itself to accumulate information, to analyse it constantly in order to notice the changes of the insurance market and to respond to them properly. Strategic planning should help an insurance company to adapt to the constantly changing market. This is exceptionally important for such Indian insurance companies that still operate under the circumstances of the transition period.

The long-term strategic plan is usually prepared for 3-5 years. It covers the main factors and means of a company over that period of time and takes cognizance of the tendencies of a company's development and long-term objectives referring to the means that are necessary to fulfil them. Every strategic plan needs certain preconditions. The scale of these preconditions depends on the changes of the insurance market over the defined period of time.

While preparing the strategic plan of an insurance company it is necessary to refer to the following main principles:

- The plan should be prepared by the people, who will later on implement it;
- The level of the planning competency should correspond to the competency of using company's recourses;
- It is necessary to assure the flexibility of the planning and possibility to adapt to the inner and outer changes of a company's environment.

The strategic marketing planning is related to the marketing researches that supply the necessary information for the reasoned decisions. It is necessary to have in mind that the everyday information of an insurer that generally is used for managing insurance risks would not always be useful for marketing purposes. While implementing marketing, insurers have to obtain the so-called specialized information. It is generally received from the specialized marketing researches.

Such researches could be considered:

- Exploratory marketing researches that help to reveal and confirm various ideas and hypotheses;
- Descriptive researches that help to receive information about various hypotheses;
- Experimental marketing researches.

Without the necessary marketing information or using imprecise, outdated data it is easy to take misconceived decisions of insurance company's activities. Meanwhile, using the data received during the marketing researches should help to reduce the uncertainty of decisions. Therefore, there is the need to collect, store and analyse various information. Generally, Western insurance companies establish information banks.

When performing marketing research, it is purposeful to denote the following stages of this activity:

- The formation of the research objectives;
- The preliminary market research based on the all accessible secondary information;
- The operative planning of the marketing research, the specification of the object and instruments (for example, survey, questionnaire research, information analysis, etc.) of the research;
- The generalization of the received results (market receptivity, forecasts of servicing possibilities, motivating of clients, probabilistic customer reaction towards new insurance service, etc.).

Information received during the marketing research should define the object of the research both in a qualitative and quantitative way. Indian insurers have to pay more attention to the analysis of macroeconomic factors as well, for the size of insurance market and its development tempo depend on those.

Insurers should analyse systematically the market of insurance products customers in order to:

- Evaluate the changes of the market and to specify the objectives and strategies of their insurance company, and to develop the new ideas of business expansion;
- Reduce uncertainty while making decisions; evaluate if these decisions satisfy the needs, requests and expectations of their clients;
- Supervise the activities of an insurance company.

In order to reach marketing effectiveness and to make reasoned decisions on their activities in the selected objective market, the Indian insurers should pay more attention not only to the general marketing researches, but also to the special, more concrete researches. Heads of insurance companies should spend some time and money to receive trusted information, to analyse and to process it as well. The introduction of marketing department and evaluation of its functions in the organizational managing structure of an insurance company. In the latter years heads of the Indian insurance companies became more interested in the organizational structure of their companies and have been taking the initiative to improve and modernize it. Nevertheless, not all companies provide place for specialized marketing departments in their organizational structure.

Sales departments are dominant in the organizational managing structure of most Indian insurance companies. In some companies sales departments' employees perform marketing functions as well. Heads of the Indian insurance companies do not pay attention to the so-called inner marketing, which requires that marketing decisions should be taken not only by the employees of the specialized marketing department, but by other employees as well, especially those, who work with clients. We think that in the short run heads of the Indian insurance companies will start establishing marketing departments, will also evaluate their place and role they play in the overall organizational structure of their companies.

They will shortly ascertain that establishing marketing departments is the necessity determined by the development of the insurance market. The main functions of a marketing department are to receive trustworthy information about the processes and phenomena that take place on the insurance market, to process the received information, to analyse it and to prepare presentations for the management, who take strategic and tactical decisions. This department should form the demand for insurance services, create communication system with the clients, organize public relations, take care of the image-building of their company and etc. It is understood that most probably it is not purposeful to establish a whole separate marketing department in a company, nevertheless, other marketing specialists, working in another departments could perform its functions.

The necessity to pay more attention to the objective groups of clients (objective markets of clients). Indian insurers should form the organizational management structures of their companies taking cognizance of the clients segments, *i.e.* the groups of clients they are working with. Most often there are two groups distinguished: organizations (legal entities) and individual (private) clients or their families (households). As experience shows the viewpoints of working with these groups differ. Therefore, heads of the Indian insurance companies while, constructing" the organizational managing structure of their enterprises should consider the specifics of rendering services to different groups (segments) of customers.

The so-called organizational managing structure of an insurance company should be formed not just as to the so-called productive, but rather practical standpoint. The insurance companies that apply marketing in their activities should specialize their work just as to the objective groups of clients (segments) they are rendering their services to. Hence, heads of the Indian insurance companies should summon additional financial, organizational and intellectual resources to be able to work with the objective groups of clients. It is also worth mentioning, that Indian insurance companies still do not pay sufficient attention to the market segmentation. The other actual problems of the Indian insurance market while applying marketing are the improvement of services quality; the image-building of insurance companies; the modernization of service sales channels just as to the newest technologies; the consolidation of interaction between the insurers and the insured, etc.

While implementing marketing Indian insurers should evaluate the specifics of insurance marketing and only just as to that organize its activities. The observance of the mentioned specifics increases the efficiency of marketing, helps to evaluate more objectively the expectations of the insurance clients. Nevertheless, the majority of Indian insurers do not observe this important thing: they identify insurance marketing as an overall marketing, *i.e.* as the traditional marketing of a production kind. First of all, it is necessary to realise that the insurers do not submit to the insured simple insurance polices, but rather the solution of concrete problems based on the insurance risks that worry them most. The implementation of this idea is simple only at first glance. Basically, it covers certain profound, essential things related to both the insurer and the psychology of the insured and their motives of behaviour.

The situation that is now in the Indian insurance market is mainly determined by the transition from centralized economics to the market economics model. Such situation invokes a problem related to the necessity to realise the functional purpose of insurance services and their culture. Many people do not understand (and do not want to understand) the essence of insurance and the social economical role of it as well as the benefits it brings. On the other hand, the majority of people receive average and small revenue. They are precautious and careful about insurance. Some people understand insurance premiums not as safety guarantee but rather as purposeless waste of money. Therefore, having evaluated such a situation, insurers should try to make more efforts to enlighten society, to elevate its mentality and change its attitude towards insurance.

Indian insurers should pay more attention to the quality of their services and to the adaptation of these services to the needs of groups of people (segments), *i.e.* to differentiate insurance services. It is necessary to have in mind, though, that high quality of services, corresponding to the needs and expectations of the insured is a major factor of the insurance market's competitiveness.

Insurers should determine criteria of quality of their services and observe them while rendering insurance services to their clients. The criteria of services' quality should be clearly understood, measured and meet the requirement of clients, as well as correspond to the insurance traditions. Since people of Indiawhen choosing an insurance company give preference to its reliability, heads of the insurance companies should apply more actively those methods of marketing that build good image of a company. Under conditions of unstable Indian insurance market the image of an insurance company should symbolize the reliability and stability of its activities. Indian insurers should take care not only of the image of their own company, but also of the general reliable image of insurance business.

There are several elements in the image structure of insurers that are essential:

- Advantages of an insurer as compared to his competitors; his financial reliability and competence, as well as the authority of heads of an insurance company in the country, region, city;
- Historically developed point of view towards insurance, people moods and social stereotypes;
- Specialization of an insurer to render certain services and his influence to the image.

The whole insurer's communication system with the insured should guarantee the conveyance of an insurance company's image to both inner and outer surroundings. This system is a basis to many of the marketing activities: starting from choosing of the logo and ending up the interior design of the company's office, from business card or secretary work to publicity campaign.

Therefore, the condition of effective marketing for an insurer is the preparation of the plan of communication with clients in order to achieve two goals: become famous and become attractive. For more exact and concrete characteri-zation of their image insurers most often use slogans, for example, you'll receive aid", guaranteed tranquillity" and soon. The important peculiarity of insurance marketing is a specially created active insurance placing (sales) of channel system. The leading Indian insurance companies, especially those of foreign capital, create this kind of system having in mind the requirements of the insurance market. Indian insurance companies should pay more attention to the so-called direct marketing, the principles of which successfully use western insurance companies.

Indian insurers when working with clients-organizations most often use personal insurance sale. Insurers should propose not an insurance policy to the insured-organizations, but rather a complex system of financial, economical management of the risk reduction. Some Indian insurance companies have started paying more attention to working with insurance agents and training them to apply marketing principles in their activities in the past years.

Nevertheless, smaller insurance companies still neglect such activities. Special information material should be prepared for agents, as well as the scenario of the discourse with clients. It would also be advisable to attract psychologists, who would teach communication skills. The leading Indian insurance companies use unconventional channels when selling their products–banks, tourist agencies, post-offices, petrol stations, etc.

Nevertheless, only minority of insurance companies uses such method. The attempts of the insurers to sell their policies in banks are determined not only by the necessity to reduce costs, but also by the fact that bank clients become insurance companies' clients as well when buying insurance policies, especially life insurance policies.

It should be noted that Indian insurance market experiences transition period, but in the nearest future it should receive intense acceleration of development. Due to this, heads of the leading Indian insurance companies start applying certain insurance marketing methods in their activities and elements. These companies prepare to organize insurance marketing activities of a superior level that would base upon marketing researches, planning and strategy formations.

Though, such companies are still not numerous. In many companies marketing is applied episodically, spontaneously, fragmentarily. The main object of such companies now is to implement in more qualified manner the elements of insurance marketing and prepare to switch to its complex and methodical application in the future. It is already advisable to employ marketing specialists in such companies, who would be occupied with preparing marketing activities plan and step-by-step implementation of marketing.

CONCLUSIONS

Insurance marketing is a development process's result of the objective management of insurance business under the conditions of the economical market. The necessity of insurance marketing application is determined by the already developed objective and subjective conditions of the Indian insurance market. It should be noted that the leading Indian insurance companies have already started paying more attention to the problems of marketing application. They started implementing separate elements and means of insurance marketing in their activities, especially those elements related to sales of insurance products and advertising. Still, marketing is not methodically and systemically applied in the Indian insurance companies.

The main tendencies of insurance marketing application in the Indian insurance companies are as follows: the mission of the insurer as one of the practical directions of insurance marketing application; strategic planning of marketing based on the marketing researches; the introduction of marketing department and evaluation of its functions in the organizational managing structure of an insurance company; the necessity to pay more attention to the objective groups of clients.

7

Role of Relationship Marketing on Insurance Market

INTRODUCTION

Insurance market like the other financial markets has a great importance for the economy of every country, as the insurers have the capacity to concentrate a large amount of the savings made by population and companies in order to be further invested in the economic activities. For our country, the insurance market is more challenging as this one is not enough developed and has recorded huge increasing rates during the last years. Nevertheless, this trend could breakdown due to the financial crisis recorded in the developed countries, which seems to have a negative impact on the worldwide economic trends.

We started our research from a diagnosis of insurance market at the level of EU countries before the crisis, in order to find information about the position of Romanian market inside the internal market of EU. Such information was very valuable for possible solutions of the identified problems.

The research was based on a short literature review and on a statistical analysis of data provided by the member states. The outcomes showed us a low development of Romanian insurance market in comparison with the majority of member states, which is a strong reason both for theoreticians and policy makers to find solutions to overpass the negative effects and to re-launch this market. Beyond the negative effects, the crisis could offer a unique chance for our country to reduce the existing differences from the rest of EU members. In this respect, we found the relationship marketing tools as the best fitted for solving the researched problem at the level of insurance service providers.

LITERATURE REVIEW

The insurance activity "is working with the risk". It tries to protect the insured people against the risks that could occur in their field of activity, even in their life, spreading the liability between the premium payers in order to make the event supportable from financial point of view.

There are many examples of risk: a homeowner faces the possibility of economic loss caused by a house fire, a driver faces a potential economic loss if his car is damaged or if might have to pay for injures caused to a third party in a car accident. Normally, only a small percentage of policyholders suffer losses. Their losses are paid out of the premiums collected from the pool of policyholders. Thus, the entire pool compensates few unfortunates as each policyholder exchanges an unknown loss for the payment of a known premium. .

Insurance companies deal on the financial market, which has a high level of regulation in many countries. In this respect, European Commission proposed in 2005 a white chapter, which contains the EU financial services policy until 2010. Completing the single market in financial services is recognised as one of the key areas for EU's future growth, essential for EU's global competitiveness. The challenge of this new strategy has been to apply a better regulatory discipline in order to create the best financial framework in the world, with real benefits for the citizens and businesses of Europe through lower capital costs, better pensions and cheaper, safer retail financial products etc.

The regulatory system is necessary because the financial service providers are themselves exposed to risks. Insurers make money in two ways: from premiums charged to customers as payment for accepted risks and from the investment of a part of premiums in various financial and non-financial products. From these incomes they pay the claims of occurred risk and other administration expenses. The investment of money in risky financial products could lead to losses for insurance companies that could affect both the security of their customers and the confidence of these ones. In fact, such a situation happened with American International Group (AIG), the biggest insurer from USA.

The marketing of insurance products are made by the own agents of insurance companies or by intermediaries (independent agents and brokers). Brokers and agents search the market in order to find clients that need insurance. Additionally, brokers use their knowledge and access to the insurance marketplace for selecting among insurance products or risk management systems the ones that are best suited to the buyer's needs and desires.

The employees of brokers and agents often practice relationship marketing, searching their prospects among their friends or relatives. Due to their particularities, the insurance services are very suitable for applying relationship marketing principles.

RESEARCH METHODOLOGY AND OUTCOMES

This research started from a very strong problem discovered on the Romanian market as result of the financial crisis that generated a worldwide economic crisis with a negative impact at the level of a great part of the economic sectors. This negative outcomes could affect the Romanian insurance market, which has had an accelerated increasing before the first crashes recorded by the American financial sector. The research methodology is based on secondary data analysis, using public sources like official statistics provided by European and national institutes. The large majority of data was of quantitative nature, contained in longitudinal and crosssectional series.

Based on such data, we tried to make a Principal Component Analysis, using many variables related to insurance market, but it cannot be isolated more than one component due to a strong direct correlation between the analysed variables. Therefore we limited the analysis to a bivariate one, taking into account pairs of relevant variables. The research outcomes showed us a huge discrepancy between the Romanian insurance market and the similar markets of the most developed countries of EU. In the same time, we can find similarities among the newest EU members including Baltic and Central and Eastern European countries.

The main weakness of our research consists in the unavailability of recent data that could reflect the impact of the economic crisis on the insurance market. For this reason, the research should be continued when new data will be available. Such an analysis could give us a complete image of the EU markets and the rearrangements of the trends in every member state.

COORDINATES OF INSURANCE MARKET IN THE EUROPEAN UNION

The EU's insurance market is one of the largest worldwide, the European insurance groups being the leaders of the world in terms of financial strength and size. All the EU countries are associated to CEA, which is an insurance and reinsurance federation. Other 6 non-EU countries are members of this organisation (Norway, Liechtenstein, Turkey, Croatia, Iceland, and Switzerland).

The insurance market of CEA members generated in 2007 premium incomes of €1122bn, employed almost one million people and invested more than €7 200bn in the economy. This market has recorded significant increases in real terms (inflation adjusted) every year since 1995, with a single exception in 2001, when the total premiums dropped with 1.7%. In 2007, in spite of a good economic growth, the insurance sector in Europe recorded only a very slight increase in total premium income of 1.2% in real terms, after two consecutive years with 6.5% increase.

In Europe, life insurance accounted for more than 60% of overall premiums in 2007. Non-life insurance products followed closely by health and accident had market shares of respectively 12% and 11% of overall insurance premiums as far as property insurance recorded more than 7%. The dynamic of the main categories of insurance show a higher increase of life-insurance (1.7%) in comparison with just 0.4% recorded by non-life insurance premium in 2007

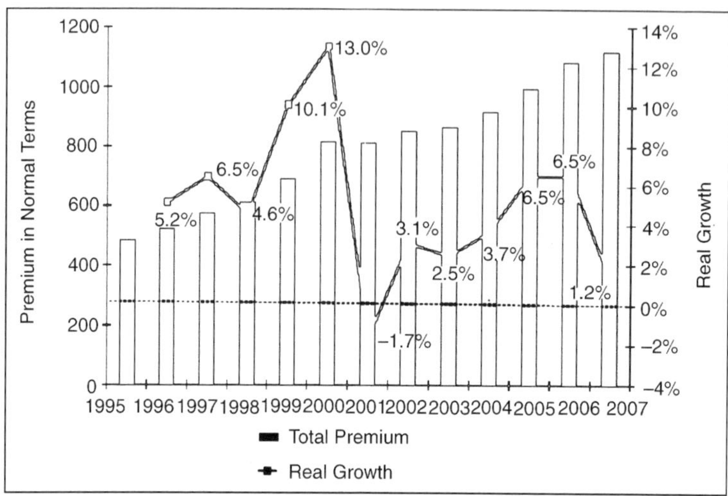

Fig. Total Premiums in Europe–1995-2007

Taking into account the figures recorded at the level of EU members (EU-27), we can find that this countries recorded 95% of the total premiums subscribed in 2007 on CEA market. In spite of this fact, there are still high discrepancies among EU countries even at the level of older members.

Thus, the countries of Euro zone represented 62% of the total premiums subscribed in EU-27. The gap is huger if we take into consideration that UK, the biggest insurance market of EU, gave 26.3% of total premiums subscribed in the CEA countries in 2007.

The analysis of statistical data at the level of EU member states indicates a strong correlation between the total subscribed premiums and the size of population on one hand and between the same variable and the number of insurance companies that activate on every local market on the other hand.

In the table above we can see that the Pearson correlation coefficient between the value of premiums and the population size is 0.825 and the same coefficient between the total premiums and the number of companies present on the local markets is 0.936. Both values indicate a direct correlation with a very high intensity. In addition, it can be found a strong direct correlation between the population size and the number of companies that activate on the market.

If we look at the top 3 countries just as to the value of premiums, the correlation is not the same, the association being an inverse one. In this respect, Germany is on the third place, even it has the highest population and UK is on the first place as premium values but on the third place as population.

Table. Top Countries According Premium Income

Country	Population (mil. People)	Premium Income (€ Million)	Share of Premium (%)
United Kingdom	60.6	295044.9	28%
France	63.2	194310.0	18%

Germany	82.4	163200.0	15%
Others	280.1	413407.8	39%
Total	486.3	1065962.7	100%

In order to identify the relative the main categories of insurance, we placed the EU members in the plane determined by the premiums subscribed in life and in non-life insurance. For comparability, data regarding the premium subscriptions were reported per capita in order to eliminate the influence of population size.

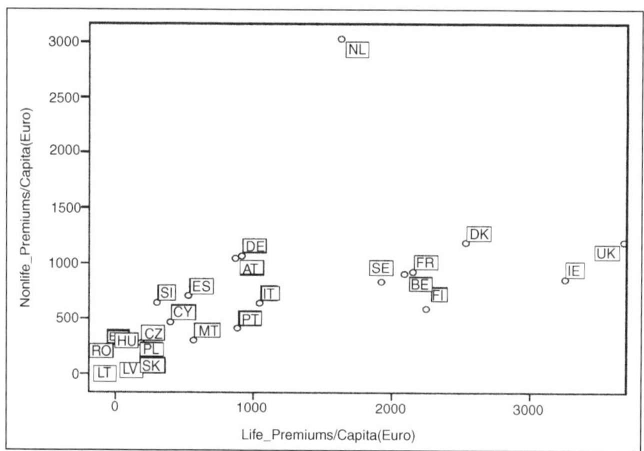

Fig. The Positions of EU Countries Just as to Life and Non-life Premiums

The highest level of life premiums per capita (21862 Euro) was recorded in Luxembourg, which was not placed on the chart from technical considerations. Excepting this country, in the chart, it can be seen the positions of UK and Ireland with the highest levels of life premiums per capita and the position of the Netherlands with the highest level of non-life premiums per capita. Denmark, Finland, France, Belgium and Sweden have also high levels of life premiums per capita. As regards non-life premiums, there is a high homogeneity among the former member countries (EU-15) excepting the Netherlands. All new EU members recorded very low levels of premium subscribed both for life and non-life purposes.

RELATIONSHIP MARKETING IN THE CRISIS PERIOD

The members of the Pan-European Insurance Forum agree that insurance industry is not immune to the effects of the current crisis even if the conventional insurers entered the crisis in a comparatively strong position because the specific characteristics of the insurance business model have protected the industry from the worst impacts of the financial turmoil. The sale of insurance products–in particular unit linked business in life-is expected to fall due to the economic slowdown.

A better regulatory system is necessary for the financial system. In this respect, large complex financial institutions have to be supervised in their entirety in order to obtain a much greater transparency for structured financial products. As well, regulators must step up their efforts to achieve convergence in accounting standards.

In our opinion, the insurers have to take their own anti-crisis measures. Such measures should be oriented mainly towards marketing strategies and activities, which need to be really focused on customer needs. In this respect, relationship marketing principles are the best suited for increasing trustworthiness of customer in the protection power of insurances and in the financial security of insurers. Generally, in the relationship marketing, companies have to establish strong relationships with their customers, to maintain them and to create a basis of mutual cooperation on long term. Furthermore, consumers desire relationship partners that they can trust. All of these ones are reasons of customer satisfaction that generate additional benefits at the level of companies.

The sale of insurance policies has all the characteristics that make it suitable for relationship marketing. It is well known a joke among insurance sellers, which states that "nobody goes to a supermarket (or other shops) in order to buy an insurance policy". In this context, the insurer agent has to contact the potential customers, to identify their necessities and to offer them insurance programmes that better fit their needs. As relationship marketing technique, the insurer could consider Multi-Level Marketing (MLM), which is still successfully used by some insurance brokers.

CONCLUSIONS

Insurance market has a high importance for the entire economy, so that it is necessary to put in practice cumulative measures to avoid as much as possible the negative effect of economic crisis. In these actions, the authorities should have a great implication but it is the insurers' duty to take their own decisions in the direction of using the relationship marketing tools.

As the crisis has a very negative impact on the trust worthiness of customers, the relationship marketing become much more than a fashion, being a powerful tool of trust building with positive effects on re-launching the insurance sales. Our research outcomes, for the Romanian market, such measures become more necessary as there is a wide gap in its relative position towards the developed countries of European Union.

The strong correlation existing between the insurance premiums and the number of population comes with additional arguments of the high potential of local market in spite of the current economic crisis. Further directions of this research should focus on the statistical data that are to be issued in order to measure the real impact of crisis and the tendencies of these data on medium and long term.

8

Insurance Distribution Channels: Markets in Transition

INTRODUCTION

The insurance marketplace is undergoing a transform-ation that may eventually lead to significant changes in how consumers purchase insurance products. A variety of distribution channels are currently used in this market place, and some insurers utilize a combination of distribution channels. These include the Internet-led channels, company-led channels, bank-led channels, and agent-led channels.

Of these distribution channels, the most discussed and anticipated channel is the Internet-led channel. The widespread diffusion of the Internet has created an explosion in the growth of electronic channels, including direct channels, electronic markets, or "electronic intermediaries over which multiple buyers and sellers do business", and other cyber me diaries. Prior to the advent of the Internet, most purchasers of insurance products used traditional agent-led distribution channels such as direct writers or independent agents. Given its reliance on traditional channels, the insurance marketplace has only recently begun to reflect this broader growth in electronic channels.

The Internet was expected to have a major negative impact on the traditional agent-led distribution channel. However, consumers have not shown a marked preference for purchasing insurance product via the Internet. Currently, less than two per cent of insurance products are purchased via the Internet. Although less frequently used, company-led distribution channels through mediums such as direct mail or telephone call centers have seen increasing growth. While an agent is still required in this setting, this person typically does not meet with the insured.

With the passage of the Financial Modernization Act of 1999, growth of the bank-led channel was predicted for the U.S. market. The results of a recent American Bank Insurance Association survey indicate that insurance represents a very small percentage of total bank revenue, but bankers predict an increase in marketing efforts.

While it is true that insurance purchasers today have more options available than they did five years ago, it is unclear if and when these channels will dominate existing insurance distribution channels. Several obvious factors that impact on a channel's adoption are consumer attitudes and preferences. In particular, it may be that consumers consider insurance products to be more complex than originally thought. Consumers still do not view even personal lines insurance products to be commodity products.

The purpose of this chapter is to discuss the transitions that are occurring in property/liability insurance distribution channels. As part of this discussion, we describe some of the factors that are impacting on the adoption of alternative channels (*e.g.*, the Internet), provide an overview of the academic literature on innovation adoption and insurance distribution channels, and comment on the near-term future for insurance distribution channels.

EXPECTATIONS V. REALITY

The growth of the Internet has led to a great deal of speculation and discussion regarding its potential impact on traditional distribution channels. For example, the meeting topic for the 2000 International Insurance Society meeting was "The Power of Leadership in the Knowledge Millennium." Part of the focus of the presentations at that meeting was on the changing channels of distribution. Some trade publications during that time period included articles suggesting that insurance agents were faced with the strong possibility of being replaced with a more efficient and less-costly Internet-led distribution channel. The same was true for travel agents during that time period. Interestingly, the experience of insurance agents and travel agents has been very different.

The travel industry has indeed seen a growth of the Internet-led distribution channel for a wide variety of travel-related purchases including plane tickets, hotel reservations, and car rentals. Examples of cybermarkets operating today include Expedia, Travelocity, and Orbitz. Additionally, sites allow consumers to make offers for various travel services including airline travel. Other sites, create an auction market for travel services.

Finally, consumers can purchase tickets online directly from airlines. As the Internet-led channel has grown for travel-related types of services, travel agents have come under increasing pressure and airlines have reduced the commissions paid to travel agents. In some cases, the agents are no longer compensated by the airlines to serve as a channel intermediary. For example, Delta Airlines recently announced that it would no longer pay commissions to travel agents. The experience of insurance agents has been much different. Recent figures suggest that online sales accounts for less than 2% of total premium volume. Although there have been some changes in the areas of commissions and production requirements, agents continue to be the primary distribution channel for insurance products.

A recent National Underwriter article reported the results of a survey of four insurance industry associations (the National Association of Independent Insurers, the National Association of Mutual Insurance Companies, the American Insurance Association, and the Alliance of American Insurers). All four of these associations indicated an expectation that the traditional agent-led distribution channel will continue to be a major distribution channel for insurers.

While the adoption rate of the Internet as a distribution channel has been low, we have seen widespread adoption of the Internet as a support channel. Insurers are using the Internet to provide general information on financial services products (*e.g.* , insurance, investments) and planning involving the use of these products, to provide specific information on the company and its product lines, to provide administrative support to its policyholders, and to serve as a prospecting and communication tool for its agent-led channel. For example, Celent Communications surveyed major U.S. property/liability insurers regarding Internet usage.

The six main usage areas were:

1. Agent access to quotes,
2. Agent extranet,
3. Policyholder account access,
4. Customer live quotes,
5. Customer quote request, and
6. Agent locator.

Of these six, the two most frequently used were the agent locator (over 60%) and the agent extranet (approximately 40%). These results clearly indicate that for property/liability insurers, the web is being used as an information or communication tool, as well as a prospecting tool for insurers' agents.

INNOVATION ADOPTION

To gain a better understanding of what factors tend to drive the adoption of one channel over another, it is helpful to examine some of the existing literature on innovation adoption and insurance distribution channels.

THE INTERNET CHANNEL

One factor that leads to the adoption of an innovation is how widespread it is. Rogers suggests that widespread diffusion of an innovation will lead to significant changes in the market channels themselves. We have seen widespread diffusion of the usage of the Internet in both the travel and insurance industries; however, the adoption patterns have been quite different.

The ability to reduce the transactions costs of interaction between buyers and sellers has always been acknowledged as a central motivation for the use of the web. Predictions of disintermediation and cybermediation are typically based on the reduced transaction costs of electronic interaction between sellers and buyers; for example, in book retailing or online stock trading.

Trust is another factor that drives or affects the adoption of the Internet-led channel. Gefen and others examined privacy and security as it relates to choosing an Internet channel. The widespread popularity of online stores or online auctions provide some indication that consumers trust the channel sufficiently to provide personal and financial information via a secure part of the channel. Additionally, secure support channels like Paypal have been created to provide secure payment channels for purchases.

Rogers presents five attributes of innovation (relative advantage, compatibility, complexity, trialability and observability). Of these, relative advantage has been shown empirically to consistently be the best predictor of adoption/usage. Choudhury surveyed auto insurance consumers to examine the relative advantage of the agent-led channel compared to the Internet-led channel.

They found that relative advantage is a multi-dimensional attribute. In addition to transactions costs, relative advantage also includes the dimensions of trust and knowledge. They also found that the purchase process for some consumers is a two-stage process.

These consumers first use the Internet to collect information on products or services. They then return to the agent to complete the purchase. This behaviour highlights the current role that the Internet plays in providing support to the agent-led channel.

OTHER DISTRIBUTION CHANNELS

It is interesting to note that cost differences do exist between traditional distribution systems, and yet these channels continue to co-exist. Posey and Yavas noted that earlier studies had shown that insurers using the independent agency system have higher costs than those employing a direct writer system. Taken to their logical conclusion these studies suggest that competition in insurance markets should have eliminated the independent agency system.

Posey and Yavas demonstrate that an equilibrium exists in which the independent agency and direct writer marketing systems can co-exist. The concept of differential services is also one that can explain why different distributions systems co-exist. Barresse examine this issue in the property/ liability insurance setting. They note that prior research suggests that insurers using independent agency distribution systems have higher expense ratios than insurers using other distribution systems.

A reasonable expected outcome for the more expensive distribution system is a loss of market share in a competitive market. In line with that conclusion, they report that independent agents' share of the auto insurance market declined from 69% in 1970 to 59% in 1990. While market share losses were noted for a more standardized insurance product like auto insurance, the same pattern was not observed in the commercial insurance setting.

Defenders of the independent agency system argue that higher expense ratios are attributable to a difference in the level of services offered to consumers. Besides the higher demand for services than in personal lines insurance, the greater complexity of commercial lines insurance over personal lines results in a greater demand for services provided by the independent agency channel. Query and Hoyt also found support for this concept of differential services. This was particularly true after controlling for whether or not the respondent had a prior claim experience.

Regan examined the distribution channel preference from a transactions cost perspective. She found that independent agents are used more often by insurers that sell more complex insurance products, while exclusive agency insurers use their agents to market more standardized products. She categorized these transactions based on frequency of exchange, complexity of the contracting environment, exogenous uncertainty and the importance of relation-specific investments that cannot be transferred to other users without the loss of value.

Other authors have examined the choice of distribution channel within the context of complexity and search costs. For example, Mayers and Smith examine the insurer's distribution channel choice and they suggest that more complex products require higher levels of service and that high value/high price types of insurance products will be best distributed by an independent agency channel. Conversely, insurance products that are more standardized may require lower levels of service. These types of products would be best suited for a direct writer type of channel.

Other more general explanations for why multiple distribution channels exist include imperfections in the markets and differences in product quality. Market imperfections are caused by price regulation, slow diffusion of information, and search costs differences. The concept of differential values suggests that the difference in product quality creates demand for different levels of service from the distribution channel. Higher value/higher price insurance products require greater service and one would expect a more costly, service rich distribution channel to be utilized for these types of products.

The results of a survey conducted by J. D. Power and Associates illustrate that there are factors other than price that drive insurance purchases. Of particular interest are the results on switching behaviour and reasons for online purchases of auto insurance. In part, the survey results highlight the importance of cost savings in the decision to switch insurers. Interestingly, what J. D. Power and Associates found was that 40% of the respondents indicated that they would not switch regardless of cost savings.

Given the fact that the auto insurance marketplace is saturated (*i.e.* , virtually all potential purchasers have insurance policies), any gain in market share is obtained at the loss of market share by other insurers. As such, the results of the survey have implications for insurers that are trying to introduce a competing channel. The 40% figure is relatively high and it indicates either the presence of inertia or the appreciation by many consumers of the value-added services provided by the current agent and/or insurer.

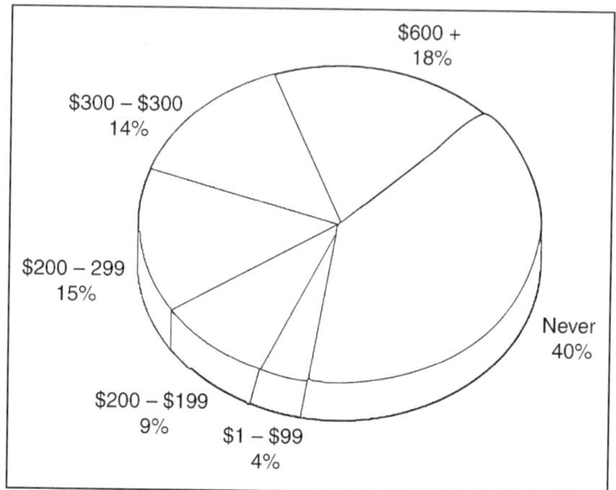

Fig. Cost Saving and Switching

The survey also provides interesting insights into consumer attitudes regarding online insurance purchases. Figure contains these results. On the question of why people buy car insurance online, only 30% of the respondents indicated that their decision to purchase online was driven by price savings. However, 34% of the respondents indicated that this decision was event or service related. This also may provide some indication of the importance of value-added service in retaining business, as well as the importance of handling claims in a manner that is satisfactory to the policyholder.

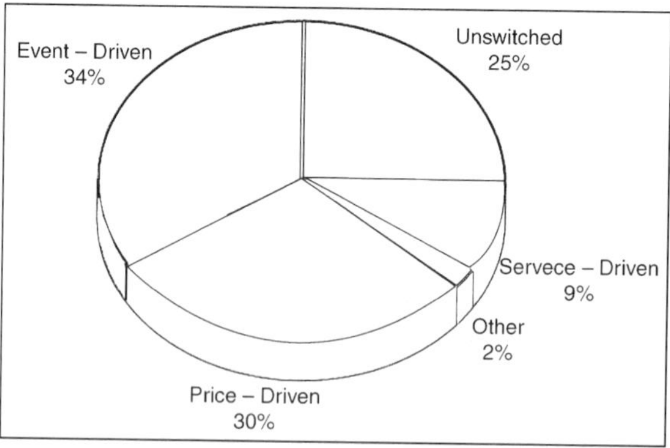

Fig. Why People Buy Car Insurance Online

DATA

We collected data on insurance distribution channels and lines of business for the top 20 property and casualty insurance groups for the years 1990, 1995 and 2000 from Best's Insurance Reports. Line of business data were used to classify each group based on its primary line of business focus, we used a breakpoint of 80% to classify the group as personal, commercial or mixed business. For example, if a group had 80% or more of its business in personal lines, it was classified as primarily personal lines. If the group had 80% or more of its business in commercial lines insurance, it was classified as primarily commercial lines. Those groups with less than 80% in either area were classified as mixed business.

Data on distribution channel usage by insurers is difficult to obtain, but what we could obtain does allow us to gain several interesting insights into some of the changes that are occurring. For the personal lines insurers, we further categorized them as either general personal lines or targeted personal lines. Among the general personal lines insurers, we observe a decline in the number of agents for captive agency types of companies. Examples of these insurers include State Farm and Allstate. State Farm reported a decline in the number of captive agents from 17,600 in 1990 to 16,000 in 2000. Allstate reported a decline in captive agents from 16,300 in 1990 to 13,000 in 2000.

We then categorized targeted personal lines insurers as either narrow focus/select risk or as narrow focus/substandard risk. Insurers categorized as narrow focus/select risk tend to pursue the low risk members of the auto insurance pool. For these types of insurers, we find that they have used and continue to use direct response channels. Examples of insurers in the narrow focus/select risk category include GEICO and USAA. Insurers classified as narrow focus/substandard risk tend to be pursuing substandard risks, but their niche has been in writing the best of the substandard risk class.

Currently, there is a movement towards expanding the targeted risk pool. In the past, insurers in this category have used independent agent and broker channels to write business; however, now they are turning to multiple distribution channels. To reach the broader market, they are adding direct response and Internet-led channels to the traditional independent agent and broker channels. An example of a company in this category is Progressive. For insurers that are primarily involved in commercial lines, there has been and continues to be a heavy reliance on independent agents and brokers to distribute insurance products. For example, Chubb had 3,300 independent agents and brokers in the year 1990, and that increased to 5,000 independent agents and 1,000 brokers in the year 2000.

Likewise, St. Paul reported 3,750 independent agents and 340 brokers in 1990, and this grew to a total of 4,700 in 2000. Overall for the insurers in our sample we observe increases in the numbers of independent agents and brokers from the year 1990 to 2000. This may in part be a result of the merger and acquisition activity among property and liability insurers (*e.g.*, the population of independent agents and brokers is spread across fewer insurers).

Insurers categorized as mixed business continue to use a variety of distribution channels, including independent agents and brokers and direct response channels. Channel activity for the mixed classification insurers continues to widen with a continued trend towards multiple distribution channels.

FUTURE TRENDS

To date, the expected disintermediation and demise of agent-led channels clearly has not occurred. This is most evident in the mixed and commercial lines areas. While there are several factors that may explain the low rate of adoption of alternative distribution channels, it may in part reflect the consumer's perception that insurance is a complex product.

As noted earlier in the chapter, complexity is one explanation for why different distribution systems co-exist. Given the low adoption rates for sales via the Internet, perceived complexity across insurance lines (personal and commercial) may continue to serve as a deterrent to Internet adoption. If the Internet is to experience significant gains as a distribution channel, then perceptions regarding product complexity will have to change.

Since there is a clear difference in complexity between personal and commercial lines, any growth of sales in the Internet-led channel will likely first occur in the personal lines area. While the Internet channel does play an increasingly important role as a distribution channel for some insurers, the major usage of the Internet channel appears to be in the service area where transactional efficiencies are readily achievable.

The current structure of the financial services industry in Europe and the United States is much different with banks in Europe playing a major role in the distribution of insurance products. The primary differences between these two markets is as much attributable to regulatory constraints as it is to consumer preferences.

The passage of the Financial Services Modernization Act of 1999 removed the regulatory barriers between insurance and banking that were created under the Glass-Steagall Act, and many predicted growth of the bank-led insurance distribution channel in the U.S. market.

The results of a recent American Bank Insurance Association survey indicates that banks are increasing their marketing efforts, but that insurance still represents a very small percentage of bank revenue. The banks participating in the survey were very large financial institutions.

While they represented only 4% of financial institutions, they held 41% of total bank assets. The percentage of banks engaged in some form of general lines insurance activity grew from 40.4% in 1999 to 45.7% in 2000. However, the revenues generated from insurance marketing are still not substantial. The survey reported that insurance revenue, as a portion of bank revenue, is less than 0.5%.

The results of the survey indicate that marketing of insurance varies significantly across banks. Thirty per cent of the respondents indicated that they do not currently market annuities, credit coverage or general lines of insurance. Twenty-two per cent of the respondents indicated that they currently market annuities or credit coverage types of products now, but they don't market general insurance (life and health or property casualty) types of products. Forty-one per cent of the respondents indicate that they market general lines, credit coverage, and/or annuity types of products.

While life and annuity products continue to be the dominant insurance products that these banks currently market, it is interesting to note the increase in efforts to market property and casualty products. Twenty-six per cent of the respondents indicated that they market auto and homeowners insurance, and an additional 17% indicated that they would market these products within the next two years. In comparison, roughly 21% of the respondents indicated marketing commercial property and casualty, and an additional 11% to 14% indicated having plans to market commercial insurance products in the next few years.

The survey does provide some mixed signals for growth by reporting that over 15% of banks report planning to distribute personal lines insurance products within the next two years, but that the number of banks reporting such plans declined by ten per cent. However, given the size and financial strength of banks operating in the United States, their efforts to market insurance products indicates the presence of a potentially formidable competitor as the bank-led channel grows in the property/liability insurance marketplace.

SUMMARY

In conclusion, our analysis makes it clear that the early predictions of widespread adoption of the Internet as an insurance marketing channel were inaccurate. Further, the predicted demise of the independent agency system and other agent-led distribution channels has not materialized. However, it is clear that insurers are continuing to experiment with alternative distribution channels. More and more insurers are utilizing multiple distribution channels as they continue to balance the needs of different groups of consumers against the cost of distributing their products and services. When it comes to insurance distribution channels one-size does not fit all.

9

Direct Marketing of Insurance

As insurers move to direct distribution and database marketing, new approaches to the business, integrating the marketing, underwriting and pricing activity will be increasingly important. Many insurers today are adopting increasingly sophisticated approaches to direct marketing, especially for automobile insurance. Large, sophisticated customer databases and sophisticated analytic approaches are used to direct marketing efforts.

The underwriting, pricing and marketing roles at these companies are evolving but are still largely segregated. Each area functions in a highly specialized area, linked to the others but still compartmentalized. Marketing analyses customers and customer lists to predict response rates and thus profitability of the marketing activity. Actuarial analyses experience data to estimate loss costs by type of insured. This is often done with special actuarial databases, making little use of more extensive customer databases.

To achieve optimal results, more integration of these three roles is needed. The actuary will need to have active hands on involvement in the marketing process, helping the marketers move beyond response prediction, to analysis of loss costs as well. This chapter explores how companies should operate in this new environment.

INTRODUCTION

Direct Marketing is increasing in importance in business in general, and in the insurance business in particular. Direct marketing is gaining share in the insurance business worldwide, with spectacular success in some areas such as U.K. auto. Database marketing techniques are increasing in sophistication, driven in part by increases in available computer power. Other Financial Services companies such as banks use these techniques well, and will bring them to the insurance markets, forcing insurers to adopt them to keep pace.

To maximize value from these techniques, they should not be viewed as simply a change in how insurance is marketed. They should be used in a way that has a broad impact on the entire operation, integrating marketing with pricing and underwriting. Direct marketers use very sophisticated analytic techniques, developed over many years of marketing a wide variety of products.

Insurance is a unique product for these techniques in many respects. One very important respect is that the cost of goods sold is a function of who buys the product. For other products, direct marketing techniques are used to manage the volume of sales and the cost of selling, with the cost of the products sold taken as a fixed assumption in the analysis. Managing the cost of goods sold is, in a sense, the focus of traditional actuarial pricing work. The actuary determines rates that will produce the targeted unit profits. The primary focus of the work is loss costs, which represent the bulk of the cost of goods sold for most types of insurance. Marketing unit costs are typically taken as an input assumption.

By integrating database marketing techniques with traditional actuarial approaches, the total profits from the business sold can be managed more effectively. Management of loss costs and marketing costs will be integrated into a single process. This integration of marketing and pricing will impact the actuary's job tremendously. Traditionally, the pricing actuary has focused on rate analysis, typically reviewing each set of rates once or twice a year. The process for doing those reviews has not changed much for many years. That work has been coordinated with other areas of the company, but not closely integrated with them on a day-to-day basis.

In a database marketing environment, actuaries will have much larger data sets to analyse, updated much more frequently. Decisions concerning rate levels will be made frequently, not just for changing filed rates, but also for managing the marketing process. The rest of this chapter describes this new environment. First, there is a brief description of current processes in a non-integrated approach. Then, direct marketing approaches in general use for all industries are described, including emerging database marketing techniques.

The chapter then goes on to describe a new objective function for insurance, one that integrates the usual direct marketing goal of maximizing business acquired per marketing dollar with the usual actuarial goals of managing the loss ratio. The goal of an integrated approach is to maximize this new objective function per dollar invested in marketing. The following sections go on to discuss how the marketing, pricing and underwriting functions should operate to accomplish that. Most of the principles discussed here generally apply to any line of business, in any country. Examples used here to illustrate these principles generally are based on U. S. private passenger automobile insurance.

TRADITIONAL APPROACHES TO PRICING, UNDERWRITING AND MARKETING

PRICING

Traditionally, actuarial pricing activity has focused on the need to review and update the rates charged. Overall rate levels are reviewed every 6 to 12 months. Indicated changes in rates are filed with state regulators and implemented when approved. The process is entirely a cost-based analysis in form, but in practice there is usually some recognition of the market (*e.g.* , competitor prices) reflected in the final rate decisions.

UNDERWRITING

The underwriting activity involves a review of individual risk applications that are received. Rating data is verified, using tools such as motor vehicle reports. Risks are evaluated based on factors not in the rating plan-*e.g.*, credit history, interactions of unusual variables.

The underwriting process results in a decision whether to accept or reject the risk. It is frequently used to make judgmental adjustment to rates-*e.g.* , assigning auto risks to one of several tiers: select, standard or non-standard. This evaluation process is increasingly being done using expert systems. Some underwriting decision rules are based on analysis of loss experience data, but many are not. Often they reflect the seasoned judgment of experienced insurance professionals as to what constitutes a good risk.

MARKETING

The objective in traditional direct marketing is to maximize sales per dollar of investment in acquiring customers. This traditional approach assumes that the cost of goods sold per unit is fixed and known. That is the case for many products commonly sole through direct marketing, *e.g.*, Ginsu Knives. But not for insurance, where the cost of goods sold is a random variable, and the expected value of that random variable is a function of who the buyer is.

Direct marketers have developed very sophisticated analytic tools for maximizing the sales generated per dollar of marketing costs. The marketing databases to which those tools are applied are increasingly large and powerful. Applied to managing marketing costs alone, these techniques impact only 10-20% of the premium dollar. If they can also be applied to manage loss costs, representing 70-80% of the premium dollar, the potential payoff is much greater.

DIRECT MARKETING TECHNIQUES

Direct marketing techniques have been well developed over many years, for many different types of products. They have increased in sophistication as computing power has become cheaper, and as increasing amounts of consumer data have become available. For those readers not familiar with the field, there are many popular books describing it. In most applications, the goal of direct marketing is to maximize the return per dollar invested in marketing-*e.g.* , in creating and mailing a direct mail campaign. The return is typically measured in terms of numbers of sales or dollar volume of sales.

Tools to manage that return include selecting who to mail to and design of marketing materials for direct mail. For other media, tools include advertising design, and choice of advertisement placement for print and radio and television. In some cases, price is also a tool. By testing different prices, the company can select which combination of price (profit margin) and response rates (sales volume) will maximize total gross margins.

Past results are the basis for analysis using those tools. For example, results of past direct mail campaigns can be used to select the best prospects for a new mailing. The results of the past campaign are analysed to determine the key characteristics of people who bought-*e.g.*, demographics, psychographics, prior buying behaviour for similar products. There are many mailing lists that can be rented to identify new prospects. This data can be added to the company's house list (the database of its own customers' past behaviour). Mathematical analyses identify prospects promising the best return per marketing dollar in the new campaign.

Similarly, results on past print, radio and television campaigns are analysed for planning future advertisement placement. The impact of variations in advertising copy is reviewed as part of that process. Marketing database tools have increased in size and power over the years. Successful direct marketers continually enrich their databases. Knowledge about customers and their buying behaviour is a key competitive advantage. Marketing databases are constantly enriched through external data sources, through customer feedback and surveys, and through customer interaction with the call center.

Sophisticated mathematical tools are used to analyse this data, to spot buying behaviour patterns that can help manage the marketing process more effectively, These tools are often based on linear regression models, enhanced by special techniques for examining interactions among variables. Sometimes advanced techniques such as Artificial Neural Networks are used. In summary, direct marketing applies sophisticated mathematical techniques to large data sets, to manage the marketing process to maximize response rates or revenue generated. Much of this approach is valid for insurance as well, but the objective function-the item being maximized-should change.

OBJECTIVE OF AN INTEGRATED APPROACH

The company's objective is to maximize the overall profit, reflecting both marketing costs and loss costs. In deciding how to invest its marketing dollars, the company will want to maximize, per dollar of marketing cost, the aggregate value of the profits generated by customers acquired.

Viewing just the next policy year, the profitability of each customer acquired can be viewed as the rate that is actually charged minus the indicated rate that should be charged to exactly meet the company's profit target. That indicated rate should cover all costs, including the cost of capital. To maximize profits, the company would want to market in a way that maximizes the aggregate value of: the profitability per target customer times the probability of acquiring that customer. Marketing, pricing and underwriting activities should coordinate to maximize that. This is a pure profit maximization criterion.

At times, the company may want to overlay other objectives on this, for example:

- Geographic coverage of urban areas at least at specified minimum levels, to meet regulatory/public policy concerns; or
- Geographic dispersion to manage catastrophe exposure

For discussion that follows, the pure profit maximization objective is assumed. The approaches discussed could easily be adapted to reflect additional considerations such as these.

A broader, longer-term profit measure, such as Lifetime Customer Value (LCV) may also be appropriate. This measures the value of an acquired customer over the lifetime of his relationship with the company. That is similar to approaches used by many life insurers to price long-term contracts, estimating the total profits over the lifetime of the policy. Embedded Value financial management approaches incorporate that view into a regular financial reporting system. In some companies/industries LCV measures often extend beyond the current product sold, to include all future expected sales to the same customer.

In direct marketing, where money is invested in acquiring new customer relationships, that view of customer profitability is appropriate. The approach discussed here could be easily adapted to reflect it, on a reasonable approximation basis. As a simple example, assume that the market will adjust over time to eliminate excess returns-*i.e.*, the excess of rates actually charged over the indicated rates-at a constant rate over 4 years. If inflation is 6% and the risk-adjusted rate of return that the company wants to earn on investments in marketing is 12%, then the present value of all excess returns could be estimated as:

$$[\text{Actual–Indicated Rates}] \times$$
$$[1 + 0.75 \times (1.06/1.12) + 0.50 \times (1.06/1.12)^2 + 0.25 \times (1.06/1.12)^3]$$

Another important issue in these analyses is how to treat expenses. What expenses should be reflected in determining these indicated rates? Many would argue that only variable costs should be reflected.

MARKETING IN AN INTEGRATED APPROACH

Insurance introduces a number of unique issues for direct marketing that are not present for most other products.

For automobile insurance, for example, we can generally say that:

- Most people will definitely buy a policy, but only one policy.
- Most people already have a policy, and inertia will lead them to renew that unless there are significant savings from switching (*e.g.*, 15 to 20% in research we have seen).

- Decisions to change insurers occur mainly at policy renewal dates, but also at the time of other significant changes such as moving to a new address, buying a new car, change in marital status. But absent one of these events, insureds are unlikely to change except at the renewal date.

In addition, there are variations in buyer behaviour in insurance that do have strong parallels in direct marketing of other products.

- Some, but not all, insureds will shop around extensively for the best price before purchasing, and price will largely determine their purchase.
- Some people have a strong preference for dealing with an agent (and perhaps strong loyalty to their current agent or company), while others will have a strong preference to purchase direct.

These factors influence the marketing process in many ways. Targeting offers to people who are at the right time to switch is important for managing cost-effectiveness of the marketing effort. Renewal dates of current policies are important data to capture on the marketing database. Mailing lists of people at key events (*e.g.* , moving) are also very useful.

Demographic factors are important indicators of propensity to buy direct, without an agent, and should influence marketing decisions. For example, Generation X is much more likely to buy direct than are Senior Citizens. Of course, each of these groups can be segmented into sub-groups more and less likely to buy direct. In traditional direct marketing, the goal is simply to maximize expected sales volumes.

For insurance, the objective function is more complex:

Probability of Aacquiring the Customer
Times
Expected Profit of the Customer if Acquired

For the first item, all of the usual direct marketing analytic approaches for targeting marketing investments will apply. In addition, insurance presents a new factor-the difference between the rate the company offers and competitor rates. While this is only one additional factor, in practice it is likely to be the most important factor in acquiring the customer.

The second item is unique to insurance. It involves comparing the rate the company offers with the best estimate of the indicated rate. Thus, insurance introduces two new elements to the direct marketing process-the rates that competitors charge, and the indicated rate that the company should charge to meet its profit goal. Both of these are unknowns, both depend on the particular customer, and both are areas where the actuary can play a key role.

COMPETITOR RATE COMPARISONS

Competitor pricing is extremely important. The difference between the company's rates and the rates of competitors should be reflected in the marketing process, since they are a prime determinant of the probability of acquiring the customer. Competitor rates include both those charged by the insured's current carrier, and the rates other insurers would charge.

In principle, rates could be compared on a case-by-case basis in selecting prospects for a mailing. This comparison could be automated, using the company's rating plan logic and competitor rating plans, if the marketing data base contains the rating variables on each prospect and competitor rating plans are known.

For prospects on the database who are not customers, estimates of competitor rates may be inferred from results on similar people who are customers. It should be relatively easy to identify categories of prospects where the company is more likely to beat competitor rates. Going beyond that to estimate competitor rates, the resulting probability of acquiring the customer and the expected profit per solicitation mailed will be much more complicated. At the simplest level, combining a sense of where the competitor rates are high with a sense of where the company's own rates are very profitable will give a good indication of where to focus marketing efforts.

The marketing process can be an important source of competitor rate data, particularly in cases where underwriting scoring systems are used to assign insureds to tiers of rates. Customer interaction processes should be designed to collect this data, as well as data that could be used purely for marketing. Also, it is useful to validate rate data from competitor rate manuals and similar sources. As for traditional direct marketing, for insurance the marketing process can provide feedback to the price-setting process. At times, the competitors' rates may be significantly above the rates charged for categories of business that are attractive. Those situations should lead to rate increases in the next rate manual change or it may indicate adjustments. If the volume in those categories is large, that may indicate doing the next rate change earlier.

PRICING IN AN INTEGRATED APPROACH

There are two sets of prices to consider in direct marketing of insurance:

1. Prices actually charged
2. Indicated prices that would be charged to cover expected losses and administrative expense

The prices actually charged will be calculated using traditional approaches. Regulatory requirements, the need to fit policy administration systems, and general public understanding of the current rating system are all reasons for not changing the formal rating plans used.

For the rate analyses submitted to regulators, where required, it will also be most practical to continue using traditional approaches. For the indicated prices, however, there are no such restrictions. The analysis and rating only needs to be understood by internal experts and management. These analyses are not generally disclosed outside the company.

Determining indicated rates, of course, involves the same actuarial principles as traditional rate analysis-adjustments for loss development, trend, rate level changes, classification relativities, etc. But when integrated into a direct marketing operation, there are important differences in the application of those principles. There is a much larger set of variables of analyse-including characteristics captured on the marketing database as well as the variables used in the rating plan. The indicated rates should be updated more frequently-*e.g.* , recalculating estimates of indicated rates for each mailing or marketing programme.

Two general types of approaches to meeting these new needs are discussed below. One involves adapting traditional actuarial approaches to these new circumstances. The other involves adapting traditional direct marketing analytic techniques for predicting response rates to the more complicated task of calculating indicated prices.

Indicated Prices using Traditional Actuarial Approaches

The simplest approach would make a few adjustments to the rates actually used (and filed with regulators where applicable).

Adjustments to those actual rates could be made for various considerations, for example:

- Judgmental adjustments to filed rates are often made for practical reasons which do not reflect better estimates of indicated rates (*e.g.* , no policy to increase beyond 20%). These adjustments should be eliminated.
- Filed rates reflect trending to the average effective date of the business to be sold using those rates. That trend is too much for early sales and too little for later ones. For direct marketing, the indicated rates could be adjusted to reflect the timing of each marketing campaign.
- Seasonality of loss experience is usually ignored in filed rates, but may be important for catastrophes or for six month policies. That can be reflected in marketing decisions.

A more precise approach would actually update the indicated rates whenever new data is available. For example, if new marketing campaigns are developed each month, the indicated rates would be updated each month, incorporating the latest available experience data. The traditional rate recalculations can be easily automated, in a way that allows actuarial and management review at the appropriate points.

Automating the process entirely without allowing for review would not be advisable. But the review process would need to be much quicker than is often the case for annual or semi-annual rate filings. It would have to be done more frequently, as part of the preparation for each marketing campaign. An even more tailored approach would incorporate in this traditional actuarial approach rating variables that are not part of the rating plan used for rates actually charged, but that do significantly impact the indicated rate. For the indicated rates, used internally only, there is no need to restrict the analysis to variables formally used in the rating plan.

Indicated Prices using Database Marketing Techniques

The alternative general approach is to adapt the tools and techniques used by direct marketers to the prediction of loss costs. Those tools are primarily variations of linear regression approaches. The use of Generalized Linear Models to analyse insurance rates is common for personal automobile insurance in the U.K., but not as widely in the U.S. These linear regression and related techniques are better suited in many ways than traditional actuarial techniques for this process, which involves large number of variables, and updating the analysis (and often even the set of variables used) very frequently. Practice, and mathematics, in this area has been highly refined through years of use in predicting response rates.

However, projecting insurance loss experience is more complex than projecting response rates. Insurance loss experience, and expected loss amounts, are more volatile than response rates or sales volumes, and generally more complex to predict (*e.g.*, more variables may be needed in the analysis.) Concepts and skills from traditional actuarial analysis of loss experience should be incorporated in using these techniques.

For example:

- Several years of experience may be needed, especially where the experience base is small, given the much larger potential number of classification factors.
- Premiums at current rates should be used for experience loss ratios, where those are the profit measures used in the analysis.
- A common actuarial approach is to limit losses, to avoid instability due to large losses. It may be desirable to test alternative levels of and approaches to capping (with broad average factors to provide for losses above the cap).
- Losses should be adjusted for loss development to ultimate, and for trend. These adjustments should be done in a way that is consistent with the cap on losses.

There are a number of theoretical issues to address in applying linear regression techniques to insurance loss data. Those are beyond the scope of this chapter. They are likely covered in the literature in areas where Generalized Linear Models are commonly used for insurance rate analysis.

No matter how sophisticated the regression techniques used to estimate indicated rates, they can only reflect the experience on policies actually written by the insurer. For a small or rapidly growing insurer, the current book may not indicate expected experience from the overall target market. Most insurers feel they have a lot of knowledge of their business beyond the experience data being analysed. Raw experience indications are tempered to reflect that, using credibility techniques. Bringing actuarial credibility techniques into use with linear regression analyses will present additional challenges.

CONCLUSION

Direct marketing and the emerging technology of database marketing are here to stay. They will increase in power and in usage, as the analytic techniques become more refined, as computer power continues to decrease in price, as customer databases become richer, and as consumers continue to become accustomed to purchasing without an agent.

Direct writers using these approaches will gain share in personal automobile insurance, and in other lines as well. Banks and other financial services industries are ahead of the insurance industry in mastering these techniques. They will enter the insurance industry, bringing these techniques with them. Insurers will need to adopt them to compete. Agent-based insurers will also need to adopt them, to help improve agent productivity and reduce marketing costs.

These new techniques should not be regarded just as enhanced marketing tools. They should fundamentally change the operations of insurers, with integration of marketing, underwriting and pricing. Insurers who do not do this will miss the full potential of these new tools. This integration offers expanded opportunities for actuaries, as the pricing actuary is drawn into the marketing team, helping to manage that process on a day-to-day basis.

It also presents a threat to those actuaries who stick to traditional approaches and roles. Companies using these new techniques will bring in marketing executives with mathematical skills comparable to most actuaries, and with a business orientation that may resonate better with top management. If actuaries do not learn and use these new techniques, and apply their unique skills to using them, they risk becoming viewed as regulatory compliance technicians, not as executives who help drive the business.

10

Insurance Marketing in the Digital Age

THE CHALLENGE

To drive organic growth, many insurance companies have significantly increased spending on marketing campaigns. Despite this, a major challenge remains in cross-selling additional lines of business, which is a significant missed revenue opportunity. Often, the opportunity is missed because, to leverage the skill sets and experience of underwriters, resources are structured on a line-ofbusiness basis. Insurance carriers unknowingly put in place cumbersome obstacles which prevent them from effectively penetrating their existing base of policyholders. It is possible to market fully to policyholders but to do so, companies need to capture data effectively.

Best practices focus on capturing three types of data-client data, transactional data, and interaction data:

1. Client data consists of specific geo-coded location, mailing addresses and other descriptive operations data (SIC or NAICS codes). This data further defines the insured's operations and provides insight into what exposures are present and how readily they might be cross sold
2. Transactional data consists of new business, renewal and endorsement transaction data to determine the degree to which the insured has actively managed their exposures
3. Interaction data provides insight into why the insured initiated the contact–what were the specific touch points that drove the insured to interact with their insurance carrier. In other words, was the motivation to lower price, buy more coverage, or submit a claim

This valuable data, including demographic and psycho-graphic elements, are presented to carriers throughout the application and renewal processes but also through customer service centers. Additional external demographic and psychographic data can be leveraged through third party data providers providing improved insights into the buyer.

With the decreasing cost of storage today, data can now be warehoused in a more cost-effective manner than ever before, which can facilitate future underwriting and marketing initiatives. Given a coordinated data strategy for account underwriting and cross-line solicitation, production underwriters can benefit immensely from both internal and external data sources.

POTENTIAL BENEFITS

Facilitated by non-traditional data capture, the cross-selling of lines of business can provide untold benefits in organic growth. This approach relies on enriching the data necessary to identify those businesses more likely to be cross-sold. In general, insurance carriers have lacked unified underwriting guidelines across multiple lines of business thus adding to missed cross-sell opportunities. Often, underwriting specialization has only focused on the improvement of line of business loss ratios. Due to the current inability for many carriers to leverage existing customer data outside of and even within their own divisions, they miss the opportunity to promote their products and service to their existing policyholder base.

Because of the distributed nature of contact between the agent/insured and the carrier, many insureds are not even aware of all the carrier's products and services. When customers experience a coordinated underwriting and marketing approach by their carrier across lines of business and across operating divisions (Commercial and Personal), they benefit from a deeper, more loyal relationship with the carrier which results in more wallet share. It is believed that these stronger relationships also improve retention rates (or "stickiness") in both Commercial and Personal Divisions.

As a result, during periods of softening rates such as the market is currently experiencing, accounts with multiple lines of business are often better protected from policyholder attrition given the depth of their relationship with a specific carrier and the unwillingness of an insured to move their full insurance schedule. Insurance companies are wise to also judiciously increase underwriting and loss control service touch points or interactions when it makes fiscal sense. When they do, and they utilize the client information retained for cross-sell models, they are better able to demonstrate loss control and underwriting insights across multiple lines of business. Deeper account penetration and more frequent touch points impact retention rates by as much as 10 points as policyholders perceive an enhanced value from these interactions.

CAPTURE VALUABLE DATA

Carriers dedicate significant dollars and resources to solicit new policyholders. Unfortunately, during the acquisition process, they often do not electronically capture marketing or application data. All too often, when marketing analysis or predictive modeling calls for additional policyholder data, insurance companies find themselves idea rich but data poor.

Why is data so important in cross-selling? Capturing data is a significant first step to gain specific insights into policyholders; and providing leverage in any future marketing and predictive modeling initiatives. Usually, carriers warehouse policyholders' "rating" component data but other demographic or marketing data may be left in cavernous filing cabinets. To fully leverage these rich marketing insights, this data must be fully harvested through detailed data-collected procedures and used in organized processes to understand and learn from these marketing diamonds in the rough.

As part of a policy's non-renewal or cancellation, it is highly beneficial to capture the reasons for such cancellation or attrition. This data will pay dividends in future predictive modeling activities, providing a reservoir of actionable data for subsequent demand analysis and pricing optimization initiatives. It is also valuable to ask the reasons for requesting a policy quotation. Ask the insured, "Why are you moving your coverage from your prior carrier?" Although at first glance this may not appear to be useful information, it can be extremely significant. Rather than assuming that the sole motive is price, the carrier can better understand the insured's true buying motivation.

Alternatively, during policy cancellation processing, question the reasons for the cancellation. This may yield reason(s) for the change which uncover valuable trends in the changing competitor landscape; potential customer service concerns; or other coverage discrepancies that can be remediated thus keeping the insured happy.

Equally important is capturing specific reasons for which a prospective policyholder decides not to accept the carrier's new business quotation. Currently, in most carriers, this information lays stagnant in a non-digital world (if captured at all). Tracking the number of quotes not written due to coverage discrepancies, pricing, or lack of supplemental risk services yields better insights of the carrier's most profitable insureds. Data collection during the policyholder's complete lifecycle provides data enhancement for future marketing programmes as well as key components for next-generation predictive modeling underwriting and pricing improvement.

MINE THE MOST PROFITABLE SLICE OF BUSINESS

Commercial/Personal insurance carriers like to think of themselves as good underwriting organizations; yet, due to a lack of insightful data, they often fail to identify the most profitable portions of their policyholder base. By identifying the demographic characteristics of the most profitable policyholders and cross-correlating this data with their likelihood to purchase additional products, insurance carriers can achieve profitable organic growth at a relatively cost-effective price. At the same time, carriers reduce acquisition costs on those customers with a high propensity to purchase more lines of business.

USE DATA TO BETTER UNDERSTAND POLICYHOLDERS

What kind of data, internal and external, might be used to build deeper understanding of clients?

Certainly, client, transaction and interaction data is already taken in via the Commercial web portal intake process and should be warehoused for future value and analysis, such as:

- Insight into why the insured is shopping their policy
- Business operations reflecting SIC/NAICS code assignments
- Specific geo-coded location data
- Other line of business policy data
- Historical loss data

Collectively, this information provides the nature and extent of risk exposure, but also can play a role in determining whether a specific insured is willing to purchase additional insurance protection.

Associated agency/broker submittal information further enriches the dataset, providing independent agency representation that often plays a key role in acceptance of an insurance policy. More in-depth data collection, such as responses to specific loss control or underwriting questions, can be embedded into the new business application. These provide even deeper insights into the buyer's critical triggers, such as price sensitivity, exposure avoidance, or an appetite for services. This holds true even if the agent is completing the application.

Policyholders who are strong believers in effective loss control are more likely to accept a reasonable rate increase if the loss control services provided by that insurer have been shown, historically, to reduce lost work days. In contrast, price-sensitive insureds may not give weight to effective loss control services, assuming that all loss control services are similar in quality resulting in a focus only on the cheapest price.

USE DATA TO BETTER UNDERSTAND MANAGEMENT

External data sources help improve the demographic/psychographic data picture of not only the company but also of the company's management. Small to mid-size companies often reflect the operational prowess (or lack thereof) of their top leaders and therefore, personal demographic/psycho-graphic variable information (mortgage size, recent bankrup-tcies/foreclosures, and household financial/demographic status) may provide additional marketing insights into the purchasing appetite/patterns of executives.

What value might there be in knowing how interested an executive is in purchasing Gucci shoes versus Nike sneakers from a local discount shoe store? Why might it be helpful to know if the top executive drives a Hummer, Honda or hybrid? Does it really matter whether they are gen X, baby boomer, grandparent or father for the 1st time? Smaller organizations often take on the personae of the top 2-3 individuals. Significant value can be derived from understanding the demographic/psychographic parameters of decision-makers and/or their households. Through clustering analysis, this information can be cross-correlated to determine the propensity to purchase additional coverage and services.

Plus, such external data can further improve insights into a propensity to purchase higher limits of insurance to protect company assets. Identifying personal lifestyle attributes may also directly affect the ultimate loss costs of these additional lines. For example, an executive who is a chronic smoker is less likely to support smoke-ender programmes and other prospective health initiatives in their organization. This executive may miss an opportunity to improve the workers' compensation case and indemnity reserves, because smokers often use workers' compensation benefits at a higher rate.

CONCLUSION

Is it cost effective to warehouse marketing-associated data from insurance applications? Is there a legitimate return on investment for the expense involved? Does it make sense to capture this data on both quoted and written business? Are there third party data sources that can further enrich a carrier's intelligence?

BY ALL MEANS–YES

With the historically inexpensive price of storage today, reasonably cheap data acquisition is within the financial grasp of most insurance companies, even smaller ones. Tactical marketing plans should leverage all policyholder acquisition and retention data; and use it within new business predictive modeling efforts. Marketing efforts should include the development and storage of new internally-and externally-sourced data.

Through cross-referencing policyholder data to rich external, intuitive psychographic data sets, carriers can enhance their understanding of policyholders.

As a result, they can:

- Better position products and services to capitalize on cross-selling opportunities
- Identify the purchasing propensities of the insured
- Understand the linkage between personal demographics and corporate risk

By introducing ways to leverage existing or new data, insurance companies can overcome the traditional limitations imposed by their underwriting organizational structures, and develop aggressive growth plans across all lines of business. Through the development of a data driven organic growth strategy, carriers can now better cultivate their data fields to drive new revenue and cross-pollinate their business.

11

Micro Insurance

NEED FOR MICRO-INSURANCE–RISKS FACED BY THE POOR

Micro-insurance is a key element in the financial services package for people at the bottom of the pyramid. The poor face more risks than the well-off, but more importantly they are more vulnerable to the same risk. Usually, the poor face two types of risks–idiosyncratic (specific to the household) and covariate (common, eg., drought, epidemic, etc.). To combat these risks, the poor do pro-active risk management–grain storage, savings, asset accumulation (specially bullocks), loans from friends and relatives, etc. However, the prevalent forms of risk management (in kind savings, self-insurance, mutual insurance) which were appropriate earlier are no longer adequate.

Poverty is not just a state of deprivation but has latent vulnerability. Microinsurance should, therefore, provide greater economic and psychological security to the poor as it reduces exposure to multiple risks and cushions the impact of a disaster. There is an overwhelming demand for social protection among the poor. Microinsurance in conjunction with micro savings and micro credit could, therefore, go a long way in keeping this segment away from the poverty trap and would truly be an integral component of financial inclusion.

DEFINING MICRO-INSURANCE

The draft chapter prepared by the Consultative Group to Assist the Poor (CGAP) working group on micro-insurance defines micro-insurance as "the protection of low income households against specific perils in exchange for premium payments proportionate to the likelihood and cost of the risk involved." The chapter deliberates on the key roles to be played by all stakeholders–insurers, regulator and the Government. The working group also agrees that the cost of such cover should be affordable.

CONSULTATIVE GROUP ON MICRO-INSURANCE CONSTITUTED BY GOI

In 2003, GoI constituted a Consultative Group on Micro-Insurance to examine existing insurance schemes for rural and urban poor with specific reference to outreach, pricing, products, servicing and promotion and to examine existing regulations with a view to promoting micro-insurance organisations with specific reference to capital requirements, licensing, monitoring and review, etc.

The report of the consultative group has brought out the following key issues:

- Micro-insurance is not viable as a standalone insurance product.
- Micro-insurance has not penetrated rural markets. Traditional insurers have not made much headway in bringing micro-insurance products to the rural poor. (In addition, the Committee feels that micro insurance has not penetrated even among the urban poor).
- Partnership between an insurer and a social organisation like NGO would be desirable to promote micro-insurance by drawing on their mutual strengths.
- Design of micro-insurance products must have the features of simplicity, availability, affordability, accessibility and flexibility.

FINDINGS OF THE UNDP STUDY REPORT

A study commissioned by the United Nations Develop-ment Programme (UNDP) titled "Building Security for the Poor-potential and Prospects for Microinsurance in India" states that 90% of the Indian population-some 950 million people-are not covered by insurance and signify an untapped market of nearly US$2 billion. This enormous "missing market" is ready for customised life and non-life insurance, but first, serious mismatches between the needs of the insured and the insurers must be overcome, pitting priorities against profits.

The UNDP report has analysed six key issues pertinent to the growth of the micro-insurance industry in India, capturing the concerns of different stakeholders as indicated below:

- There are specific reasons for low demand for insurance in spite of intense need. Suppliers have their own concerns which helps to explain why there have been so little efforts at market development. Consequently, the rural market is characterized by limited and inappropriate services, inadequate information and capacity gaps.
- There are challenges in product design, which has resulted in a mismatch between needs and standard products on offer. Efforts at product development/diversification have been limited.
- Pricing, including willingness to pay and the availability of subsidies, influence the market. In the absence of a historical data base on claims, premium calculations are based on remote macro aggregates and overcautious margins. Building and sharing claims histories can help in aligning pricing decisions with actuarial calculations, thereby reducing prices.

- Difficulty in distribution is one of the most cited reasons for absence of rural insurance. The high costs of penetrating rural markets, combined with underutilization of available distribution channels, hinder the growth of rural insurance services. This adds to costs, both, managerial and financial. Like inclusive credit, inclusive insurance is expected to be a "low ticket" business, requiring volumes for viability.
- Cumbersome and inappropriate procedures inhibit the development of this sector.
- Contrasting perspectives of the insured and the insurers, lead to low customization of products and low demand for what is available.

The UNDP report further states that micro-insurance solutions should, therefore, attempt at addressing key issues that will improve customer satisfaction (demand-supply gaps, appropriate products and pricing), provide distribution efficiencies for better outreach and remove procedural hassles facilitating easier renewals and claim settlements. With a view to reduce costs, the report has also suggested that the premia payable on micro-insurance be exempted from payment of service tax, which will also enable greater penetration in rural markets.

ENABLING ENVIRONMENT FOR MICRO-INSURANCE IN THE INDIAN CONTEXT

Helping the rural poor systematically manage financial risks to their livelihoods and lives through micro-insurance offers innovative ways to combat poverty in India. The timing of the UNDP study is strategic as policy interest has been renewed in energizing the rural insurance market in India.

The following factors could provide the needed impetus to push micro-insurance to the "next level" in terms of growth and outreach:

- The widening, deepening and upscaling of micro-finance interventions has provided the institutional precincts on which the edifice of micro-insurance could be built in rural areas.
- There are a wide range of developmental programmes being supported by the Government like the SGSY, the NREGP, etc., which have facilitated the improvement of income levels of many rural households. The GoI-package of "Doubling Flow of Agricultural Credit" has also enabled greater institutional credit flow for agriculture and allied activities. However, what is of concern is that all these interventions, though ambitious in stated intent, only incidentally address risk, if at all. The most vulnerable rural population-in particular, women-are largely excluded from the insurance market. This only amplifies the felt need of this segment for protection of their lives/income-generating assets against various perils. At present, the Personal Accident Insurance Scheme (PAIS)

which is being provided as a bundled offering along with the Kisan Credit Card (KCC) Scheme and the Rashtriya Krishi Bima Yojana (RKBY) for insuring crops, are, probably, the only borrowal-linked riskmitigation mechanisms available to rural households. Further, many State Governments are offering health insurance facilities to the rural poor (eg., Yeshaswini Scheme of the Government of Karnataka) which have also generated considerable acceptance and awareness about insurance products in the rural areas.

- In October 2004, the RBI permitted RRBs to undertake insurance business as a "corporate agent" without risk participation. As RRBs have a network of branches in rural areas, they could play an important role in increasing outreach.
- Though the 2005 IRDA regulations on micro-insurance have some restrictive aspects, they have also a number of positive features. Its most innovative feature is legally recognizing NGOs, MFIs and SHGs as "micro-insurance agents. " This has the potential of significantly increasing rural insurance penetration.
- Many commercial banks have partnered foreign insurance companies for providing life insurance policies. Thus, banking outlets (which number close to 70,000) and more than 1 lakh cooperative societies could provide the needed outreach to purvey micro-insurance facilities, without any further addition to transaction costs.

ADDRESSING DIFFERING PERSPECTIVES IN MICRO-INSURANCE

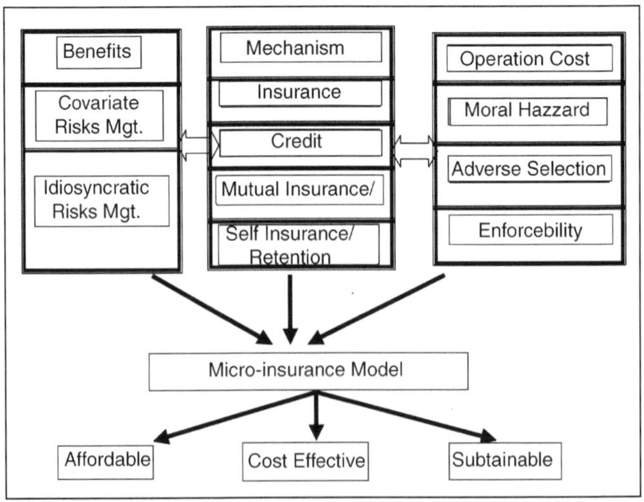

As already indicated, there are contrasting perspectives which have traditionally impeded the growth of this sector globally. The same is true of the Indian experience also. The competing perspectives of the insured, *viz.*, need, affordability and willingness vis-à-vis the insurer's, *viz.*, insurability, profitability and deliverability continue to be the core dilemma in micro-insurance thru' institutional sources. Further, the core problems in institutional insurance, *viz.*, moral hazard, adverse selection and poor infrastructure which results in high claims costs, administrative costs and consequently inadequate coverage have to be addressed effectively, for enabling the growth of an affordable, cost-effective and sustainable model.

DELIVERY MECHANISM: MICRO-INSURANCE MODELS

A key concern in the pricing of an insurance product is the element of cost of acquisition and its delivery. Obviously, the delivery costs have to be contained to keep the cost of insurance sufficiently low to attract the poor and to incentivise the insurer to venture into this segment viewing it as a genuine market opportunity.

The Committee studied four different models for delivering micro-insurance services to the targeted clientele:

- *Partner–Agent Model*:
  - Insurers utilize MFIs' delivery mechanism to provide sales and basic services to clients.
  - There is no risk and limited administrative burden for MFIs.
- *Full Service Model*:
  - The provider is responsible for all aspects of product design, sales, servicing, and claims assessment.
  - The insurers are responsible for all insurance-related costs and losses and they retain all profits.
- *Community Based Model*:
  - The policy holders own and manage the insurance programme, and negotiate with external health care providers.
- *Provider Model*:
  - The service provider and the insurer are the same, *i.e.*, hospitals or doctors offer policies to indivi-duals or groups.

LEVERAGING EXISTING NETWORK FOR MICRO-INSURANCE

It would be difficult for the insurers to establish a vast network for distribution of micro-insurance products. They need to utilize existing Government organizations, banks, MFIs, NGOs and SHGs to increase the outreach of micro-insurance to the poor. The advantages of these entities are that they find greater acceptability among the financially excluded, and with a better understanding of their needs are well equipped to advise them on the choice of products.

In India with a vast rural population characterized by challenges and complexities, it makes sense to latch on to an existing mechanism operating in these segments to lower costs and to help the insurer to leverage on the faith already generated by the entity. Hence it would be prudent to choose a partner-agent model for delivery where the insurer underwrites the risk and the distribution is handled by an existing intermediary. This model keeps the cost of insurance attractive enough for the poor to enter and remain in its fold even while addressing the concern of the insurers about the low returns of micro-insurance.

LINKING MICRO-CREDIT WITH MICRO-INSURANCE

It is becoming increasingly clear that micro-insurance needs a further push and guidance from the Regulator as well as the Government. The Committee concurs with the view that offering microcredit without micro-insurance is bad financial behaviour, as it is the poor who suffer on account of such bad product design. There is, therefore, a need to emphasise linking of microcredit with micro-insurance. Linking micro-insurance with micro-finance makes good business sense. Further, as it helps in bringing down the inherent risk cost of lending, the Committee feels that NABARD should be regularly involved in issues relating to rural and micro insurance to leverage on its experience of being a catalyst in the field of micro-credit.

IMPLEMENTATION STRATEGY FOR MICRO-INSURANCE

Keeping in view the various issues dealt with earlier in this Chapter, the Committee has identified five major areas for formulation of strategies for effective implementation of micro-insurance programmes.

HUMAN RESOURCES REQUIREMENT AND TRAINING

As indicated earlier, the UNDP report states that there is a huge untapped market–of around 950 million people and nearly US$2 billion–for insurance in India. IRDA may consider putting in place an appropriate institutional structure for deciding on service packages including premia and formulating strategies for effective promotion of micro insurance. There is also a felt need for development, of both fulltime and part-time staff, thru' effective training in insurance marketing and servicing concepts.

OPERATIONS AND SYSTEMS

To address the requirements of the huge market potential available, appropriate systems should be evolved for tracking client information, either manually or using technology. While a technology platform may take time for setting up, in the long-run, the same will be cost-effective and reliable. Similarly, the procedures for premium payments, claims and other services should be formalized along with increased customization of products to stimulate demand.

DEVELOPMENT OF ADEQUATE FEEDBACK MECHANISM

Keeping in view the diverse nature of market requirements, suitable mechanisms to collect market intelligence, collating and interpretation of the same, in a formally structured manner, is important for product development and process refinement.

Insurance companies should go beyond devising new products to improving their processes for building awareness, marketing enrollment, premium collection, claim settlement and renewal. For this they need use innovative channels such as business correspondents, SHGs, NGOs and MFIs as also cooperatives and mutual associations. Further, the use of technology such as mobile phones and ATMs for premium collection should be encouraged to keep transaction costs low.

DEVELOPMENT OF DATA BASE

High costs of penetration and acquisition often leads to higher pricing of products, thereby impacting client outreach and market depth. Building up historical data base on risk profiles, claims, settlement ratios, etc., will facilitate in better pricing of products, based on actual rather than presumed risks.

Besides enabling cost reduction, warehousing of such data will make the market more transparent for entry of more operators. The IRDA and the Government should help in provision of data such as human mortality and morbidity, weather parameters and livestock mortality/morbidity, on a timely, large sample and regular basis. This will lead to finer pricing on actuarial basis and eventually cut costs of insurance.

CONSUMER EDUCATION, MARKETING AND GRIEVANCE HANDLING

The micro-insurance sector is unique in the sense that there is an ongoing challenge to explain the concept and benefits to the insured. Creating awareness thru' use of pictorial posters, local folk arts and street theatres might be useful to explain the mechanisms of insurance. Local community-based organisations could organize premium collections, as they have better access to the local people. To make it more acceptable to the people, micro-insurance products, apart from covering only risks, should also provide an opportunity for providing long term savings (endowment).

IRDA'S REGULATIONS ON MICRO-INSURANCE

Building on the recommendations of the consultative group, IRDA notified Micro-Insurance Regulations on 10th November 2005 with the following key features to promote and regulate micro-insurance products.

The regulations focus on the direction, design and delivery of the products:

- A tie-up between life and non life insurance players for integration of product to address risks to the individual, his family, his assets and habitat,
- Monitoring product design through "file and use",
- Breakthrough in distribution channels with inclusion of NGOs, SHGs, MFIs and PACS to provide micro-insurance, with appropriate compensation for their services,

- Enlarged servicing activities entrusted to micro-insurance agents,
- Issue of policy documents in simple vernacular language.

Currently the IRDA regulations do not favour composite insurance (*i.e.*, life and non-life insurances by the same company) and also limit the agency tie-up to one life and one non-life insurer. However, in recognition of the uniqueness of micro insurance, these regulations enable life and non-life companies to tie-up for offering a combined policy in rural areas.

Further, the IRDA has allowed insurers to issue policies with a maximum cover of ₹ 50,000 for general and life insurance under these regulations. The regulations have also eased the norms for entry of agents relating to training and pre-recruitment examination. As an attraction, remuneration to agents has also been leveled across the term of the policy.

Another striking feature of the regulation is the provision of extending coverage to the family as a unit as against the system of insurance coverage to individual lives. The insurer has to take IRDA's prior approval for launching micro-insurance products through the "file and use" mode. The maximum cover will be ₹ 30,000 per annum for a dwelling and contents or livestock or tools or implements or other named assets or crop insurance against all perils. For individual and group health insurance, the maximum cover is ₹ 30,000 per annum per individual. For personal accident policies the maximum ₹ 50,000 per annum and is open to 5-70 age group.

In case of life micro-insurance products, the cover amount for term insurance ranges between ₹ 5,000-50,000 for a minimum term of five years and maximum of 15 years. The entry age for this product is kept between 18-60. Endowment insurance policy provides cover for ₹ 5,000-30, 000 for a minimum five years and maximum 15 years for people aged between 18 and 60. Further, an insurer can collect the premium for both life and general insurance components directly from the consumer or agents.

At the time of opening of the insurance sector, IRDA had decided that all insurers, including the new entrants, should fulfill certain obligations to spread insurance in rural areas. Specific regulations have been issued prescribing targets in terms of quantum of policies to be written in the rural sector consistent with the years of their operations and also certain quantified target for coverage of lives in the social sector.

With a view to encouraging the insurers to meet these obligations and give a fillip to micro-insurance products, IRDA also decided that all micro-insurance products may be reckoned for the purpose of fulfillment of the social obligation and where such policy are issued in rural area they could also be reckoned for rural sector obligation. IRDA has also proposed to benchmark the above obligations with reference to quantified limits of sums assured under micro-insurance policies. The approach would ensure the faster development of the micro-insurance market and take the insurance penetration to rural areas.

The Committee wholly subscribes to the initiatives of IRDA in widening outreach of micro-insurance products to the rural poor and recommends that the same may be implemented with renewed zeal as providing micro-insurance is a necessary and essential adjunct in the inclusive process. The IRDA should continue to impose Rural and Social Sector Obligations but there should be no unreasonable caps on premiums and channel commissions. This is in line with the de-tariffing process in other sectors also. In the long run, it is only when the insurance companies find it profitable to serve this market that they will do so on their own.

OTHER RECOMMENDATIONS

Micro-insurance in India is a new concept and in the real sense, is yet to be tested for its conduciveness to the needs of the target segment. The most significant constraint is the lack of base line data on potential claims that can help the insurers to design or price products. The consumption and saving patterns are also a critical aid to assess the insurance needs. The issue of moral hazard and adverse selection is a matter of concern for the insurer. Spreading awareness among this segment of insurable population and capacity building of the delivery organisations are major challenges.

PRODUCT DEVELOPMENT/PROCESS RE-ENGINEERING

Customised product development to suit the varying requirements of the local populace is a pre-requisite. The processes/procedures are to be streamlined and simplified, to facilitate easier access for the rural poor. Information should be made available in vernacular for easy understanding of the terms on offer.

BUILDING DATA BASE

With a view to bringing down product costs, building data base of claim histories, risk profiles, etc., are to be undertaken. This will also help in aligning pricing decisions with actuarial calculations.

USING EXISTING INFRASTRUCTURE

Micro-insurance service providers can use the existing banking infrastructure and also adopt the agency-mode (NGOs, SHGs, NBFCs, etc.) for providing services, thereby leveraging on the existing physical branch network and reducing costs.

USE OF TECHNOLOGY

The technology platforms being envisioned to facilitate financial inclusion should enable micro-insurance transactions also. Towards this end, there is a need to integrate the various modules-savings, credit, insurance, etc.-into the technology framework so that holistic inclusive efforts are possible in the rural areas.

REVIEW OF EXISTING SCHEMES

There are a large number of group life and health insurance schemes which are run by various central ministries and State Governments. The level of actual coverage in terms of claims preferred and settled in such schemes is disturbingly low. These schemes should be reviewed by an expert group set up by the IRDA. However, with reference to specific segments, the Committee makes the following recommendations.

LIFE INSURANCE

A wide range of products are available but penetration is really limited in rural areas. The procedural requirements at the time of entry and in case of claims settlement are cumbersome. The commission structure for agents is also heavily weighed in favour of getting new policies with very little incentive to service existing policies. In this regard, Micro Insurance Guidelines (MIG) 2005 issued by IRDA has provided for equal commission throughout the life of a policy and this will now remove the disincentive in servicing existing policy holders.

HEALTH INSURANCE

In case of Health Insurance, penetration level is even much lower than Life Insurance. The two categories *viz.*, Critical Illness and Hospitalisation are the main product segments. Some State Governments have developed Health Insurance schemes which are still in very early stages. The Committee has observed that mutual health insurance models have advantages of its members performing a number of roles such as awareness creation, marketing, enrolment, premium collection, claims processing, monitoring, etc.

Under this arrangement, the costs of offering small-ticket health insurance gets significantly reduced. The high covariant risks such as epidemics will have to be taken care of by a mutual entity taking reinsurance for such risks. IRDA has also suggested that the capital requirements for stand-alone health insurance companies be reduced to ₹ 50 crore as against ₹ 100 crore for Life Insurance Companies and the Committee endorses the same.

CROP INSURANCE

This is a very important risk mitigation arrangement for small and marginal farmers. However, the present scheme suffers from very serious implementation problems. Leaving the discretion to notify crops/regions to state governments has contributed to adverse selection. Further, claims settlement based on yield estimation has been cumbersome and the sampling area for crop cutting experiments is very large. An alternative model based on weather insurance has been attempted.

Farmers are happier with it because of quick settlements. On the down side premium rates are very high. Further, due to low density of weather stations, the problem of large area averaging is a critical factor even with weather insurance. To counter this, there is a need for having a large number of smaller weather stations. The Committee recommends that policies be evolved to make crop insurance universal, *viz.*, applicable to all crops/regions and pricing actuarial.

LIVESTOCK INSURANCE

As in Life Insurance, the problem lies in the process of enrollment and claims settlement. Several pilots indicate that the involvement of local organisations like SHGs, dairy co-operatives, NGOs and MFIs improves the quality of service, reduces false claims and expedites claims settlement. The Committee recommends that these experiences be studied and adopted by insurance companies.

ASSET INSURANCE

This could cover a wide range including residential buildings, farm and nonfarm equipments and vehicles. For poor households, insurance for a hut, irrigation pump, a handloom or a bullock cart could have considerable economic significance. Products are available but penetration levels are negligible. The main constraint seems to be lack of distribution channels appropriate for lower income groups. The Committee again recommends that involving local NGOs, MFIs, SHGs, etc. as distribution channels as well as facilitators of claim settlements would be quite useful.

INVENTORY OF MICRO-INSURANCE SCHEMES–ILO

The ILO (2004) has recently prepared an inventory of micro-insurance schemes operational in India:

- The inventory lists 51 schemes that are operational in India.
- Most of the schemes were launched in the last 4-5 years.
- 43 schemes for which the information is available cover 5.2 million people.
- Most insurance schemes (66%) are linked with micro finance services provided by specialised institutions or non-specialised organisations. 22% of the schemes are implemented by community-based organisations and 12% by health care providers.
- Life and health are the two most popular risks for which insurance is demanded; 59% of schemes provide life insurance and 57% of them provide health insurance.
- Most schemes (74%) operate in 6 southern states of India:
  - Andhra Pradesh (27%),
  - Tamil Nadu (23%),
  - Karnataka (17%)
  - Kerala (8%).
  - Maharashtra (12%) and
  - Gujarat (6%) account for 18% of the schemes.

12

Marketing Mix

INTRODUCTION

Indian insurance market is likely to spectator the deep changes in the sphere of all the four programmes of marketing mix. The customer driven market would result a lot of flexibilities and innovations in products, pricing, distribution channels and communication mechanisms.

The Insurance Regulatory and Development Authority (IRDA) with its developmental and regulatory guidelines are likely to endorse competition, fairness and reliability and at the same time protect insured against excessive, inadequate or unfairly discriminatory rates while efforts for intensification of the existing distribution channels and making them more effective will continue.

Introduction of new intermediaries like insurance brokers, new boulevard like banc assurance and utilization of electronics media and internet would call for new strategies. Communication to create more awareness and greater demand for insurance products will continue to assume high importance. At the same time, unfair or misleading advertisements will be discouraged and necessary checks and controls will be in place.

REVIEW OF LITERATURE AND RESEARCH METHODOLOGY

Marketing strategies for insurance products in the emerging scenario would be understood in terms of the following steps: Market Research, Segmentation, targeting, Positioning, Implementation, and Control.

In context to this, a brief account of reviews about the studies which have served a main base for the present study is given below:

- Gupta, examined that the insurance sector reforms are a part of the Government's priorities. A package of reforms is very much in the offing. There is an immediate need of a regulatory framework to open up the insurance industry.
- Mittal, analytically examined the global market to observe how the new sense of competition which will come to the market after the liberalization will affect the non-life insurance markets structure and

operation in India. Jha, commented that improvement in life span and advancement in medical science had changed the customers' needs for insurance products worldwide. The focus of the insurers in matured market of the west had shifted to pension, health care and protection products. Hasanbanu, and Nagajyothi, concluded that there is significant relationship between age, educational qualification, gender, occupation and income of respondents and their level of investment with taking LIC policies and further concluded that there is no significant relation between marital-status, family type and family size and their level of investment with taking LIC policies.

To study the nature, pattern and process of marketing mix in the insurance companies in India.

To achieve the aforesaid objective the following hypothesis are set:

- There is no significant difference between the respondents of various age groups regarding the variables of marketing mix.
- There is no significant difference between male and female respondents concerning the variables of marketing mix.
- There is no significant difference between the respondents of various qualifications about the variables of marketing mix.
- There is no significant difference between the respondents of various hierarchies as regards to the variables of marketing mix.
- There is no significant difference between the public company and private companies respondents regarding the variables of marketing mix.

The study incorporates primary data and a total of 95 executives at various positions in private as well as public life insurance company are examined during the study. The sample included in the study is drawn from U.T. of Chandigarh, states of Delhi and Haryana. In order to fulfill the objective, demographic variables (age, sex, qualification, hierarchy level, type of organization and marital status) are included in the study.

For primary data collection, structured questionnaire is prepared which is based on; three-point scale (rarely, sometimes and regularly/always) is used. A score of 1 for the response 'rarely', 2 for 'sometimes' and 3 for 'regularly/ always' is assigned. Initially factor analysis is applied to raw data after checking the correlation between the variables of marketing mix in life insurance industry in India. Then for each factor a combined score is obtained.

Finally, one-way ANOVA and T-test is applied to test the significance of the study:

- Age-wise analysis:
  - 20-30 years,
  - 30-40 years and
  - 40 years and above years,
- Qualification-wise analysis:

  - Graduate,
  - Postgraduate and
  - M. Phil. /Ph. D.
- Hierarchy-wise analysis:
  - Junior,
  - Middle, and
  - Senior,
- One-way ANOVA is used to test the significance whereas for Sex-wise analysis:
  - Male, and
  - Female.
- Organization-wise analysis:
  - Public, and
  - Private Organization

T-test is used to test the significance. In order to know the nature, process and pattern of marketing mix, nine dimensions (MM 1 to MM 9) are set to analyse marketing mix in life insurance industry.

The descriptions of those variables are as:

- *MM 1*: It represents that the concept of marketing mix understood and used by the marketing department of insurance industry.
- *MM 2*: It represents that the marketing department attempt to quantify the level of expenditure in insurance industry.
- *MM 3*: It represents that the elasticity of various mix ingredients are studied by marketing personnel's in life insurance industry.
- *MM 4*: It denotes that the review of marketing mix by the marketing department in life insurance industry.
- *MM 5*: It expresses that the careful analysis is carried out to develop an optimum mix and most economic mix.
- *MM 6*: It explains that the life insurance companies attempt to analyse its competitor's mix.
- *MM 7*: It represents that the life insurance companies adjusts its marketing mix in relation to specific segments.
- *MM 8*: It denotes that the other departments understand the mix concept and they are invited to take parting its development.
- *MM 9*: It expresses that the life insurance company do briefing about mix plan to outside contractors (such as research/advertising agencies).

DESCRIPTIVE AND STATISTICAL INFERENCES

DESCRIPTIVE INFERENCES

Table expressed the opinion of 95 respondents of different age groups, sex, qualifications, hierarchies and organizations. In total, 38 respondents belongs to age group 20-30 years, 37 respondents belongs to 30-40 years age group and 20 respondents belongs to 40 years and above age group. 80 respondents are male executive and only 15 respondents are female executives. The predominance respondents are graduate followed by 33 respondents who are postgraduate and only 26 respondents possess M.Phil./Ph.D. degrees. Hierarchy-wise analysis revealed that major part of 95 respondents is on senior position, 31 respondents on middle position and 25 respondents on junior position. Preponderance belongs to LIC and 38 respondents belong to privatcompanies.

	Demographics	**MM1**			**MM2**			**MM3**			**MM4**			**MM5**		**MM6**			**MM7**			**MM8**			**MM3**			
		R	S	R/A	R	S	R/A	R	S	R/A	R	S	R/A	R	S	R	S	R/A	R	S	R/A	R	S	R/A	R	S	R/A	Total
Age (Years)	20-30	14	12	12	2	30	6	22	4	12	4	12	22	26	12	8	20	10	12	20	6	6	14	18	6	22	10	38
	30-40	3	10	24	5	18	14	7	12	18	2	10	25	11	26	4	12	21	17	6	14	7	6	24	7	17	13	37
	40 years and above	2	6	12	4	6	10	2	6	12	0	6	14	10	10	0	10	10	6	4	10	4	4	12	4	10	6	20
	Total	19	28	48	11	54	30	31	22	42	6	28	61	47	48	12	42	41	35	30	30	17	24	54	17	49	29	95
Sex	Male	16	25	39	11	44	25	26	17	37	4	24	52	37	43	10	37	33	27	24	29	13	21	46	13	43	24	80
	Female	3	3	9	0	10	5	5	5	5	2	4	9	10	5	2	5	8	8	6	1	4	3	8	4	6	5	15
	Total	19	28	48	11	54	30	31	22	42	6	28	61	47	48	12	42	41	35	30	30	17	24	54	17	49	29	95
Qualification	Graduate	7	9	20	2	24	10	11	9	16	0	11	22	11	22	4	11	18	14	4	15	5	6	22	5	14	14	33
	Postgraduate	2	13	18	5	16	12	8	7	18	0	11	22	11	22	4	11	18	14	4	15	5	6	22	5	14	14	33
	M. Phil./ Ph. D.	10	6	10	4	14	8	12	6	8	6	6	14	18	8	2	16	8	4	14	8	8	6	12	8	14	4	26
	Total	19	28	48	11	54	30	31	22	42	6	28	61	47	48	12	42	41	35	30	30	17	24	54	17	49	29	95
Hierarchy	Junior	2	10	13	6	14	5	6	11	8	0	8	17	11	14	4	10	11	12	3	10	6	4	15	6	9	10	25
	Middle	7	10	14	2	17	12	13	6	12	2	12	17	19	12	8	11	12	6	15	10	6	7	18	6	23	2	31
	Senior	10	8	21	3	23	13	12	5	22	4	8	27	17	22	0	21	18	17	12	10	5	13	21	5	17	17	39
	Total	19	28	48	11	54	30	31	22	42	6	28	61	47	48	12	42	41	35	30	30	17	24	54	17	49	29	95
Organization	Public	6	21	30	9	34	14	16	14	27	4	18	35	28	29	10	25	22	21	13	23	13	5	39	13	24	20	57
	Private	13	7	18	2	20	16	15	8	15	2	10	26	19	19	2	17	19	14	17	7	4	19	15	4	25	9	38
	Total	*19*	*28*	*48*	*11*	*54*	*30*	*31*	*22*	*42*	*6*	*28*	*61*	*47*	*48*	*12*	*42*	*41*	*35*	*30*	*30*	*17*	*24*	*54*	*17*	49	29	95

MM1

Greater part of respondents believed that the concept is properly understood and regularly implemented in life insurance companies followed by 28 respondents are of view that the concept is sometimes understood and implemented and only few respondents believed that the concept is not understood and implemented in toto. Age-wise analysis depicted that predominance of respondents are of 30-40 year age group followed by 14 respondents who belong to 20-30 year age group. The main part (81.25 per cent) of 48 respondents is male and rest is female.

Major part (41.67 per cent) of 48 respondents are graduate followed by 37. 50 per cent possess postgraduate degree and rest possess M. Phil. /Ph. D. Degree. Majority (43.75 per cent) of 48 respondents is at senior position, 29.17 per cent at middle position and 27.08 per cent at junior position. Major respondents of 48 respondents belong to public sector and rest (37.5 per cent) belongs to private sector.

MM2

The best part (54 respondents) sometimes are of opinion that marketing department in life insurance companies attempted to quantify the level of expenditure while 30 respondents have expressed their views as life insurance companies regularly attempted to quantity the level of expenditure. Only 11 respondents believed that marketing department in life insurance companies rarely quantifies the level of expenditure.

MM3

As many as 42 respondents expresses their views that marketing department of life insurance industry regularly determine elasticity of various mix ingredients, followed by 31 respondents who thinks that marketing department rarely understand the elasticity of various mix and only 22 respondents are of view that an attempt is made sometimes to identify elasticity of various mix by marketing department in life insurance companies.

MM4

Preponderance respondents viewed that marketing department of life insurance companies reviewed its marketing mix regularly followed by 28 respondents who opinions that marketing department sometimes review its marketing mix. Very few respondents viewed that marketing department rarely review its marketing mix in life insurance companies.

MM5

A high portions opinioned that careful analysis is carried out regularly in order to identify the most effective and most economical mix. Almost equal respondents viewed that careful analysis is carried out sometimes in order to identify the most effective and most economical mix.

MM6

41 respondents expressed their views that life insurance firms regularly consider the understanding of competitor's mix very carefully whereas 42 respondents are of opinion that companies do analyse its competitors' mix sometimes, and only 12 respondents observes that company rarely attempt to analyse its competitor's mix.

MM7

Most of (35 respondents) respondents are of opinion that life insurance companies rarely adjust its marketing mix in relation to specific segment followed by 30 respondents who are of opinion that life insurance companies adjust sometimes the components of mix whereas the same proportion (30 respondents) are opinioned that the mix is adjusted regularly.

MM8

54 respondents recognized that other departments regularly shows their involvement and participation in development of marketing mix while 24 respondents believed that other departments advise sometimes the marketing department in this regard. Only 17 respondents believed that other departments rarely show their involvement and participation in this regard.

MM9

49 respondents viewed that companies sometime provides provide full details of their marketing mix plans to outside contractors while 29 respondents viewed that companies regularly provides full details about mix plans. Only 17 respondents deny that company rarely provides any idea to outside contractors.

RELATIONSHIP BETWEEN VARIABLES OF MARKETING MIX

In order to understand the relationship between various dimensions of marketing mix of life insurance companies, correlations are calculated. Table indicates the correlation between various dimensions of marketing mix. The value of correlation for various dimensions of marketing mix ranges between $p< 0.05$ to 0.01.

The result suggests positive correlation between MM 1, MM 2, MM 3, MM 4, MM5, MM 6, MM 8 and MM 9.

The value of significance level ranges between $p<0.05$ to $p<0.01$. In general, it can be concluded that increase in one variable would lead to increase in rest positively related variables.

Table. Correlation Analysis between the Variable of Marketing Mix

Variables		MM1	MM2	MM3	MM4	MM5	MM6	MM7	MM8	MM9
MM1	Person Correlation	1	.262(*)	.629(**)	.292(**)	.601(**)	.417(**)	– .220(*)	.553(**)	.400(**)
	Sig. (2 -tailed)		.010	.000	.004	.000	.000	.032	.000	.000
MM2	Person Correlation	.262(*)	1	.441(**)	.055	.316(**)	.597(**)	–.143	.231(*)	.211(*)
	Sig. (2 -tailed)	.010		.000	.595	.002	.000	.168	.024	.040
MM3	Person Correlation	.629(**)	.441(**)	1	.232(*)	.592(**)	.473(**)	.038	.325(**)	.383(**)
	Sig. (2 -tailed)	.000	.000		.024	.000	.000	.716	.001	.000
MM4	Person Correlation	.292(**)	.055	.232(*)	1	.319(**)	.335(*)	.207(*)	.730(**)	.709(**)
	Sig. (2 -tailed)	.004	.595	.024		.002	.001	.044	.000	.000
MM5	Person Correlation	.601	.316(**)	.592(**)	.319(**)	1	.659(**)	.115	.499(**)	.521(**)
	Sig. (2 -tailed)	.000	.002	.000	.002		.000	.265	.000	.000
MM6	Person Correlation	.417(**)	.597(**)	.473(**)	.335(**)	.659(**)	1	.178	.374(**)	.436(**)
	Sig. (2 -tailed)	.000	.000	.000	.001	.000		.084	.000	.000
MM7	Person Correlation	– .220(*)	–.143	.038	.207(*)	.115	.178	1	.164	–.100
	Sig. (2 -tailed)	.032	.138	.716	.044	.265	.084		.111	.335
MM8	Person Correlation	.553(**)	.231(*)	.325(**)	.730(**)	.499(**)	.374(**)	.164	1	.824(**)
	Sig. (2 -tailed)	.000	.024	.001	.000	.000	.000	.111		.000
MM9	Person Correlation	.400(**)	.211(*)	.383(**)	.709(**)	.521(**)	.436(**)	–.100	.824(**)	1
	Sig. (2 -tailed)	.000	.040	.000	.000	.000	.000	.335	.000	

INTERPRETATION OF FACTOR ANALYSIS FOR MARKETING MIX

After calculating high relationship between the variables of marketing mix, Factor Analysis is carried out to investigate the linear relationship of some underlying factors. Requesting principal components analysis and specifying in a rotation the output of Factor Analysis is obtain. Table provides output of the Factor Analysis for this problem, the rotated factor matrix comprising all nine variables, the per cent of variance, cumulative per cent of variance and the Eigen values of all factors having Eigen values of 1 or more than 1.

It is seen from the cumulative per cent of variance column that three factors extracted together account for 76.0783 per cent of total variance (information contained in the original 9 variables). This is a pretty good bargain, because from the 9 variables 3 underlying factors are extracted in an economised fashion. Total 76 per cent of information is retained by the three factors extracted; only 24 per cent of information is lost out of 9 original variables.

Table. Rotated Factor Matrix

Variables	Mix Ingredient	Mix Development	Mix Adjustment
MM1	0. 594241	0. 428493	-0. 38691
MM2	0. 761522	-0. 06519	-0. 10173
MM3	0. 770685	0. 215734	-0. 07806
MM4	0. 052312	0. 880292	0. 188221
MM5	0. 723687	0. 404106	0. 081795
MM6	0. 806814	0. 235322	0. 247171
MM7	0. 017497	0. 084309	0. 960976
MM8	0. 253025	0. 895827	0. 041604
MM9	0. 257215	0. 872779	-0. 13395
Eigen value	4. 169578	1. 522032	1. 155125
Percentage of Variance	46. 32864	16. 91147	12. 83472
Cumulative Per cent	46. 32864	63. 24011	76. 07483

Table for rotated factor matrix, it is noticed that variable numbers MM1, MM2, MM3, MM5, MM6 have loading of 0. 595241, 0. 761522, 0. 770685, 0. 723689 and 0. 806814 on Factor 1. This suggests that Factor 1 is a combination of these five original variables. Keeping in view the nature of the variables, Factor 1 is naming as Mix Ingredient. Further, it is noticed that variable number MM4, MM8 and MM9 have loading of 0. 880292, 0. 895827 and 0. 872779 on Factor 2. This suggests that Factor 2 is a combination of these three original variables.

Keeping in view the nature of these variables, Factor 2 is naming as Mix Development. Further, it is noticed that variable MM7 have loading of 0. 960976 on Factor 3. This suggests that Factor 3 is comprises single variable. Keeping in view the nature of this variable, Factor 3 is naming as Mix Adjustment. Table depicted that Mix Ingredient is found most important factor followed by Mix Development and Mix Adjustment.

After reducing original data by applying factor analysis, statistical tools One-way ANOVA (on age, qualification and hierarchy) and t-test (on sex and organization) is applied to draw concrete results. These tests are applied on three factors namely, Mix Ingredient, Mix Development and Mix Adjustment (Factor1, Factor2, and Factor3) those come out because of factor analysis.

ONE-WAY ANOVA FOR AGE-WISE ANALYSIS

Table. One-way ANOVA For Age-wise Analysis of Executive Respondents

Factors	Age	N	Mean	Std. Deviation	F Value	Sig. Level
Mix	20-30 Years	38	2. 032	0. 527		
Ingredient	30-40 Years	37	2. 454	0. 463	7. 114	0. 001

	40 Years and above	20	2. 460	0. 528		
Mix	20-30 Years	38	2. 297	0. 619		
Development	30-40 Years	37	2. 415	0. 665	0. 358	0. 700
	40 Years and above	20	2. 400	0. 629		
Mix	20-30 Years	38	1. 842	0. 679		
Adjustment	30-40 Years	37	1. 919	0. 924	1. 261	0. 288
	40 Years and above	20	2. 200	0. 894		

Table depicted that the mean values for Factor 1 (Mix Ingredient) are 2.032, 2. 454 and 2. 460 with values of S. D. 0.527, 0. 463 and 0.528 respectively for the respondents of age groups of 20-30, 30-40 years, and 40 years and above. The value of F is 7. 114 at 0.001 significant level. To conclude, it can be said that there is significant difference (the value of significant level for F-test is less than 0.05) between the opinions of respondents of various age groups regarding Mix Ingredients. The mean values for Factor 2 (Mix Development) are 2.297, 2.415 and 2.400 with S.D. 0.619, 0.665 and 0.629 respectively for different age groups. The value of F is 0.358 at 0.700 significant level.

To sum up, it can be extracted that there is no significant difference (the value of significant level for F-test is greater than 0.05) between the opinions of respondents of various age groups regarding Mix Development. The mean values for Factor 3 (Mix Adjustment) are 1.842, 1.919 and 2.200 with values of S.D. 0.679, 0.924 and 0.894 respectively for the respondents of various age groups. The F value is 1.261 at 0.288 significant level. To fathom out, it can be extracted that there is no significant difference (the value of significant level for F-test is greater than 0.05) between the opinions of respondents of various age groups regarding Mix Adjustment.

Age-wise analysis for executive respondents investigates that hypothesis is not fully accepted because respondents of various age groups show significantly different opinion about Mix Ingredient.

T-TEST FOR SEX-WISE ANALYSIS

Table. T-Test for Sex-wise Analysis of Executive Respondents

Factors	Sex	N	Mean	Std. Deviation	Value of T-test	Sig. (2-tailed)
Mix Ingredient	Male	80	2. 285	0. 552	–0. 055	0. 957
	Female	15	2. 293	0. 489		
Mix Development	Male	80	2. 383	0. 611	0. 648	0. 518
	Female	15	2. 267	0. 769		
Mix Adjustment	Male	80	2. 025	0. 842	2. 146	0. 035
	Female	15	1. 533	0. 640		

Table reveals that the mean value for male and female respondents for Mix Ingredients is 2. 285 and 2. 293 with the value of S. D. 0. 552 and 0. 489 respectively. The value of t-test is -0. 055 at 0. 957 significant level. In simple words, it is concluded that mean difference between the male and female respondents regarding Factor 1 is not significant (the value of significant level for ttest is greater than 0. 05). The mean value for Mix Development is 2.383 and 2.267 with S. D. 0.611 and 0.769 respectively for both male and female respondents.

The t-value is 0.648 at 0.518 significant level. To sum up, it can be extracted that there is no significant difference (the value of significant level for t-test is greater than 0.05) between the opinions of male and female respondents regarding Mix Development. Lastly, the value of mean for male and female respondents regarding Mix Adjustment is 2.025, 1.533 with S. D 0.842 and 0.640 respectively.

The t-value is 2.146 at 0.035 significant level. Surprisingly, here both male and female respondents have significantly different (the value of significant level for ttest is less than 0.05) opinion regarding Mix Adjustment. Analysis observes that hypothesis is also not fully accepted because male and female respondents have significantly different opinion about Mix Adjustment.

ONE-WAY ANOVA FOR QUALIFICATION-WISE ANALYSIS

Table. One-way ANOVA for Qualification-wise Analysis of Executive Respondents

Factors	Qualification	N	Mean Deviation	Std. Value	F Level	Sig.
Mix Ingredient	Graduate	36	2. 294	0. 529		
	Postgraduate	33	2. 418	0. 503	2. 487	0. 089
	M. Phil. /Ph. D.	26	2. 108	0. 569		
Mix Development	Graduate	36	2. 444	0. 530		
	Postgraduate	33	2. 485	0. 603	3. 233	0. 044
	M. Phil. /Ph. D.	26	2. 102	0. 748		
Mix Adjustment	Graduate	36	1. 722	0. 779		
	Postgraduate	33	2. 030	0. 951	2. 361	0. 100
	M. Phil. /Ph. D.	26	2. 154	0. 675		

The respondents of various qualifications regarding Mix Ingredient have means values 2.294, 2.418 and 2.108 with S.D. 0.529, 0.503 and 0.569 respectively. The F value is 2.487 at 0.089 significant level. To fathom out, it is said that the opinion of respondents of various qualifications is not significantly different (the value of significant level for F-test is greater than 0.05). The mean value for respondents of various qualifications regarding Mix Development is 2.444, 2.485 and 2.102 with S.D. 0.530, 0.603 and 0. 748 respectively. The value of F is 3. 233 at 0. 044 significant level.

In concrete terms, it can be abstracted that respondents of various qualifications have different opinion regarding Mix Development (the value of significant level for F-test is less than 0.05). The mean values for Mix

Adjustment are 1.722, 2.030 and 2.154 with the values of S.D. 0.779, 0.951 and 0.675 respectively for the respondents of various qualifications. The F Value is 2.361 at 0.100 level of significant. It can be interpreted that there is no significant difference (the value of significant level for F-test is greater than 0.05) between the opinions of respondents of various qualifications. Analysis of executive respondents on various qualification depicted that hypothesis is not fully accepted because respondents of various qualifications have significantly different opinion about Mix Development.

ONE-WAY ANOVA FOR HIERARCHY-WISE ANALYSIS

Table. One-way ANOVA for Hierarchy-wise Analysis of Executive Respondents

Factors	Hierarchy	N	Mean Deviation	Std. Value	F Level	Sig.
Mix Ingredient	Junior	25	2. 264	0. 423		
	Middle	31	2. 206	0. 642	0. 761	0. 470
	Senior	39	2. 364	0. 521		
Mix Development	Junior	25	2. 400	0. 682		
	Middle	31	2. 247	0. 566	0. 812	0. 447
	Senior	39	2. 436	0. 659		
Mix Adjustment	Junior	25	1. 920	0. 954	1. 218	0. 301
	Middle	31	2. 129	0. 718		
	Senior	39	1. 821	0. 823		

The mean values for junior, middle and senior level respondents regarding Mix Ingredient are 2.264, 2.206 and 2.364 with the S. D. 0.423, 0.642 and 0.521 respectively. The F Value is 0.761 at 0. 470 level of significant. In general sense, it can be extracted that there is no significant difference (the value of significant level for F-test is greater than 0.05) between the opinions of respondents of various hierarchies.

The mean value for Mix Development is 2.400, 2.247 and 2.436 with S. D. 0.682, 0. 566 and 0. 659 respectively, for junior, middle and senior level respondents. The F-Value is 0.812 at 0.447 significant level. In general sense, it can be extracted that there is no significant difference (the value of significant level for F-test is greater than 0.05) between the opinions of respondents of various hierarchies regarding Mix Development.

Lastly, the mean value for Mix Adjustment is 1.920, 2.129 and 1.821 with S. D. 0.954, 0.718 and 0.823 respectively, for junior, middle and senior level respondents. The F Value is 1.218 at 0.301 significant level. To abstract, it can be extracted that there is no significant difference (the value of significant level for Ftest is greater than 0.05) between the opinions of respondents of various hierarchies regarding Mix Adjustment. Above analysis justified that hypothesis is fully accepted that there is no significant difference between the opinions of respondents at various hierarchies regarding variables of marketing mix.

T-TEST FOR ORGANIZATION-WISE ANALYSIS

Table. T-Test for Organization-wise Analysis of Executive Respondents

Factors	Organization	N	Mean	Std. Deviation	Value of T-test	Sig. (2-tailed)
Mix Ingredient	Public	57	2. 284	0. 517		
	Private	38	2. 289	0. 580	-0. 046	0. 963
Mix Development	Public	57	2. 374	0. 69		
	Private	38	2. 350	0. 548	0. 178	0. 859
Mix Adjustment	Public	57	2. 035	0. 886		
	Private	38	1. 816	0. 730	1. 266	0. 209

The mean values for Mix Ingredient for the public and private organizations are 2.284 and 2.289 with S. D. 0.517 and 0.580 respectively. The t Value is -0.046 at 0.963 significant level. The mean values regarding Mix Development is 2.374 and 2.350 with S. D. 0.691 and 0.548 respectively for respondents of public and private companies. The value of t is 0.178 at 0.859 significant level.

Further, the mean values for Mix Adjustment is 2.035 and 1.816 with S. D. 0.886 and 0.730 respectively for respondents of public and private companies. The value of t is 1.266 at 0.209 significant level. To abstract, it can be extracted that there is no significant difference (the value of significant level for t-test is greater than 0.05) between the opinions of respondents of public and private companies regarding Mix Ingredient, Mix Development and Mix Adjustment.

Organization-wise statistical analysis revealed that hypothesis is fully accepted that there is no significant difference between the opinions of private and public company respondents regarding variables of marketing mix.

CONCLUDING REMARKS

In this chapter, various dimensions of marketing mix are measured. The analysis is done by five demographic variables namely, age, sex, qualification, hierarchy and organization.

The main findings are as following:

- Factor Analysis depicted that Mix Ingredient is found as most important factor followed by Mix Development and Mix Adjustment. It can also be extracted that there is no significant difference between the opinions of respondents of various hierarchies regarding Mix Adjustment. It can be extracted that there is no significant difference between the opinions of respondents of public and private companies regarding Mix Ingredient, Mix Development and Mix Adjustment.
- Further, age-wise, sex-wise and qualification-wise analysis reveals that the difference is found significant between the opinions of

respondents regarding Mix Ingredient, Mix Development and Mix Adjustment respectively. Analysis observes that hypothesis is also not fully accepted because male and female respondents have significantly different opinion about Mix Adjustment.

- Analysis of executive respondents on various qualification depicted that hypothesis is not fully accepted because respondents of various qualifications have significantly different opinion about Mix Development. Analysis justified that hypothesis is fully accepted that there is no significant difference between the opinions of respondents at various hierarchies regarding variables of marketing mix. Organization-wise statistical analysis revealed that hypothesis is fully accepted that there is no significant difference between the opinions of private and public company respondents regarding variables of marketing mix.

On the basis of analysis following suggestions could be made:

- The insurance firms should focus on the concept of marketing m2ix and they should implement the concept, insurance firms should quantify the level of expenditure for its mix ingredients, insurance firms should study elasticity of mix ingredients, insurance firms should carry out careful analysis in order to identify most effective and most economic mix, insurance firms should analyse its competitors' mix while implementing marketing mix, insurance firms should review whole mix in detail and so that each segment gets its own assemblage of mix components, insurance firms should review its marketing mix on regular basis, marketing department of insurance firms should call other functional department while developing marketing mix, and marketing department should provide the detail of their thinking on the subject supported by mix plan.

13

Market Segmentation and Positioning

INTRODUCTION

Ever wondered why marketers only target certain markets or how these markets are identified? Think about universities for a moment: how do they identify which students to communicate with about degree schemes? What criteria do they use? Do they base it on where you live, your age, your gender, or is it just about your entrance scores? Do they market to postgraduate and undergraduate audiences differently, what about international and domestic student groups—is this difference important for the effective marketing of higher education services to prospective students?

In this chapter, we consider the way organizations determine the markets in which they need to concentrate their commercial efforts. This process is referred to as market segmentation and is an integral part of marketing strategy. After defining the principles of market segmentation this chapter commences with an exploration of the differences between market segmentation and product differentiation, as this helps clarify the underlying principles of segmentation.

Consideration is also given to the techniques and issues concerning market segmentation within consumer and business-to-business markets. The method by which whole markets are subdivided into different segments is referred to as the STP process. STP refers to the three activities that should be undertaken, usually sequentially, if segmentation is to be successful. These are segmentation, targeting, and positioning, and this chapter is structured around these key elements.

THE STP PROCESS

The growing use of the STP process has occurred as a direct result of the prevalence of mature markets, the greater diversity in customer needs, and the ability to reach specialized or niche segments. As such marketers are increasingly segmenting markets and identifying attractive segments (*i.e.* who to focus on and why?), in order to identify new product opportunities, develop suitable positioning and communications strategies (*i.e.* what message to communicate), and effectively allocate resources to key marketing activities (*i.e.* how much should we spend and where?).

Organizations will often commission segmentation research when they want to re-scope their marketing strategy, investigate a declining brand, launch a new product, or restructure their pricing policy. Organizations operating in highly dynamic environments seek to conduct segmentation research at regular intervals, to keep in touch with changes in the marketplace. STP refers to the three activities segmentation, targeting, and positioning.

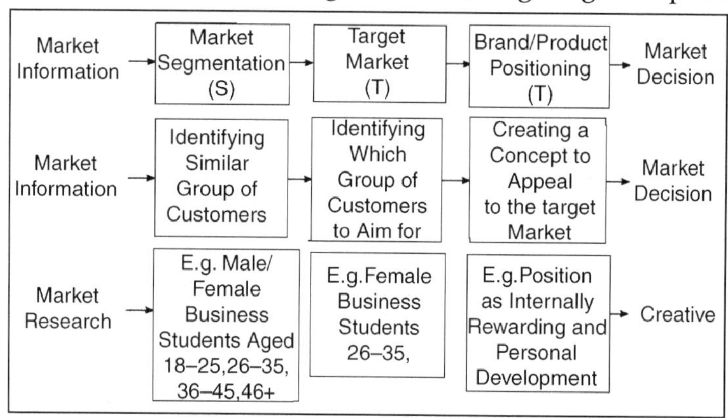

Fig. The STP Process

Key benefits of the STP process include:

- Enhancing a company's competitive position by providing direction and focus for marketing strategies such as targeted advertising, new product development, and brand differentiation. For example, Coca-Cola identified through market research that its Diet Coke brand (also marketed as Coca-Cola Lite) was regarded as 'girly' and 'feminine' by male consumers. As a direct result the company developed a new product, branded Coke Zero, which is targeted at the health-conscious male segment of the soft drinks market.
- Examining and identifying growth opportunities in the market through the identification of new customers, growth segments, or new product uses. For example Arm and Hammer was able to attract new customers when existing consumers identified new uses for their baking soda. Lucozade also changed the positioning and targeting from its original marketing strategy positioned for sick children and rebranded to target athletes as an energy drink.
- More effective and efficient matching of company resources to targeted market segments promises the greatest return on marketing investment (ROMI). For example, financial institutions like HSBC and Barclays and large retailing multinationals such as Tesco and ASDA Wal-Mart are utilizing data-informed segmentation strategies

to effectively target direct marketing messages and rewards to customers they have classified as offering long-term value to the company, *i.e.* they are profitable customers.

THE CONCEPT OF MARKET SEGMENTATION

Market segmentation is the division of a market into different groups of customers with distinctly similar needs and product/service requirements. Or to put it another way, market segmentation is the division of a mass market into identifiable and distinct groups or segments, each of which have common characteristics and needs and display similar responses to marketing actions.

Market segmentation was first defined as 'a condition of growth when core markets have already been developed on a generalised basis to the point where additional promotional expenditures are yielding diminishing returns'. There is now widespread agreement that they form an important foundation for successful marketing strategies and activities.

The purpose of market segmentation is to leverage scarce resources; in other words, to ensure that the elements of the marketing mix, price, distribution, products and promotion, are designed to meet particular needs of different customer groups. Since companies have finite resources it is not possible to produce all possible products for all the people, all of the time. The best that can be aimed for is to provide selected offerings for selected groups of people, most of the time. This process allows organizations to focus on specific customers' needs, in the most efficient and effective way. As Beane and Ennis eloquently commented, 'a company with limited resources needs to pick only the best opportunities to pursue'.

The market segmentation concept is related to product differentiation. If you aim at different market segments, you might adapt different variations of your offering to satisfy those segments, and equally if you adapt different versions of your offering, this may appeal to different market segments. Since there is less competition, your approach is less likely to be copied and so either approach will do. An example in the area of fashion retailing might be if you adapt your clothing range so that your skirts are more colourful, use lighter fabrics, and a very short hemline, for instance, this styling is more likely to appeal more to younger women.

If alternatively, you decide to target older women, then you might need to change the styling of your skirts to suit them by using darker, heavier fabrics, with a longer hemline. This is exactly what Marks and Spencer did to attract a younger female shopper into their M&S stores and compete more directly with Next and Debenhams for share of this market. The company launched a range of female clothing called Per Una, and three years on the fashion range has been a huge success reportedly generating annual sales of nearly £230 m—more than 10 per cent of the total womenswear sales at M&S. If you start by adapting new product variants, you are using a product differentiation approach. If you start with the customer's needs, you are using a market segmentation approach. This is illustrated more clearly in Figure using offering rather than product to indicate that the same concept may apply to a service.

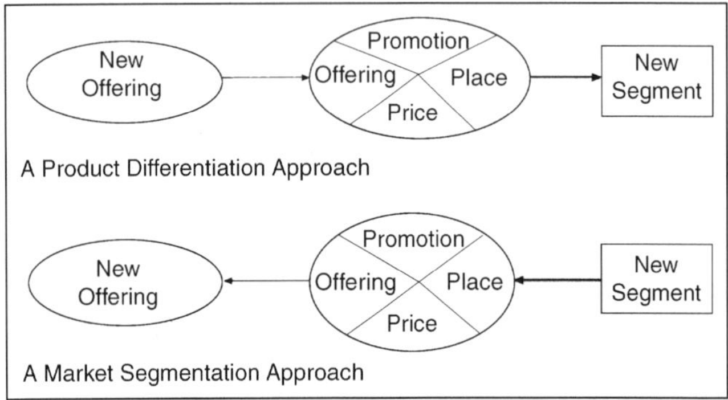

Fig. The Difference between Market Segment and Product Differentiation

A relational marketing perspective would replace the marketing mix—the 4Ps—either with the 7Ps or with a discussion of the need to design, develop, and deliver the customer experience. The concept of market segmentation was first proposed as an alternative market development technique in imperfectly competitive markets, that is, in markets where there are relatively few competitors selling an identical product.

Where there are lots of competitors selling identical products, market segmentation and product differentiation produce similar results as competitors imitate your strategic approach more quickly and product differentiation approaches meet market segment needs more closely.

With an increasing proliferation of tastes in modern society, consumers have increased disposable incomes. As a result, marketers have sought to design product and service offerings around consumer demand (market segmentation) more than around their own production needs (product differentiation) and they use market research to inform this process.

THE PROCESS OF MARKET SEGMENTATION

The intricacies involved in market segmentation are said to make it an exacting activity. Griffith and Pol argue this point on the basis of multiple product applications, greater customer variability, and problems associated with the identification of the key differences between groups of customers.

However, there have been numerous attempts to define and describe business segmentation, using a variety of variables and ranging from the severely product-based to customer needs-based orientation. There are two main approaches to segmenting markets. The first adopts the view that the market is considered to consist of customers which are essentially the same, so the task is to identify groups which share particular differences. This is referred to as the breakdown method. The second approach considers a market to consist of customers that are all different, so here the task is to find similarities. This is known as the build-up method.

The breakdown approach is perhaps the most established and well recognized and is the main method used for segmenting consumer markets. The build-up approach seeks to move from the individual level where all customers are different, to a more general level of analysis based on the identification of similarities. The build-up method is customer oriented as it seeks to determine common customer needs. The aim of both methods is to identify segments in the market where identifiable differences exist between segments (segment heterogeneity) and similarities exist between members within each segment (member homogeneity). This is displayed in Figure.

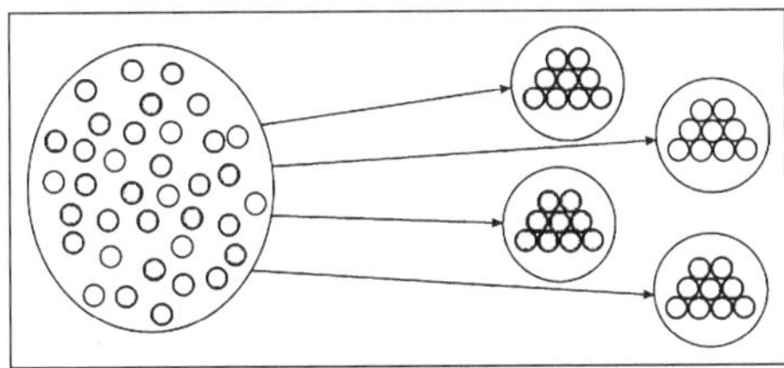

Fig. Segment Heterogenelty and Member Homogenlty

Other segmentation researchers have distinguished between a priori or post hoc segmentation methods. In the former, segments are predetermined using the judgement of the researchers beforehand (*i.e.* a priori).

This approach typically progresses along seven stages encompassing the following steps including:

1. Selection of the base (a priori) for segmentation (*e.g.* demographics, socio-economics).
2. Selection of segment descriptors (including hypotheses on the possible link between these descriptors and the basis for segmentation).
3. *Sample Design*: Mostly using stratified sampling approaches and occasionally a quota sample.
4. Data collection.
5. Formation of the segments based on a sorting of respondents into categories.
6. Establishment of the profile of the segments using multivariate statistical methods (*e.g.* multiple discriminate analysis, multiple regression analysis).
7. Translation of the findings about the segments' estimated size and profile into specific marketing strategies, including the selection of target segments and the design or modification of specific marketing strategy.

With the post hoc approach, the segments are deduced from the research and instead pursue the following process:

- *Sample Design*: Mostly using quota or random sampling approaches.
- Identification of suitable statistical methods of analysis.
- Data collection.
- *Data Analysis*: Formation of distinct segments using multivariate statistical methods (*e.g.* cluster analysis, CHAID).
- Establishment of the profile of the segments using multivariate statistical methods (*e.g.* factor analysis) and selection of segment descriptors (based on the key aspects of the profile for each segment).
- Translation of the findings about the segments' estimated size and profile into specific marketing strategies, including the selection of target segments and the design or modification of specific marketing strategy.

Segmentation in business markets should reflect the relationship needs of the parties involved and should not be based solely on the traditional consumer market approach, which is primarily the breakdown method. Through use of both the breakdown and the build-up approaches, a more accurate, in-depth, and potentially more profitable view of industrial markets can be achieved.

However, problems remain concerning the practical application and implementation of B2B segmentation. Managers report that the analysis processes are reasonably clear, but it is not clear how they should 'choose and evaluate between the market segments' which have been determined.

Much segmentation theory has been developed during the period when transactional marketing was the principal approach to marketing, rather than the more relational approaches adopted in today's service-dominated environment. Under these circumstances, the allocation of resources to achieve the designated marketing mix goals was of key importance.

Freytag and Clarke have quite rightly identified that market segmentation is not a static concept. In other words, those customers who make up the various segments have needs which may change, and consequently, those customers may no longer remain members of the particular segment to which they originally belonged. Market segmentation programmes must therefore use customer data which are current.

The segmentation process will therefore vary just as to the prevailing conditions in the marketplace and the changing needs of the parties involved, not simply the needs of the selling organization.

MARKET SEGMENTATION IN CONSUMER MARKETS

To segment consumer goods and service markets, we use market information we have collected based on certain key customer-, product-, or situation-related criteria (variables). These are classified as segmentation bases and include profile (*e.g.* who are my market and where are they?); behavioural (*e.g.* where, when, and how does my market behave?); and psychological criteria (*e.g.* why does my market behave that way?). These differing types of segmentation bases are depicted in Figure.

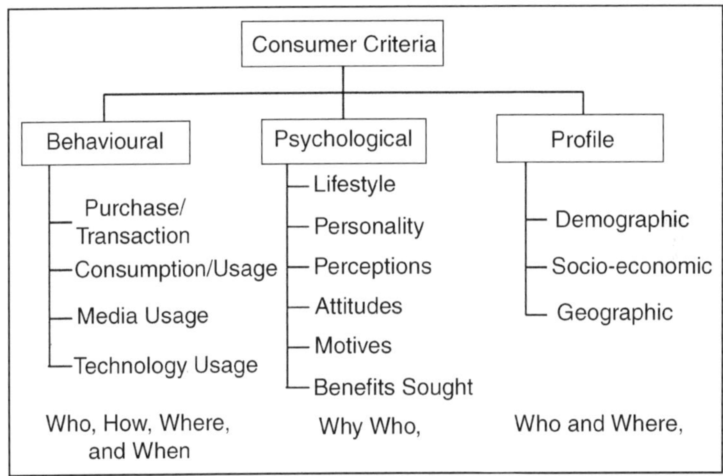

Fig. Segmentation Criteria for Consumer Market

A fourth segmentation criterion that can be added is contact data, a customer's name and full contact details beyond just their postcode (*e.g.* postal address, e-mail, mobile and home telephone number). The data are useful for tactical-level marketing activities such as addressable direct marketing.

Table. Segmenting Criteria for Goods and Services Markets

Base Type	Segmention Criteria	Explanation
Profile	Demographic	Key variables concern age, sex, occupation, level of education, religion, social class, and income characteristics, many of which determine a potential buyer's ability to purchase a product or service.
	Lifestage	Lifestage analysis is based on the principle that people need different products and services at different stages in their lives (*e.g.* childhood, adulthood, young couples, retired).
	Geographic	In many situations the needs of potential customers in one geographic area are different from those in another area. This may be due to climate, custom,or tradition.

	Geodemographic	This approach to segmentation presumes that there is a relationship between the type of housing and location that people live in and their purchasing behaviours.
Psychological	Psychographic (lifestyles)	Analysing consumers' activities, interests, and opinions, we can understand individual lifestyles and patterns of behaviour, which in turn affect their buying behaviour and decision-makingprocesses. On this basis, we can also identify similar product and/or media usage patterns.
	Benefits sought	By understanding the motivations customers derive from their purchases it is possible to have an insight into the benefits they seek from product use.
Behavioural	Purchase/ transaction	Data about customer purchases and transactions provides scope for analysing who buys what, when, how often, how much they spend, and through what transactional channel they purchase. This provides very rich data for identifying 'profitable' customer segments.
	Product usage	Segments are derived from analysing markets on the basis of their usage of the product offering, brand, or product category. This may be in the form of usage frequency, time of usage, and usage situations.
	Media usage	Data on what media channels are used, by whom, when, where, and for how long provides useful insight into the reach potential for certain market segments through differing media channels, and also insight into their media lifestyle.

Table illustrates the key characteristics associated with each of the main approaches to consumer market segmentation. An important consideration when selecting the differing bases for segmentation is the trade-off between ease and cost of measurement or data acquisition and the degree to which the criteria for which data has been acquired can provide an accurate snapshot of current and future customer behaviour, especially its predictability of customer choice behaviour.

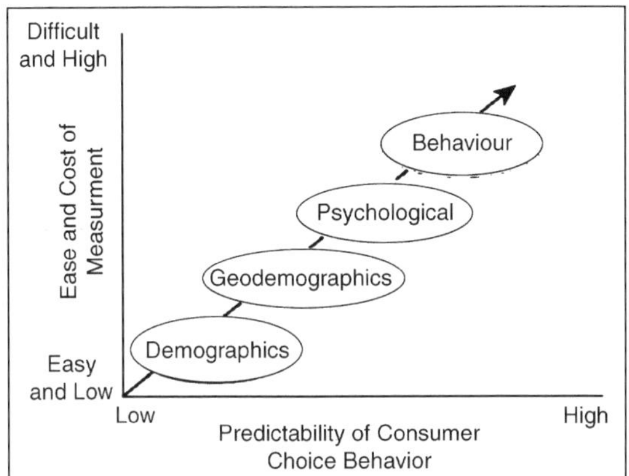

Fig. Considerations for Segmentation Criteria Accessibility and use

As is depicted in Figure demographics and geodemo-graphics are relatively easy to measure or the data to obtain; however, these bases suffer from low levels of accurate predictability of a customer's future behaviour. In contrast, behavioural data, what a customer does, their product usage, purchase history, and media usage, although more difficult and costly to acquire (although with changes in technology this cost/accessibility is changing), provides a more accurate predictability of future behaviour.

This is founded on the notion that humans are creatures of habit and behavioural trends. Therefore the brand of toothpaste you purchased on the last three occasions is more than likely going to be the brand of toothpaste you purchase next time. However, this is also influenced by a customer's susceptibility to marketing communications such as sales promotions (media usage and response behaviour) and market environment.

PROFILE CRITERIA

A core customer-related method of segmenting consumer goods and service markets is using criteria to profile who the market is and where they are. This is called profile segmentation criteria and includes using demographic methods (*e.g.* age, gender, race), socio-economics (*e.g.* determined by social class, or income levels) and geographic location (often using sophisticated postal or zip code systems). For example, a utility company might segment households based on geographical area to assess brand penetration in certain regions; or a financial investment fund might segment the market based on age, employment, income, and asset net worth to identify attractive market segments for a new investment portfolio. All these are examples of segmentation based on profile criteria.

Demographic

Demographic variables relate to age, gender, family size and lifecycle, generation (such as baby boomers, Generation X, etc.), income, occupation, education, ethnicity, nationality, religion, and social class. These relate to the profile of a consumer and are particularly useful in assisting marketing communications and media planning, simply because media selection criteria have been developed around these variables.

Age is a common way of segmenting markets and is the first way in which a market is delineated. Children are targeted with confectionery, clothes, music, toys, and food simply because their needs and tastes are radically different from older people.

For example, Yoplait Dairy Crest (YDC) has launched Petits Filous Plus probiotic yogurt drinks to extend the brand and increase its appeal among 4 to 9 year olds and inform parents that 'one Petits Filous Plus yogurt drink consumed every day as part of a balanced diet can help maintain kids' wellbeing'.

In the drinks market we often see the use of age. For example, the popular chocolate drink Milo is targeted to children and teenagers as an after school chocolate energy drink. In contrast Red Bull is positioned as an energy drink for young adults. In the travel industry we see organized tours and holidays for the 18–35s, with the differing needs of senior citizens met by brands such as Saga Holidays which are exclusively targeted at the over 50s. Stena Stair Lifts provide products to meet the needs of physically disadvantaged older consumers.

Gender differences have also spawned a raft of products targeted at women such as:

- Beauty products and fragrances;
- Magazines;
- Hairdressing; and
- Clothes.

Products targeted at men include:

- Magazines;
- Grooming Products; and
- Beverages.

Some brands develop products targeted at both men and women, for example fragrances and watches. Increasingly marketers are also recognizing the importance of segments that have not traditionally been targeted by certain product categories, such as insurance products designed for women and beauty products for men.

An example of a product designed just as to the combination of age and gender is Dove's new Dove ProAge product range. These products reflect the unique needs of women in their later years, continuing Dove's campaign for Real Beauty by launching a new series of products with television and print advertisements targeted to women in their fifties.

Income or socio-economic status is another important demographic variable because it determines whether a consumer will be able to afford a product. This comprises information about consumer personal income, household income, employment status, disposable income, and asset net worth. Many companies target affluent consumers offering high-end exclusive product offerings.

Targeting low-income earners can also be profitable. Discount stores such as Dollar Dazzlers, Crazy Clarks, and Pound Stretcher make a considerable impact on the retail market by developing an offer for low-income market segments. The socio-economic distinction in marketing strategies is also increasingly apparent in the development of differing retail brand labels of large multinational retailers like Tesco, ASDA Wal-Mart, and Coles Myer. For example, Tesco Finest is developed for markets with more disposable income in contrast to Tesco Value, which is marketed to the more price-conscious and low-income market segment.

Lifecycle

The lifestage approach to segmenting markets is based on the premise that people at different stages in the lifecycle need different products and services. Adolescents need different products from a single 26-year-old person, who in turn needs different products from a 26 year old who is married with young children. For example, Tesco, ASDA Wal-Mart, and Sainsbury's have all invested in the development of product lines targeted at singles with high disposable incomes and busy lifestyles with their 'meal for one' ranges. This is in contrast with the 'family value' and 'multi-packs' targeted at families. However, as families grow and children leave home so the needs of the parents change and their disposable income increases.

Holidays and automobiles are key product categories that are influenced by the lifestage of the market. Historically the family lifecycle consisted of five categories through which individuals and households would progress: single bachelor, newly married, married with children, empty nester, and solitary survivor. However, since this classification was developed, society has changed and continues to change in values, beliefs, and family lifecycle.

Table. BMRB-TGI Lifestage Segmentation Groups

Lifestage Group	Demographic Description
Fledglings	15–34, not married and have no son or daughter; living with own parents
Flown the nest	15–34, not married, do not live with relations Nest builders 15–34, married, do not live with son/ daughter
Mid-life	35–54, not married, do not live with relations independents
Unconstrained couples	35–54, married, do not live with son/daughter

Playschool	Live with son/daughter and youngest child 0–4 parents
Primary school	Live with son/daughter and youngest child 5–9 parents
Secondary school	Live with son/daughter and youngest child 10–15 parents
Hotel parents	Live with son/daughter and have no child 0–15
Senior sole	55+ not married and live alone decision makers
Empty nesters	55+, married, and do not live with son/daughter
Non-standard	Not married, live with relations, do not live with families son/daughter, and do not live with parents if 15–34
Unclassified	Not in any group

A more modern lifecycle classification was developed with support from the British Market Research Bureau (BMRB) called the Target Group Index (TGI) or BMRB-TGI Lifestage Segmentation Product which classifies 12–13 lifestage groups based on age, marital status, household composition, and children (*e.g.* if they have children and the child's age). These groups are presented in Table.

Geographics

This approach is useful when there are clear locational differences in tastes, consumption, and preferences. For example, what do you put on your toast in the morning: Vegemite, Marmite, jam, or jelly? Or perhaps you don't east toast at all and prefer cold meats or noodles for your morning meal. These consumption patterns provide an indication of preferences just as to differing geographic regions. Markets can be considered by country or region, by size of city or town, postcode, or by population density such as urban, suburban, or rural.

For example, it is often said that American beer drinkers prefer lighter beers, compared with their UK counterparts and particularly compared with German beer drinkers, who prefer a much stronger drink. In contrast Australians prefer colder more carbonated beer than the UK or the USA. In the UK there are generalizations which state that Scottish beer drinkers prefer heavy bitters, northerners in England prefer mild bitter, drinkers in the west prefer cider, and in the south, lager is the preferred drink.

In addition to product selection and consumption, geographic segmentation is important with regard to retail location, advertising with regard for media selection, and recruitment. For example, to the armed forces recruits from differing geographic areas have certain demographic attributes. Furthermore, low-cost retail formats might be used for retail outlets in low-income regions. Direct sales operations (*e.g.* catalogue sales) can use census information to develop better customer segmentation and predictive models.

Geodemographics

Geodemographics is a natural outcome when combining demographic and geographic variables. The 'marriage' of geographics and demographics has become an indispensable tool for market analysis. Fusing census data with demographic information, especially socio-economic data, can lead to a rich mixture of 'who lives where' and 'what they are like'. Consumers can be classified by where they live, which is often dependent on their stage in life and their lifestyle. Two of the best known UK geo-demographic systems are ACORN and Mosaic.

ACORN

Table. ACORN Geodemographic Categories

Category	Group	Type
Wealthy achievers	Wealthy executives	01-Affluent mature professionals, large houses
		02-Affluent working families with mortgages
		03-Villages with wealthy commuters
		04-Well-off managers, larger houses
	Affluent	05-Older affluent professionals greys
		06-Farming communities
		07-Old people, detached houses
		08-Mature couples, smaller detached houses
	Flourishing Families	09-Larger families, prosperous suburbs
		10-Well-off working families with mortgages
		11-Well-off managers, detached houses
		12-Large families and houses in rural areas
Urban	Prosperous Prosperity Professionals	13-Well-off professionals, larger houses and converted flats
		14-Older professionals in detached houses and apartments
	Educated Urbanites	15-Affluent urban professionals, flats
		16-Prosperous young professionals, flats
		17-Young educated workers, flats
		18-Multi-ethnic young, converted flats
		19-Suburban privately renting
	Aspiring Singles	20-Student flats and cosmopolitan sharers
		21-Singles and sharers, multi-ethnic areas
		22-Low-income singles, small rented flats
		23-Student terraces
Comfortably	Starting out	24-Young couples, flats and terraces off
		25-White-collar singles/sharers, terraces
	Secure	26-Younger white-collar couples with families mortgages
		27-Middle-income, home-owning areas
		28-Working families with mortgages
		29-Mature families in suburban semis

		30-Established home-owning workers
	Moderate	31-Home-owning Asian family areas
	Settled	32-Retired home owners suburbia
		33-Middle-income, older couples
		34-Lower-income people, semis
	Prudent	35-Elderly singles, purpose-built flats
	pensioners	36-Older people, flats
Moderate	Asian	37-Crowded Asian terraces means communities
		38-Low-income Asian families
	Post-industrial	39-Skilled older family terraces
	Families	40-Young family workers
	Blue-collar	41-Skilled workers, semis and terraces roots
		42-Home-owning, terraces
		43-Older rented terraces
Hard	Struggling	44-Low-income larger families, semis pressed
	Families	45-Older people, low income, small semis
		46-Low income, routine jobs, unemployment
		47-Low-rise terraced estates of poorly off workers
		48-Low incomes, high unemployment, single parents
		49-Large families, many children, poorly educated
	Burdened	50-Council flats, single elderly people singles
		51-Council terraces, unemployment, many singles
		52-Council flats, single parents, unemployment
	High-rise	53-Old people in high-rise flats
	Hardship	54-Singles and single parents, high-rise estates
	Inner city	55-Multi-ethnic purpose-built estates
	Adversity	56-Multi-ethnic, crowded flats

One system of measurement of consumer lifestyles, developed by the British market research group CACI, is known as ACORN—A Classification of Residential Neighbourhoods—shown in Table, which demonstrates how these postcode areas are broken down into 5 lifestyle categories, 17 groups, and 56 types. ACORN is a geodemo-graphic tool used to identify and understand the UK population and the demand for products and services.

Marketers use this information to improve their understanding of customers and target markets, and determine where to locate operations, field sales forces, retail outlets, and so on. ACORN can also be used to determine where to send direct marketing material and host billboard and other advertising campaigns. In total, ACORN categorizes all of Britain's 1. 9 million UK postcodes, using over 125 demographic statistics within England, Scotland,

Wales, and Northern Ireland, and 287 lifestyle variables. The classification technique operates on the principle that people living in similar areas have the same needs and lifestyles, that is 'birds of a feather flock together'.

MOSAIC

In contrast, MOSAIC is a geodemographic segmentation system developed by Experian and marketed in over twenty countries worldwide. MOSAIC was originally constructed using the 1990 census, and is now based on the 2000 census data and updated on an annual basis. The resulting segmentation system consists of sixty segments which are presented as twelve separate groups. MOSAIC is based on the premise of assigning lifestyle groups to differing geographic catchment areas. For example, using MOSAIC, Figures show the area catchment profiles by income and household composition around Bristol, UK.

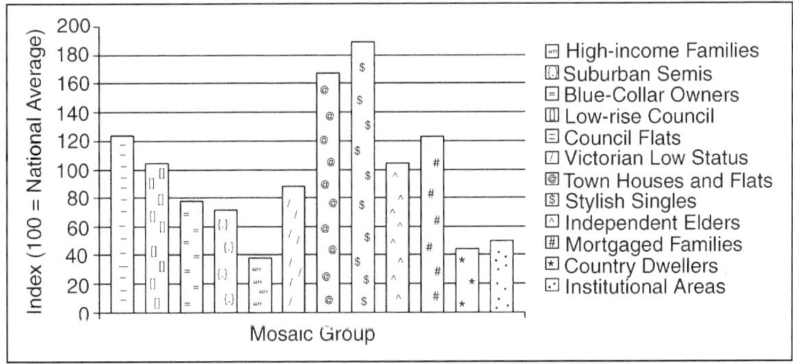

Fig. Thirty-minute Off-peak Drivetime by MOSAIC Group

Fig. Area Catchment Profile

PSYCHOLOGICAL CRITERIA

Psychological criteria used for segmenting consumer product and service markets include using attitudes and perceptions (*e.g.* negative feelings about fast food); psychographics or the lifestyles of customers (*e.g.* extrovert, fashion conscious, high achiever), and the types of benefits sought by customers from products and brands and their consumption choices.

Psychographics

Psychographic approaches rely on the analysis of consumers' activities, interests, and opinions, in order to understand consumers' individual lifestyles and patterns of behaviour.

Psychographic segmentation includes an understanding of the values that are important to different types of customers. A traditional form of lifestyle segmentation is AIO, based on customer Activities, Interests, and Opinions. These provide useful insight into what makes people 'tick'. Taylor Nelson Sofres (TNS) in 2003 developed a UK Lifestyle Typology based on lifestyles and classified the following types of lifestyle categories: belonger, survivor, experimentalist, conspicuous consumer, social resistor, self-explorer, and the aimless.

For example, the Accor hotel group used value-based segmentation to develop the brand. The Dorint-Novotel was repositioned to attract those who value personal efficiency.

This involved changing the service offering by introducing efficiency-related facilities such as automated checkouts, car hire facility, 24-hour food, and wireless computing. The Dorint-Sofitel brand was repositioned by introducing fine art for the walls, real fires, fine wines, live piano in the reception, libraries, and more experienced concierge staff. This was designed to appeal to those who valued classical (styling), customization, and passion.

Benefits Sought

The root of this approach to market segmentation lies in the idea that we should provide customers with exactly what they want, not based on how we design products and services for them, but based on the benefits that they derive from the goods/services that they use. This may sound obvious but consider what the real benefits, both rational and irrational are of different goods and services that people derive from purchasing mobile phones and sunglasses or of something you have bought recently.

For example, a major airline might well segment the airline passenger market on the basis of the benefits they seek from transport. Typically, the industry does this by differentiating between the first-class passenger (who is given substantial extra luxury benefits in their travel experience), the business-class passenger (who gets some of the luxury of the first-class passenger), and the economy-class passenger (who gets none of the luxury of the experience but still enjoys the same flight). This is also a useful segmentation base with respect to new and emerging technologies.

Table. Benefits and Concerns Motivating Web use

Motivation	Description
Social escapism	The benefits of the web as a pleasurable, fun, and enjoyable activity that allows one to escape
Transactional security and privacy	Concerned about giving of personal and transactional-based information and thus privacy and security concerns
Information	The benefits of the web for self-education and information needs
Interactive control	The interactive benefits of the self-directed and interactive control that users have with web usage
Socializations	The social benefits of the web as a facilitator of interpersonal communication and activities
Non-transactional privacy	Concerned about privacy in general rather than the security and privacy issues related to web transactions
Economic	The economic benefits of collection of information for learning and information purposes as well as for shopping and buying motivations

Marketers are increasingly identifying the key benefits and motivations of electronic technology adoption and use. For example the benefits of convenience, accessibility, and handset durability dominate mobile handset adoption for blue-collar trade workers; teenagers seek novelty through games and ringtones and innovation through the latest trends in handset design; and white-collar workers seek multifunction-ality, with the device acting as a mobile, an organizer, and a storage device. Korgaonkar and Wolin explored web users' motivations and concerns, identifying the presence of seven motivations and concerns regarding web use. The motivations described in Table suggest that consumers use the web for many more reasons than to retrieve information or to communicate and that motivations play a more significant role in determining actions with respect to usage than demographics alone.

BEHAVIOURAL CRITERIA

Product-related methods of segmenting consumer goods and service markets include using behaviouristic methods (*e.g.* by product usage, purchase, and ownership) as bases for segmentation. Observing consumers as they utilize products and media can be an important source of new product ideas, and can lead to ideas for new product uses or product design and development. Furthermore, new markets for existing products can be indicated, as well as appropriate communi-cation themes for product promotion. Purchase, ownership, and usage of products and media are three very different behavioural constructs we can use to help profile and segment consumer markets.

Product Usage

A company may segment a market on the basis of how often a customer uses its products or services, categorizing these into high, medium, and low users, by usage rate. This can be used to develop service specifications or marketing mixes for each of these groups of users. For example heavy users of public transport might be targeted differently from heavy users of private vehicles or car pooling activities.

Consumer product use can be investigated from three perspectives:

1. Social interaction perspective examines the symbolic aspects of usage and the social meanings attached to the consumption of socially conspicuous products such as a car or house. For example, Greenpeace launched a television campaign targeting owners of four-wheel drive cars or 'Gas Guzzlers', highlighting the environmental social stigma of this car purchase.
2. Experiential consumption perspective investigates emotional and sensory experiences as a result of usage, especially consumer experience such as satisfaction, and 'fantasies, feelings and fun', the hedonic consumption of products. For example, the Oxo gravy campaign concentrates on the usage of Oxo as bringing families together, emotionally appealing to consumers and expressing family values like love, sharing, time together.
3. Functional utilization perspective examines the functional usage of products and their attributes in different situations. For example, when the product is used, how often, and in what contexts.

Service providers may segment the market on the basis of the purchase behaviour of their customers. This might involve segmentation on the basis of loyalty to the service provider, or length of relationship, or some other mechanism. Usage of soft drinks can be considered in terms of purchase patterns (two bottles per week), usage situations (parties, picnics, or as an alcohol substitute), or purchase location (supermarket, convenience store, or wine merchant).

Lifestage analysis is based on the principle that people have varying amounts of disposable income and different needs at different stages in their lives. Their priorities for spending change at different trigger points and these points or lifestages do not occur at the same time. One method of segmenting service customers defines four segments based on propensity to switch suppliers: definitely will not switch, probably will not switch, might switch, and definitely will switch.

The services literature points out that customers often stay with a service provider even when they are dissatisfied and this is particularly true in retail banking for current accounts, for example, where customers seldom can see the point in shifting their funds from one account to another for very limited gains. Customers only shift suppliers when they perceive the service to be poorly priced, when inconvenienced by the service provider, when there is a core service failure (*e.g.* a hotel room is inadequately cleaned), when service encounters fail (*e.g.* arriving at a hotel with a pre-booked room and finding no room is available), when there is a poor response to service failures (*e.g.* in a hotel when complaining about the poor cleaning), competition (a rival hotel chain offers better rates), ethical problems, and when they have to (for example, the hotel customer is forced to move to another city and a Marriot Hotel is not available, for example, but a Hilton is).

Transaction and Purchase

The development of electronic technologies has facilitated the rapid growth in the collection of consumer purchase and transactional data, providing an additional consumer characteristic upon which to base market segmentation. The collection of purchase data has been enabled through the installation of electronic-pointof- sale (EPOS) computing systems, coupled with standardized universal product codes (UPC) in the USA or European article numbers (EAN) in Europe and the growth of integrated purchasing systems (*e.g.* web, in-store, telephone).

These have enabled retailers to track more accurately who buys what, when, for how much, in what quantities, and with what incentives (*e.g.* sales promotions). This provides companies with the ability to monitor purchase patterns in differing geographic regions, times, or seasons of the year, for differing product lines, and increasingly for differing market segments.

Transactional and purchase information is very useful for marketers to assess who their most profitable customers are. This is through an analytical formula called the RFM analysis. RFM analysis is based on the principle postulated in 1897 by an Italian economist, Vilfredo Pareto. Pareto's Principle ascertains that '80% of a company's profits are usually delivered by just 20% of their customers'. As such there is a significant need to segment markets and create precisely targeted marketing programmes for those most profitable to the company.

RFM analysis is a method by which marketers can identify market segments comprising customers that are most profitable. RFM stands for recency, frequency, and monetary value. Thus, those customers who purchased from you most recently, purchase from you frequently, and spend a high unit value per purchase (or the life of their relationship with you) would be classified as profitable customers. The acquisition of purchase data per customer through electronic technologies either in-store or online provides increased effectiveness of profitable segment identification.

However, one thing to note is that transactional data is just behaviour and although it might provide some insight into useful purchase trends, it will not be able to shed deeper insight into why those trends in purchase and consumption are occurring. With the rise in loyalty card schemes such as the famous Tesco Clubcard or customer reward programmes such as the many airline frequent flyer clubs and the precision of ACORN and MOSAIC geodemographic databases, we are seeing the merging of transactional and purchase data with customer profile and psychological data. This provides the bases for more effective targeting of marketing strategies to specific and defined market segments.

Media Usage

The understanding and profiling of audience media usage is central to the process of communications planning. From the 1950s television viewing information was collected by organizations such as Arbitron in the USA and AGB Ltd in the UK, providing a basis for classic studies of television viewing. Similar developments occurred with radio and print, which made possible formal studies of listening and readership. In more recent years, web usage data has been collected by market researchers such as Media Metrix, A. C. Nielsen, and NetRatings, to help profile web users. Table for an example of web user segmentation based on usage characteristics.

Table. Segmenting the Web user

User Segment	Usage Characteristics
'Quickies' 8%	• Usage occasions are short (1 min) • Visit two or few familiar sites • 15 seconds per page acquiring specific information or sending e-mail
'Surfing' 23%	• Usage occasions are the longest, averaging 70 minutes • Hit 45 sites in a typical session on the web • 1 minute or more per page • Shopping, online communities, and news sites grab their attention
'Just for facts' 15%	• Usage occasions involve looking for specific information from known sites • 9 minutes usage occasion duration • Rapid page views like quickies (30 seconds per page) • Visit transaction and time-consuming sites • Not interested in visiting for entertainmentfor self-education and information needs
'Information, please' 17%	• Usage occasions average 37 minutes and are used to build in-depth knowledge of a topic • Gathering broad information from a range of sites • Jump among linked sites without using a search engine
'Single mission' 7%	• Users who want to complete a task or gather specific information

	• Average session is 10 minutes with a 1. 5 minute page view • Venture to unfamiliar sites with e-mail sites rarely visited
'Loitering' 16%	• Leisurely visits to familiar sticky sites such as news, gaming, telecommunications • Average 33 minutes in duration with 2 minute page views
'Do it again' 14%	• Usage occasions are 14 minutes long and 2 minute pages views • Strong focus in session on familiar places with users spending 95% of session at site previously visited • Visit favourite sites for auctions, games, and investments

The logic of segmenting on the basis of frequency of readership, viewership, or patronage of media vehicles can be found in media research conducted in the 1970s. For example, Urban suggested that heavy and light magazine readership might respond differently to ads with different creative appeals. Potter *et al.* attempted to identify the profiles of five usage segments for VCRs.

As further discussed by Chatterjee, Hoffman, and Novak, segmenting users on the basis of their usage frequency of the media and its vehicles yields insights on whether the publisher attracts and retains consumers that are more or less responsive to an advertiser's communication. This information provides an important input when evaluating the efficiency and effectiveness of media. Furthermore, Chatterjee identify that differences in frequency may lead to differences in response to repeated passive ad exposures, competing ads of other sponsors, and prior ad exposure.

Frequency of media usage has been the predominant measure of media usage experience. However, Olney, Holbrook, and Batra also identified viewing time as an important dependent variable in a model of advertising effects. This is consistent with Holbrook and Gardner's argument that duration time is a critical outcome measure of consumption experiences and may be a useful behavioural indicator of experiential versus goal-directed orientations. The differing types of media usage are depicted in Table.

Table. Types of Media Usage

Usage Type	Definition	Example
Usage frequency	How often the medium is used within a certain timeframe.	How many times a week television is watched or the web is accessed.
Usage variety	The different motivations for use (motivational	The number of different motivations for using a

	variety) and different situations (situational variety) in which the medium is used.	VCR (*e.g.* recording, playing movies); the number of locations from where the web is accessed (*e.g.* home, work).
Breadth of use	The number of different types of media vehicles purchased or used in a category within a given timeframe.	The number of different brands of magazines read by the consumer within a 3-month period; the number of different types of television programmes viewed in a week.
Depth of use	The total number of media channels within a category used within a certain timeframe.	The total number of magazines purchased or subscribed to or the total number of websites visited.
Duration of use	Length of time for which the media device is used.	The number of hours the web is used in a typical web session.
Usage time	The time when the media device is used or accessed.	The differing times of day the radio or television is watched.

SEGMENTATION IN BUSINESS MARKETS

Wind and Cardozo referred to market segmentation in business-to-business markets as the identification of 'a group of present or potential customers with some common characteristic which is relevant in explaining their response to a supplier's marketing stimuli'.

Table. Segmentation Bases used in Business Markets

Base Type	Segmentation	Explanation Base
Organizational	Organizational	Grouping organizations by their characteristics size relative size (MNCs, international, large, SMEs) enables the dentification of design, delivery, usage rates or order size, and other purchasing characteristics.
	Geographic	In many situations the needs of location potential customers in one geographic area are different from those in another area.
	Industry type	Standard industrial classifications (SIC codes)

		(SIC) are codes used to identify and categorize all types of industry and businesses.
Buyer	Decision-making unit structure (DMU)	The attitudes, policies, and characteristics purchasing strategies used by organizations provide the means by which organizations can be clustered.
	Choice criteria	The types of product/services bought and the specifications that companies use when selecting and ordering products and equipment may also form the basis for clustering customers and segmenting business markets.
	Purchase situation	This approach segments buyers on the way in which a buying company structures its purchasing procedures, the type of buying situation, and whether buyers are in an early or late stage in the purchase decision process.

However, B2B market segmentation has not been as well researched and documented as that in consumer markets. Abratt and Weinstein sought to extend our understanding, the latter making comparisons of both markets' characteristics.

Recalling the simple principle that 80 per cent of profits are usually delivered by just 20 per cent of customers, there is a significant need to segment markets and create precisely targeted marketing programmes. There are two main groups of interrelated variables used to segment businessto- business markets as presented in Table.

The first set of variables involves organizational character-istics, such as organizational size and location. Those seeking to segment markets where transactional marketing and the breakdown approach dominate would be expected to start with these variables. The second group is based upon the characteristics surrounding the decision-making process of buyer characteristics. Those organizations seeking to establish and develop particular relationships would normally be expected to start with these variables, and build up their knowledge of their market and customer base.

ORGANIZATIONAL CHARACTERISTICS

These factors concern the buying organizations that make up a business market. There are a number of criteria that can be used to cluster organizations, including size, geography, market served, value, location, industry type, usage rate, and purchase situation. We discuss the main three categories used. These are presented in Figure.

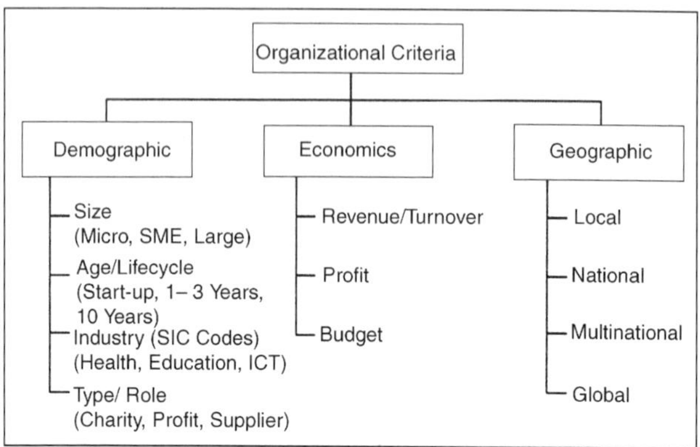

Fig. Organizational Characteristics

Organizational Size

By segmenting organizations by size it is possible to identify particular buying requirements. Large organizations may have particular delivery or design needs based on volume demand. For example, the large multiple retailers such as America's Wal-Mart and Britain's Tesco pride themselves on purchasing goods in large quantities so as to allow them to offer cheaper-priced goods. The size of the organization may have an impact on the usage rates of a good or service, so organizational size is likely to be linked to whether an organization is a heavy, medium, or low buyer of a company's products or services.

Geographic Location

Targeting by geographic location is one of the more common methods used to segment business-to-business markets, and is often used by new or small organizations attempting to establish themselves. This approach is particularly useful since it allows sales territories to be drawn up around particular locations which salespersons can easily service.

Such territories may based on European regions, for example, Scotland, England, and Wales, Scandinavia, Western Europe and Eastern Europe, and the Mediterranean. Alternatively, they might be based on specific regions within a country: for example, in the UK sales territories might be based on counties or individual nations within the UK. However, this approach is increasingly less useful as the internet and associated websites increase the channels for distribution and communicating product and service offerings.

SIC Codes

Standard Industrial Classification (SIC) codes are often used to get an indication of the size of a particular market. They are easily accessible and standardized across most Western countries, *e.g.* UK, Europe, and the USA. However, some have argued that SIC codes contain categories which are too broad to be useful. Consequently, SIC codes have received limited application although they do provide 'some preliminary indication of the industrial segments in (a) market'.

The Standard Industrial Classification (SIC) system was first introduced into the United Kingdom in 1948 to classify business establishments by the type of economic activity that they conducted. The classification has been revised on at least five occasions since then because, over a period of time, new products and the new industries that produce them emerge.

The need to take account of changes in industrial structures and industries is equally applicable to all international classifications and so they are revised from time to time to bring them up to date. A new International Standard Industrial Classification of All Economic Activities was agreed in the Statistical Commission of the United Nations in February 1989 and in 1990 the European Communities' Internal Market Council followed suit by passing a regulation to introduce a new statistical classification system.

CUSTOMER CHARACTERISTICS

These factors concern the buyers within the organizations that make up a business market. There are a number of criteria that can be used to cluster organizations based on customer characteristics including by decision-making unit, by purchasing strategies, by relationship type, attitude to risk, choice criteria, and purchase situation.

Decision-making Unit

An organization's decision-making unit may have specific requirements that influence their purchase decisions in a particular market. There may be policy factors, purchasing strategies, a level of importance attached to these types of purchases, attitudes towards vendors and towards risk, all or some of which may help segregate groups of organizations for whom particular marketing programmes can be developed/refined and delivered.

Organizations may establish certain policies that govern purchasing decisions. A business may require specific delivery cycles to support manufacturing plans. Increasingly organizations require certain quality standards to be met by their suppliers and membership of particular quality standards organizations is required as evidence of these thresholds having been reached.

Policy may dictate that the reputation of all their suppliers is critical and that contracts can only be signed with organizations that meet certain internally determined criteria. For example, if a proposed supplier is currently contracted to a significant competitor it may be a sufficient signal to open negotiations.

The relationship between organizations is obviously a critical factor. Whilst this is considered in greater depth, the attitudes and relationships between the people that represent organizations can be used as a means of segmentation. Segmentation might be based on the closeness and level of interdependence that may already exist between organizations. This could be measured in terms of a continuum from partners to unknowns.

Organizational attitude towards risk, and the degree to which an organization is willing to experiment through the acquisition of new industrial products, can vary a great deal. This variance is partly a reflection of the prevailing culture and philosophy, leadership, and managerial style. The extent to which the buying organization resists or embraces change is in turn reflected in the speed with which new product decisions are made, as well as the nature of the products selected and choice of suppliers.

The starting point of any business-to-business segmentation is a good database or customer relationship management system. It should contain customer address and contact details, along with a detailed purchase and transaction history. In an ideal world, it will also include the details of those buyers present in the customer company's decision-making unit structure.

Choice Criteria

Business markets can be segmented on the basis of the specifications of product/service that they choose. For example, an accountancy practice may segment its clients on the basis of those that seek 'compliance' type accounting products such as audits and tax submission work, companies that require management accounting services, and companies that require a complex mix of both.

A computer manufacturer may segment the business market for computers on the basis of those requiring computers with strong graphical capabilities (*e.g.* educational establishments, publishing houses) and computers with strong processing capabilities (*e.g.* scientific establishments). Companies do not necessarily need to target multiple segments, they might simply target a single segment, as Silverjet—the UK airline company—has done with the business flyer from London to New York.

Purchase Situation

There are three factors associated with the purchase situation. First, the structure of the buying organization's purchasing procedures: is it centralized, decentralized, flexible, or inflexible? Second, what type of buying situation is present:

- New task (*i.e.* buying for the first time), modified rebuy (*i.e.* not buying for the first time, but buying something with different specifications from previously), or straight rebuy (*i.e.* buying the same thing again)? Third, what stage in the purchase decision process have target organizations reached; are buyers in early or late stages and are they experienced or new? The marketing programme will need to consider, and attempt to answer, these questions in order to be successful.

For example, a large services project management consultancy company like Serco in the UK might segment the market for service project management services into public and private services and focus specifically on fulfilling large government contracts which are put out to tender in an exercise where a group of selected buyers are offered the opportunity to bid for an exclusive franchise to deliver agreed services for a defined period of time. The service provider with the best bid is then selected accordingly by the tendering organization, using its own, sometimes secret and unpublished, choice criteria, and an exclusive contract is written for the winning supplier.

Typically in segmenting business markets, a service provider may use a mix of macro-and micro-industrial market segmentation approaches, by defining the customers a company wants to target using a macro-approach such as standard industrial classification or geographic region, and then further segmenting using the choice criteria for which they select a company. In other words, multi-stage market segmentation approaches can be adopted.

TARGET MARKETS

The second important part of the STP process is to determine which, if any, of the segments uncovered should be targeted and made the focus of a comprehensive marketing programme. Ultimately, managerial discretion and judgement determines which markets are selected and exploited and which others are ignored.

Kotler suggested that in order for market segmentation to be effective, all segments must be:

- *Distinct*: Is each segment clearly different from other segments? If so, different marketing mixes, to use the traditional approach to marketing, will be necessary.
- *Accessible*: Can buyers be reached through appropriate promotional programmes and distribution channels?
- *Measurable*: Is the segment easy to identify and measure?
- *Profitable*: Is the segment sufficiently large to provide a stream of constant future revenues and profits?

This approach to the evaluation of market segments is often referred to by the DAMP acronym, making it easier to remember. Another approach to evaluating market segments uses a rating approach for different segment attractiveness factors, such as market growth, segment profitability, segment size, competitive intensity within the segment, and the cyclical nature of the industry (*e.g.* whether or not the business is seasonal, *e.g.* retailing, or dependent on government political cycles as some large-scale defence contracts are). Each of these segment attractiveness factors is rated on a scale of 0–10 and loosely categorized in the high, medium, or low columns, based on either set criteria, or subjective criteria, dependent on the availability of market and customer data and the approach adopted by the managers undertaking the segmentation programme.

Table. Examples of Segment Attractiveness Factors

Segment Attractiveness Factors	High (10–7)	Rating Medium (6–4)	Low (3–0)
Growth	+2. 5%	+2. 5% ×–2. 0%	<2. 0%
Profitability	>15%	10–15%	<10%
Size	<£5m	£1m–£5m	<£1m
Competitive	Low	Medium	High
Cyclicality	Low	Medium	High

Other examples of segment attractiveness factors might include segment stability (*i.e.* stability of the segment's needs over time), mission fit (*i.e.* the extent to which dealing with a particular segment fits the mission of your company, perhaps for political or historical reasons), and a whole host of other possibilities.

Once we have determined which segment attractiveness factors we intend to use, we can then weight the importance of each segment attractiveness factor and rate each segment on each factor using the classifications in Table. This provides us with the segment attractiveness evaluation matrix shown in Table.

Table. Example of a Segment Attractiveness Evaluation Matrix

Segment Attractiveness Factors	Weight	Segment 1 Score	 Total	Segment 2 Score	 Total	Segment 3 Score	 Total
Growth	25	6	1. 5	5	1. 25	10	2. 5
Profitability	25	9	2. 25	4	1. 0	8	2. 0
Size	15	6	0. 9	5	0. 9	7	1. 05
Competitive intensity	15	5	0. 75	6	0. 9	6	0. 9
Cyclicality	20	2. 5	0. 5	8	1. 6	5	1
Total	100	5. 9		5. 65		7. 45	

Decisions need to be made about whether a single product is to be offered to a range of segments, whether a range of products should be offered to multiple segments or a single segment or whether one product should be offered to a single segment. Whatever the decision, a marketing strategy should be developed to meet the needs of the segment and reflect an organization's capability with respect to its competitive strategy and available resources. A segmentation exercise will have been undertaken previously as part of the development of the marketing strategy. The marketing communications strategist will not necessarily need to repeat the exercise. However, work is often necessary to provide current information about such factors as perception, attitudes, volumes, intentions and usage, among others. It is the accessibility question that is paramount: how can the defined group be reached with suitable communications? What is the media consumption pattern of the target audience? Where can they get access to our product and purchase it?

TARGETING APPROACHES

Once identified, the organization needs to select its approach to target marketing it is going to adopt. Four differing approaches can be considered. These include undifferentiated, differentiated, concentrated or focused, and customised target marketing approaches.

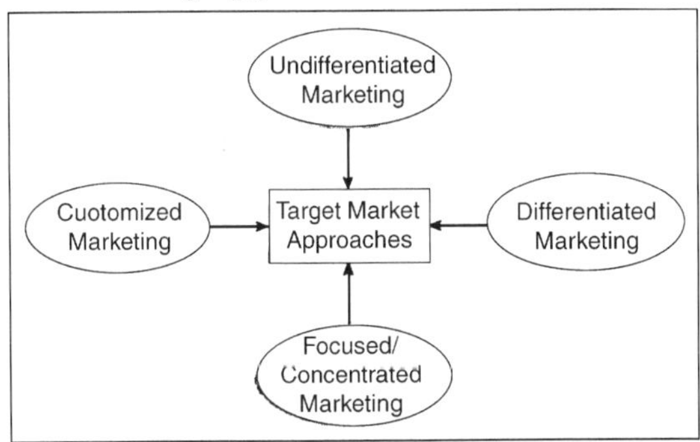

Fig. Target Marketing Approaches

In an undifferentiated approach there is no delineation between market segments, and instead the market is viewed as one mass market with one marketing strategy for the entire market. Although very expensive, this targeting approach is often selected in markets where there is limited segment differentiation. For example, the Olympics is marketed at a world market, or certain government services. The UK postal service uses an undifferentiated marketing strategy, targeting everyone, although the Post Offices do differentiate between other products and services.

A differentiated targeting approach recognizes that there are several market segments to target, each being attractive to the marketing organization. As such, to exploit market segments, a marketing strategy is developed for each segment. For example, Hewlett Packard has developed its product range and marketing strategy to target the following user segments of computing equipment: home officer users; small and medium businesses; large businesses; and health, education, and government departments.

The clothing brand Levi's uses multiple marketing strategies to target the trendy/casual, the price shopper, the tradition-alist, the utilitarian, and the mainstream clothing shopper. A disadvantage of this approach is the loss of economies of scale due to the resources required to meet the needs of many market segments. A concentrated or niche-marketing strategy recognizes that there are segments in the market, but implements a concentrated strategy by focusing on just a few market segments. This is often adopted by firms that either have limited resources by which to fund their marketing strategy, or are adopting a very exclusive strategy in the market. Jordan's the cereal company originally used this approach to target just consumers interested in organic food products.

This approach is also used a lot by small to medium and micro-sized organizations, given their limited resources: the local electrician, for example, focusing on the residential market or the cement manufacturer who targets the building market. The final approach is a customised targeting strategy in which a marketing strategy is developed for each customer as opposed to each market segment. This approach is more predominant in B2B markets (*e.g.* marketing research or advertising services) or consumer markets with high-value highly customised products (*e.g.* purchase of a custom-made car). For example, a manufacturer of industrial electronics for assembly lines might target and customise its product differently from Nissan, Unilever, and Levi's, given the differing requirements in assembly line processes for the manufacture of automobiles, foodstuffs, and clothing.

MARKET SEGMENTATION: SOME LIMITATIONS

While market segmentation is a useful process in allowing an organization to aggregate customer needs into distinct groups, it is not a perfect process.

Market segmentation has been criticized for the following reasons:

- Because the process involves approximating product/service offerings to the needs of customer groups, rather than providing an individual customised offering, there is a chance that our customers' needs are not being fully met. Customer relationship marketing processes, and software, are increasingly allowing companies to develop customised approaches to individual customers.
- There is insufficient consideration of how market segmentation is linked to competitive advantage. Whilst the product differentiation concept is clearly linked to the need to develop competing offerings, market segmentation has not tended to stress the need to segment on the basis of differentiating the offering from competitors.
- It is unclear how valuable segmentation is to the manager. Suitable processes and models to indicate how to measure the effectiveness of market segmentation processes are not yet available.

The processes involved in the target marketing process are not as precise as many authors imply. Dibb suggest segmentation plans in business to business markets often fail because businesses fail to overcome barriers encountered when implementing their plans. These include infrastructure barriers, process issues, and implementation barriers.

INFRASTRUCTURE BARRIERS

Infrastructure barriers concern culture, structure, and the availability of resources preventing the segmentation process from ever starting. For example, there may be a lack of financial resource or political will to collect the market data necessary for a segmentation programme, or even worse, an organizational culture which is rigidly product oriented.

PROCESS ISSUES

Process issues relate to the lack of experience, guidance, and expertise concerning the way in which segmentation is undertaken and managed. There are many and various statistical methods which allow us to determine whether there are different distinct groups of customers within our mass of market data. Typically, market research agencies and in-house market research teams use market data and statistical software packages to undertake this task. However, because the different statistical methods provide different results, care must be taken in determining which method to use and how to interpret these results when they are produced.

IMPLEMENTATION BARRIERS

Implementation barriers concern the way in which an organization can move towards a new segmentation model. This may be due to a move away from a business model based on products (*e.g.* engine sizes for fleet buyers), to one based on customer needs. Goller, Hogg, and Kalafatis support this view, suggesting that there is insufficient information and practical guidance for managers for segmentation strategies to be implemented successfully. It may be that the established ways of doing business becomes a barrier to moving over to a new approach. The practical issues involved in moving a business from one type of segmentation are often overlooked yet these invariably impede organizations from developing their segmentation policies.

POSITIONING

Having segmented the market, determined the size and potential of market segments, and selected specific target markets, the third part of the STP process is to position a brand within the target market(s). Positioning is important because it is the means by which goods and services can be differentiated from one another and so give consumers a reason to buy. Positioning encompasses two fundamental elements.

The first concerns the physical attributes, the functionality and capability that a brand offers. For example, a car's engine specification, its design, and carbon emissions. The second positioning element concerns the way in which a brand is communicated and how consumers perceive the brand relative to other competing brands in the marketplace. This element of communication is vitally important as it is 'not what you do to a product, it is what you do to the mind of a prospect' that determines how a brand is really positioned in a market. Kotler brings these two elements together when he says that 'Positioning is the act of designing the company's offering and image so that they occupy a meaningful and distinct competitive position in the target customers' minds.' Position-ing therefore is about a product's attributes and design, how the product is communicated, and the way these elements are fused together in the minds of customers.

It is not just the physical nature of the product that is important for positioning, and it is not just communication that leads to successful positioning. Claims (through communication) that a shampoo will remove scurf and dandruff will be rejected if the product itself fails to deliver on these attributes. Positioning therefore is about how customers judge a product's value relative to competitors and its ability to deliver against the promises made.

THE POSITIONING CONCEPT

In order to develop a sustainable position it is important to understand the market in which the product is to compete and to understand the way in which competitor brands are competing. In other words, what is the nature of the competition in the market and what tangible and intangible attributes are customers looking for when buying these types of products?

At a simple level, positioning takes place during the target market selection process. Strategic groups are the various clusters of brands that compete directly against each other. For example, in the car market, Ford, Toyota, and Mercedes each have brands that compete against each other in the high-end luxury car market. This strategic group consists of Jaguar, Lexus, and the S-Class respectively, amongst others.

The specification and design of these cars are based on the attributes that customers in this segment deem to be important and are prepared to pay for. However, designing a car that includes key attributes alone is not sufficient. Successful positioning of each of these car brands is important in order that customers perceive how each brand is different and understand the value that each represents.

Key to this process is the identification of the attributes that are considered to be important. These attributes may be tangible (for example, the gearbox, transmission system, seating, and interior design) and intangible (for example, the reputation, prestige, and allure that a brand generates). By understanding what customers consider to be the ideal standard or level that each attribute needs to attain and how they rate the attributes of each brand in relation to the ideal level, and each other, it becomes possible to see how a brand's attributes can be adapted and communicated to become more competitive.

Through market research we can identify what factors (attributes) are the key drivers of a consumer's preference for a brand. For example, from a sample of 1, 521 female teenagers that were surveyed it was identified that being trendy and stylish, having a good range of clothing, and a good brand reputation, were the most important factors for this target market when selecting a preferred brand of fashion retailer.

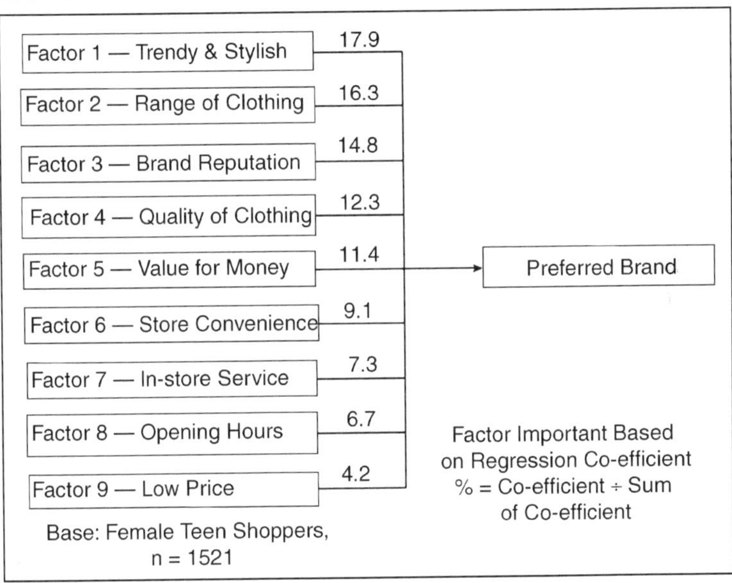

Fig. Drivers of Preferred Brand of Fasion Retaller

Using this list of drivers wc can further depict on what we call a perceptual map how the different competing brands of fashion retailers in the market are positioned just as to these drivers.

PERCEPTUAL MAPPING

Understanding the complexity associated with the different attributes and brands can be made easier by developing a visual representation of each market. These are known as perceptual maps and they are used to determine how various brands are perceived just as to the key attributes that customers value. In addition, is it possible to determine and map how customers see an ideal brand, based on the key attributes, and from this see how far away a brand is from occupying the ideal position.

Perceptual mapping represents a geometric comparison of how competing products are perceived. One thing to note is that the closer products/brands are clustered together on a perceptual map, the greater the competition. The further apart the positions, the greater the opportunity for new brands to enter the market, simply because the competition is less intense. For example, in fashion retailing there are numerous brands in the marketplace all competing with each other across differing core attributes, brand reputation, store presence, price, and clothing quality or trendy and stylish.

To show how the differing brands might be positioned relative to each other using the attribute scores for each brand of fashion retailer we can measure and map the brand positioning for the respective brands. Figure shows the positioning of a number of fashion retailers using the dimensions of price, store presence, and trendy and stylish.

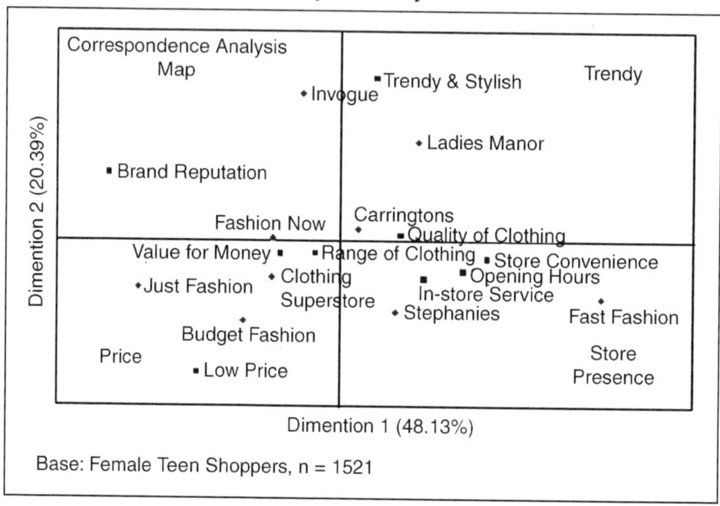

Fig. Marketing Brand Positioning: All Brands

Given the distance between the differing brands on the perceptual map, Figure shows us that there is a relatively high level of differentiation in brand positioning between the retailing brands Invogue and Fast Fashion. However, in contrast there is a low level of differentiation between Budget Fashion and Just Fashion.

Given the distance of the differing brands from each attribute, Figure also shows us that Invogue and Ladies Manor are more closely associated with the attribute of trendy and stylish; Budget Fashion, Just Fashion, and the Clothing Superstore with the attributes of price and value for money; and Stephanie's and Fast Fashion with the attributes of in-store service, opening hours, and store convenience.

Determining attribute importance and mapping the brands across these attributes, we can discover how our brand and competing brands are perceived in the marketplace. It is very rare that using just two attributes adequately reflects the diversity of opinion and preferences of the target market. Using multidimensional scaling techniques it is possible to add further attributes and create a composite picture of the main segments that constitute a market.

Perceptual mapping can provide significant insight into how a market operates. For example, it provides marketers with an insight into how their brands are perceived and it also provides a view about how their competitors' brands are perceived. In addition to this substitute products can be uncovered, based on their closeness to each other. All of the data reveal strengths and weaknesses that in turn can assist strategic decisions about how to differentiate on the attributes that matter to customers and how to compete more effectively in the target market.

POSITIONING STRATEGIES

Understanding how brands are positioned provides important inputs not only to the way a brand performs but also to the marketing communications used to support a brand. Through communications, and especially advertising, information can be conveyed about each attribute and in doing so adjust the perceptions customers have of the brand.

For example, Carrington's might want to reposition the perception the market has of its brand from range and quality of clothing to be more trendy and stylish; Fashion Now reposition more on in-store service and convenience; and Budget Fashion and Just Fashion might want to maintain their current positioning of low price, affordable, but also good value for money. Following any necessary adjustments to the product, marketing communications would emphasize these attributes and hope to further differentiate the fashion retailers across their brands' perceived positioning.

Marketing communications can be used in one of two main ways to position brands, namely to position a brand either functionally or expressively (symbolically). Functionally positioned brands emphasize the features and benefits, whilst expressive brands emphasize the ego, social, and hedonic satisfactions that a brand can bring. Both approaches make a promise: with regard to, for example, haircare, a promise to deliver cleaner, shinier, and healthier hair (functional) or hair that we are confident to wear because we want to be seen and admired, or because it is important that we feel more self-assured (expressive). Within each of these two main approaches there are numerous sub-strategies, some of which are presented in Table.

Table. Product Positioning Strategies

Position	Strategy	Explanation
Functional	Product	The brand is positioned on the basis of the features attributes, features, or benefits that the brand has relative to the competition. For example, Volvos are safe; Weetabix contains all the vitamins needed each day; and Red Bull provides energy.
	Price	Price can be a strong communicator of quality quality, typified by the lager Stella Artois, which is positioned as 'reassuringly expensive'. A high price denotes high quality, just as a low price can deceive buyers into thinking a product to be of low quality and poor value.

	Use	By informing when or how a product can be used, it is possible to create a position in the minds of the buyers. For example, Kellogg's have tried to reposition their products to be consumed throughout the day, not just at breakfast. After Eight chocolate mints clearly indicate when they should be eaten.
Expressive	User	By identifying the target user, messages can be communicated clearly to the right audience. So, Flora margarine was for men, and then it became 'for all the family'. Some hotels position themselves as places for weekend breaks, as leisure centres, or as conference centres.
	Benefit	Positions can also be established by proclaiming the benefits that usage confers on those that consume. Top Shop position themselves on the benefits users gain by being seen to be fashionable. The benefit of using Sensodyne toothpaste is that it enables users to drink hot and cold beverages without the pain associated with sensitive teeth and gums.
	Heritage	Heritage and tradition are sometimes used to symbolize quality, experience, and knowledge. Kronenbourg 1664, 'Established since 1803', and the use of coats of arms by many universities to represent depth of experience are designed to convey trust, permanence, and longevity.

REPOSITIONING STRATEGIES

Markets change and some change quickly. Technology, customer tastes, and competitors' new products are some of the reasons for these changes. If the position adopted by a brand is strong, if it was the first to claim the position and the position is being continually reinforced with clear, simple messages, then there may be little need to alter the position originally adopted.

However, most marketers need to be alert and be prepared to reposition their brands as the relative positions occupied by brands, in the minds of customers, will be challenged and shifted around on a frequent basis. However, repositioning is difficult to accomplish, often because of the entrenched perceptions and attitudes held by buyers towards brands and the vast (media) resources required to make the changes.

Repositioning is essentially a task that revolves around the product and the way it is communicated. There are four main ways to approach repositioning a product. The choice of approach depends on each individual situation facing a brand.

In some cases the brand needs to be adapted before relaunch:

- Change the tangible attributes and then communicate the new product to the same market. Regent Inns repositioned themselves in 2007, ahead of the public place smoking restrictions. The primary positioning on bar and restaurant brands such as Walkabout, Jongleurs, and Old Orleans moved to food, while lighting and seating changes were made to change the atmosphere and ambience. The brands' logos were refreshed and then communicated to the target audience through a mix of media.
- Change the way a product is communicated to the original market. When the World Golf Village in Florida was first developed, the retail, commercial, residential resort failed to attract sufficient purchasers. The scheme was repositioned using communications to convey not a 'golf only development' message but one that emphasized a well-balanced, developing premium community.
- Change the target market and deliver the same product. On some occasions repositioning can be achieved through marketing communications alone, but targeted at a new market. For example, Lucozade was repositioned from a drink for sickly children, a niche market with limited volume sales growth, to an energy drink for busy, active, and sports-oriented people. This was achieved through heavyweight advertising campaigns.
- Change both the product (attributes) and the target market. For example, the Indian company Dabur needed to develop but had to reposition itself as an FMCG company, rather than retain its earlier position as an Ayurvedic medicine manufacturer. To do this it had to develop new product offerings and new packaging, it dropped the umbrella branding strategy, and adopted an individual branding approach. This was then communicated, using leading Bollywood actors and sports stars, to reach their various new markets.

14

Marketing of Critical Illness Insurance

THE CONCEPT

Critical illness insurance is the payment of a lump sum in the event of the person insured suffering a condition covered under the policy.

WHAT IS CRITICAL ILLNESS INSURANCE

Critical illness insurance is the payment of a lump sum in the event of the person insured suffering a condition, such as cancer or heart attack, covered under the policy. In the individual market, the aim is to provide a lump sum payment at a time when finances may be strained. The benefits may be used to meet expenses which are not covered under personal or state disability cover, such as experimental or special medical treatment, home modifications, or bridging finance for a business. In the business market, the policy is often used in relation to buy-sell agreements in partnerships, to enable the remaining partners to buy out a partner suffering from a critical illness.

Due to the payment of benefits on survival of a serious illness, critical illness is classified as a "living" benefit. It is either linked to life cover or is a stand-alone benefit. In combination with life cover it is usually referred to as an "accelerated" or "pre-payment" benefit, meaning the payment of all or part of the life cover prior to death.

"Stand-alone" indicates that critical illness is a benefit in its own right with no link to life cover. This is often in the form of an independent product, but it can be a rider benefit, sometimes known as "additional payment" to distinguish it from "pre-payment". In most markets, stand-alone covers are a later and less common development designed as a cheaper alternative for people who already have adequate life cover or for those who wish to maintain a significant level of life cover irrespective of serious illness.

WHAT IS SPECIAL ABOUT CRITICAL ILLNESS COVER

- *Clear Need*: The chances of contracting and surviving a critical illness prior to retirement are reasonably high. Special medical treatment is costly and state healthcare provision is being continually reduced.

- *Broad Scope*: A wide range of medical conditions can be covered.
- *Simplicity*: Paying out a lump sum on diagnosis of a specified illness is easy to understand, and the lump sum can be used in any way the beneficiary desires.

WHY MIGHT A COMPANY THINK OF OFFERING CRITICAL ILLNESS COVER

Critical illness can increase sales by providing a full product range because it fills gaps which exist even in comprehensive life, disability and medical plans. A product will, however, only provide good sales volumes in a market where it meets the requirements of the parties involved in the transaction. For an insurance product, this means meeting the requirements of the client, the intermediary and the insurer. In this section we look at how critical illness cover meets the needs of these three parties.

The Client

In general terms, insurance deals with protecting individuals against events which have a low probability of occurring, but whose financial effects can be devastating. Products where the insured event is perceived as having a relatively high probability of occurring are easy to market, and indeed often sell themselves. Products such as motor and home contents insurance are examples of this. Many clients perceive that the chances of suffering a critical illness condition are high. Whether this is correct or not is a different issue but, as such, critical illness cover addresses clients' fears in relation to what they perceive as a high probability event. These fears are often non-specific in financial terms, although mortgage protection is a common objective. The product provides clients with peace of mind. Specific client needs and target markets.

The Intermediary

Critical illness insurance enables the intermediary to deal with clients' fears and to leave him or her feeling that these clients' needs have been addressed.

The Insurer

Insurers write this type of business in response to market demand. In most markets, the market price level enables insurers to make adequate profits. Critical illness products may also increase an insurer's competitiveness by covering a broader range of client needs, and by appearing innovative in comparison to competitors' offerings.

HOW MIGHT A MARKETING BRIEF LOOK

It is common practice for the product development area of life companies to submit a marketing brief for approval by executive management. It concludes the research stage of the product development process before the company embarks on the design stage. The brief usually summarizes the initiating idea or "hypothesis", and the results of the market research carried out to test the hypothesis. It concludes with the recommendations based on the research results.

WHAT ARE THE MAIN PRODUCT-DESIGN ISSUES

Range of Conditions Covered

The concept of critical illness insurance is very simple: the person insured must suffer a condition covered under the policy and the insurer must then pay out. The main question then is which conditions should be covered.

Many policies around the world cover just the "Big Seven" conditions, these being:

1. Heart attack
2. Cancer
3. Stroke
4. Heart surgery or bypass surgery
5. Kidney failure
6. Organ transplant
7. Multiple sclerosis

In most countries, however, there has been considerable pressure to increase the list. This may be for marketing reasons as expectations escalate or where intermediaries, for example in the UK, express concern that a client suffering from a condition not covered by the policy would have a claim against them for improper advice or negligence.

The marketing consequences of constantly updating a product are obvious:

- Marketing material must be constantly revised. Apart from the time and effort involved, frequent updates also run the risk of appearing gimmicky or even morbid.
- Staff and intermediaries must be constantly retrained.
- Existing clients are rarely happy when they find out about it. This can lead to strained relations between insurer and intermediaries, should clients complain to their intermediaries.

To address this issue, total and permanent disability (TPD) is often included as a catch-all. This does, however, increase the complexity of the product with issues such as "own or any occupation" definition and longer benefit deferment periods on conditions such as multiple sclerosis and loss of sight.

Premium Rates

An important issue affecting the marketing message is whether premiums are guaranteed or not. Around the world, most products have no premium rate guarantees. For example, in Australasia products are generally yearly renewable and the premium therefore increases with age. In contrast, in the UK the premium remains level and does not increase with age. Most policies written to date are, however, periodically reviewable so that the premium can be increased if claims experience is poor.

The marketing message is considerably strengthened with guaranteed premiums (*i.e.* no reviewability clause), but premiums are around 20% more expensive than with the reviewability clause. Whether this margin will prove sufficient is a cause of concern to the insurers who feel that the current scarcity of claims data does not enable them to identify trends in the incidence of critical illness events. Furthermore, incidence data of some illnesses outside the "Big Seven" is scarce. With yearly renewable premiums, this is not an issue as the underlying rates can be increased far more easily.

CONSUMER NEEDS

The four great motivators are said to be greed, fear, love and obligation. To a degree, critical illness speaks to all of them. However, specific consumer needs and target markets vary just as to the local market. To obtain a true understan-ding of the market dynamics, research must be carried out locally. The market described here is the UK one, based on the findings of consumer research commissioned by Munich Re in 1997, which explored attitudes to disability products as well as critical illness.

This research was basically qualitative and aimed to "identify what the main issues are, explore them in depth, help build an understanding of how and why people think as they do, and provide guidance as to how their needs–rational and emotional–can best be met". It arrived at the conclusion that consumers would prefer a contract which is likely to be both affordable and provide peace of mind in the long term.

GENERAL

People would like flexible policies where they can vary their cover as their needs change. The market would benefit greatly if long-term illness and disability had greater prominence in consumers' minds, a recent example being the implications of requiring longterm care. Many people were unaware of the existence of either cover. There was also a degree of confusion as to what each cover actually provides among those who were aware of them, and even among those who held one of these products.

BASIC ATTITUDES TO INSURING AGAINST SERIOUS ILLNESS AND DISABILITY

- Low priority among the under-40s. They think it unlikely they will need such insurance in the foreseeable future, and feel the money could be better spent on other things.
- The over-40s see this insurance as potentially more relevant, but many are put off by its high expected costs and lower priority than other things.

- One widespread deterrent to purchase is concern about how eligibility for benefit would be defined. There are worries about arguments with insurance companies "looking for a let-out". Simple, straight forward, non-arguable criteria are what people are looking for.

Triggers which overcome this attitude and activate purchase are:

- Becoming self-employed, or taking a job with less in-built income protection
- Taking out a mortgage (and being pressurized by the lender)
- Visits from insurance salesmen or financial advisers
- The need to be able to finance children through higher education
- Becoming the sole breadwinner when the spouse retires or ceases work

The main things people look for are:

- Peace of mind
- Replacing current income and thus maintaining living standards as far as possible
- Not falling behind with mortgage payments
- Financing expenses arising from having to live with a serious illness or disability

ATTITUDES TO CRITICAL ILLNESS COVER

Critical illness cover is attractive to a number of people. They like its wide range and feel they have a relatively high chance of being eligible for benefit. The price of cover was a major negative, particularly for the over-40s. The possibility of "easy money" (*i.e.* payment for conditions that don't have long-lasting effects) was widely recognized and alienated some, as well as attracting others.

Different people see critical illness cover as offering them different things. For some, it is mainly about providing facilities necessitated by the long-term effects of illness or disability, or providing compensating pleasures for them. For others, it would act as a replacement for lost income. Yet another (smaller) group of people see it as a form of life insurance "where they still pay out if you don't die". Two groups of people became apparent, one whose needs and preferences are well catered for by existing critical illness products, and another (a particularly male group) whose needs are not, and who would be more interested in a product with innovations such as:

- Eligibility based on a general definition such as "serious degenerative illness", provided that the application of the definition to a particular case was in the hands of a consultant rather than the insurer
- Benefit payments varying just as to the severity of the condition. This would provide cover when they really need it rather than the chance of a "lottery win"
- Regular reviews of premiums and coverage to take account of developments in medical science and practice

TARGET MARKETS

Theoretically everyone is a potential consumer of critical illness products because they can be sold to single people, not just those with dependants. In practice, critical illness is usually aimed at relatively affluent people aged 25 to 55. Financial services in general make use of lifestage marketing because they identify "trigger" points in people's lives. It is therefore worth looking first at target markets for critical illness within the context of the five main identifiable lifestages before addressing the separate business insurance market.

YOUNG SINGLES

Typical financial products targeted at this segment are cashpoint cards and passbooks with bank accounts, credit cards and unsecured loans. Critical illness is one of the few areas where life insurance is of relevance to single people. This is a growing market. For example, just as to Eurostat, 8% of people lived alone in the European Union in 1981. By 1999 this figure had risen to 11% and it is forecast to rise to 13% by 2010.

The earliest age at entry depends to a certain extent on the local legal framework, but in the UK most products start at age 18, although some start at 16 to cater for the "serious school boy" market, for example, where children are expected to join the family business.

A recent development in this field is the promotion of single-sex plans, such as female critical illness plans which offer women a means of preserving their independence come illness. The main difficulty experienced here is in offering a reasonable price for the most frequent, and therefore most expensive, cover. Even if other illnesses are excluded, the price differential can be small in comparison to the reduction in range of benefits.

YOUNG COUPLES/FAMILIES

Typical financial products for this segment are mortgages, most forms of insurance, unsecured loans and department store cards. The number of couples without children is on the increase in both the EU and the US. Critical illness is one of the few areas where life insurance relates to couples without dependants.

The number of couples outside marriage is also on the increase. The 1999 National Marriage Project report, nearly half of people aged 25 to 40 in the US have at some point set up a joint household with a member of the opposite sex outside of marriage. It is expected that a married couple stick together through a major illness. However, couples outside marriage may have a greater need for critical illness protection because this expectation is not present. Singles are more likely to feel they have a right to a life of their own and not be tied to someone requiring long-term medical care.

A particular trigger for critical illness in this segment is house purchase. A major fear of consumers is not so much death or that they lose their job, but that they lose their home. Fixed-term critical illness riders are therefore a logical addition to mortgage-related products, such as endowments and decreasing term. The transparent need, pre-set sum insured and the fact that the critical illness premium forms a relatively small part of the overall mortgage payments have all combined to make this a sales success in the UK, where over 50% of all critical illness sales are mortgage-related.

MATURE FAMILIES

Typical financial products targeted at this lifestage are life and health insurance products, and savings. Alongside life cover, critical illness forms part of the safety net protecting wealth accumulation and preparation for retirement during the peak earning period. There may also be a need for protection of the financial commitments to elderly dependants. Another area in this lifestage may be cover to protect payment of private school or higher education fees.

OLDER FAMILIES

Typical financial products targeted at this life stage are investments and competitive motor insurance.

RETIRED COUPLES/SINGLES

Typical financial products targeted at this segment are schemes to maximize income, immediate annuities and guaranteed acceptance plans. This lifestage has traditionally not been targeted for critical illness by life offices because of the lack of experience and because the scope for anti-selection is high. The maximum entry age on critical illness plans is therefore usually around 55 and the maximum end age 65.

Nonetheless, the need for critical illness cover remains; indeed it may even be at its most obvious to the consumer. Widows, widowers and divorcees in this lifestage are acutely aware of illness, but feel entitled to retain their ambitions and independence. Some companies have therefore extended their scope to accept applicants over 70 at outset.

BUSINESS INSURANCE

These applications are usually addressed by life cover and some form of disability cover, such as TPD or long-term disability (LTD). Critical illness cover represents a valuable additional benefit because the effect of serious illness on the business can be very similar to that of a case of disability or a death.

Individual Policies

Key person, creditor and partnership insurance are common forms. For example, the members of a partnership may need to be able to buy out the share of another member in the event of his/her suffering an illness or injury that prevents them from contributing in the long term to the success of the partnership. There is the added element of uncertainty as to when or even whether the person concerned will recover and return to work. Critical illness also covers the eventuality that the partner who suffered a serious illness can return to work but instead wishes to be bought out due to the health risks associated with returning to work.

The Self-employed

The self-employed do not participate in the standard benefits available to company employees. Critical illness not only offers the ability to cover major expenses in the short term but also the possibility of financing a subsequent change in employment if necessary.

Group

This is a market that has not been heavily penetrated to date. The marketing of these contracts needs, of course, to present a convincing case as to the value to the employer of offering a group critical illness cover to its employees. A common sales technique is to draw an analogy with the cost of insuring the company's motor fleet.

Particular advantages to the employer are:

- In some markets critical illness is a relatively cheap option.
- The employer is seen to provide a benefit of perceived high value.
- Unlike disability income products, the employer is not tied into a long-term commitment to the disabled employee. The employer may be able to sever links in a manner which is seen to be generous.

However, in many markets, employers have the upper hand and there tends to be no compelling reason why the employer should incur the cost of this form of cover in addition to the cost of other more traditional forms of group covers.

Other disadvantages from the employer perspective are:

- The employer may not want to see substantial payouts to employees who are back at work soon after suffering a serious illness.
- The employer may be concerned that in some cases the payout will be a disincentive to return to work.
- The employer may be concerned that the payout may be disproportionate to the severity of the condition suffered.
- The employer may be concerned that some conditions are not covered.

None of these problems are insurmountable and can be addressed through the product design process, such as "scaled" benefits to make them more appropriate. Another approach is to offer group critical illness cover as a voluntary, employee-paid benefit. The marketing of the product then becomes straightforward.

MARKETING MATERIAL

PRODUCT NAME

Some companies are content to use the generic name. They find this is acceptable to their clients and intermediaries. Others, however, prefer to use an individual product brand name. Which route is taken depends on the results from research of clients and intermediaries, principally whether there are significant negative associations with a generic term and/or competitive advantage to be gained from establishing a branded product.

Generic

There are some markets where critical illness is known as "dread disease". For the same reason that life insurance is not presented to clients as "death" insurance, "critical illness" represents a more acceptable description. However, even critical illness itself is sometimes replaced in marketing material with alternatives such as "serious illness", "trauma" or "crisis" cover.

Brand

Most products are designed to appeal to as broad an audience as possible; for example, the living benefit element is emphazied with names such as "Lifestyle" or "Lifecare". Those which target a particular market segment naturally differentiate themselves in the product name. Examples are "Smart Lady" (women), and "Mortgage Cover Plus" (mortgage-related).

CLIENT BROCHURE

This introduces the idea that anyone can suffer from a critical illness condition. It will also set out the choices available to the client in terms of conditions covered, indexation of sum insured and premium, etc. If the critical illness cover is an acceleration of a life insurance benefit, the life insurance benefit itself will have to be marketed and the concept of an acceleration benefit explained before launching into the marketing of the critical illness cover.

TECHNICAL GUIDE

This is largely based on the product specification finalized during product development. It provides the intermediary with all relevant product details and options in one document.

Key points regarding critical illness cover are:

- Whether the benefit is an acceleration benefit or a stand-alone benefit
- Choice of conditions covered
- Options relating to indexation of sum insured and premiums
- Commission rates and clawback rules
- Policy limits (maximum and minimum sums insured, premiums, ages, etc.)

- Non-medical limits and underwriting requirements
- Whether multiple claims are permitted, such as on policies with "staggered" or "scaled" benefits where only a percentage of the sum insured is paid on certain illnesses.

POLICY CONDITIONS

Key points regarding critical illness are that:

- It must be clear that only the medical conditions specified under the policy are eligible for payment. There can be no room for subsequent discussion of what constitutes a "critical" illness.
- Exact definitions of the illnesses covered must be given. The wording must be readily understandable and leave no room for subjective interpretation by policyholder and insured. Standard wordings exist in some markets and Munich Re can provide suggested definitions.
- The trigger point for the benefit must be clearly stated in order to avoid misinterpretation or potential dispute.

KEY FEATURES

The key features document explains in plain language and in question-and-answer format the main aspects of the policy. In the UK it is a legal requirement to provide the proposer with product key features at the earliest opportunity to enable them to fully understand the product and compare it with others prior to purchase. A customer-specific key features document must also be produced once individual details are known and the client is proceeding with the policy. The main information to be provided here concerns the premium, *e.g.* whether it is level or increasing, guaranteed or reviewable.

FLYER

Beyond the general rules applicable to flyers there are no special considerations regarding critical illness. They typically emphasize the positive benefits, such as reduced stress and future well-being, rather than threaten with illness statistics.

PROPOSAL FORM

Critical illness brings a new dimension to the underwriting questions on the proposal form. Rather than amend an existing proposal form to include critical illness, we recommend producing a special critical illness proposal form in order to satisfy the needs of all parties concerned. This is especially important in the case of a stand-alone product. It can, however, lead to practical difficulties with intermediaries using the wrong forms, especially when they deal with several insurers.

The specific questions depend of course on the product and market, but the following is a checklist of general questions which must be answered from the proposal form:

- Is it clear which type of cover is being taken out, *i.e.* accelerated or stand-alone?
- Are the critical illnesses covered under the policy also asked after? For example, "Have you ever had a heart attack?".
- Occupation, including precise duties?
- Name and address of the proposer's medical consultant?
- Family medical history?
- Smoker status, both now and in the past? If smoker, type and level of consumption?
- Daily alcohol consumption, both now and in the past?
- Previous hospitalizations, operations, special investigations or medical treatment?
- Any current medication?
- Previous cover? The proposer should be asked to comment on any previous critical illness as well as sickness cover or any simultaneous proposals.

SALES

TRAINING

The concept of critical illness insurance is different to that of the standard life insurance products most intermediaries are familiar with. It is very important that they understand the rationale behind the product, the needs it addresses and how to sell it to clients. The tools that are used in the sale of life insurance or income protection products do not work in a critical illness context. In particular, critical illness is about coming to terms with a complete change in lifestyle, as opposed to standard life products which generally aim at maintaining a given lifestyle.

The most effective sales training technique is to persuade intermediaries of the need for cover in their own personal circumstances and, if appropriate, even to actually sell the product to them at the launch seminar. This gives intermediaries the belief in the product as well as the back-office administration that enables them to sell it with confidence to their clients. It also establishes credibility with clients who ask agents "Do you have this cover?".

Insurers whose intermediaries have not bought into the product concept have experienced various problems:

- Clients have failed to understand the policy and its terms and conditions. In particular, the range of conditions covered, the moratorium (stand-down or no-pay period) and the survival period have caused claims to be refused. This has given rise to relationship problems between the insurer and the intermediary and the intermediary and the client.

- Sales have been inappropriate–*i.e.* they have not met clients' needs.
- In particular, intermediaries have tried to sell cover at too high a level. This has been prohibitively expensive for clients, who, rather than take a lower amount of cover, have taken out alternative covers.

SALES ARGUMENTS

The key to successful sales of critical illness is the ability to convince clients that it can happen to them. There are two basic ways of achieving this with critical illness products: the "statistical" and the "lifestyle" approaches. In practice, most marketing material contains elements of both. Which is most suited to a particular market depends on the characteristics of that market. Local market research must be done to determine the most suitable approach.

The Statistical Approach

The fundamental critical illness sales aid is establishing the probability of contracting a critical illness, both in general terms, such as "One in every three people will have a critical illness" or "You are five times more likely to contract a critical illness than die before retirement", and in particular:

- Cancer, *e.g.* "1 in 3 men develop a life-threatening cancer"; "A new case of cancer is diagnosed every 4 minutes"; "Every year over 330, 000 people in Germany have a heart attack or contract cancer"
- Heart attack, *e.g.* "1 in 2 Canadian heart attack victims are under age 65"; "75% of males survive more than 5 years after a heart attack"
- Stroke, *e.g.* "Every year in the UK there are 100, 000 strokes. 75% are still alive a year later"

Closer examination of these examples reveals a key message to be conveyed through statistics, that of the chances of surviving a critical illness. The message boils down to "What can be worse than death?". The effectiveness of this sales aid is increased by ascertaining the particular concerns of the target market and obtaining the relevant statistics from local medical institutions. The sales message is then easily communicated and understood.

Many clients buy on the strength of probability, often referred to as the "windfall" or "lottery" principle. An interesting technique of making critical illness both concrete and quantifiable to customers is to first ask them how they would value their life if they felt they might have a heart attack, and then to ask them how they would value their life if they know they will have a heart attack.

Using statistics to persuade clients of the need for critical illness insurance can be very effective, but the line between effective marketing and scare tactics is a fine one. Going too far can result in improper marketing, adverse publicity and ultimately restricting sales. Insurers must take care to abide by the advertising standards in force.

The Lifestyle Approach

This approach requires the client to acknowledge that there is a risk that he or she could suffer from a critical illness condition, but does not attempt to quantify it.

Having established that the risk exists, the three main lifestyle arguments for critical illness cover are:

- Quality of life
- Adapting lifestyle
- Financial commitments

Quality of Life

A life-threatening disease destroys the existing quality of life. It can even be seen as starting a new life. One of the strongest arguments for critical illness cover is not the financial impact, but the psychological.

Just as regaining dignity after a serious illness is as important as the physical recovery, the assurance that a dramatic and unforeseeable change in the quality of life is covered brings the security and peace of mind that people need. A highly effective sales technique is to ask clients to assess the impact of an event and see whether he/she is insured for it:

The client probably has insurance for the house, car or summer holiday, but the effect on his/her living standard is on the low side. On the other hand the effect of a critical illness is undoubtedly high, and yet there may be no cover at all beyond the direct medical costs covered by health insurance.

Adapting Lifestyle

There is an expectation that married couples are obliged to stick together whatever the changes in circumstances. However, a probing question for single people is "If you had a stroke, would you expect your partner to stay with you?" Many modern couples would respect the partner's right to their own life and would not expect this. Critical illness can provide the freedom to move to a small, convenient flat with an attendant nurse, or to adapt the existing environment to cope with the change in circumstances.

Financial Commitments

"Jane contracted asbestosis last year. Fortunately she died." What could be worse than death? The loss of income and cost of the treatment cycle would have financially ruined both her and her partner. People often joke that they are "worth more dead than alive!", but it costs more to live than to die. Critical illness cover provides the financial safeguards. The use of true examples where critical illness cover has worked and also where cover was absent is an important element in making the need immediate and real to consumers and agents. For example: "Thank goodness James had taken out serious illness cover because at least we don't have to worry about money. We can afford private nursing for him, and I can get on with bringing up the children in the way that we always wanted. "

The payment of school fees is a typical concern of the critical illness target market. A parent having a heart attack may mean that children will not receive private education due to savings having been used up as bridging finance or to cover extra treatment expenses. This sale is simple to make and quantify. Even without such a major expense to focus on, the cost of bringing up children after the loss of

"CASH IF YOU DO, CASH IF YOU DON'T"

The approaches in this section have so far dealt with the need for protection against critical illness, *i.e.* the assumption that insuring against risk is the client's main motivation. However, critical illness covers can also be added to savings plans to protect against the risk that the saver cannot make contributions to the plan after suffering a critical illness condition. This enables the savings plan to meet its primary purpose, such as retirement planning or children's education, even if the saver is unfortunate enough to suffer from a critical illness condition. Hence the tag "cash if you do (suffer from a critical illness condition), cash if you don't".

THE FACT-FIND

The fact-find document is a tool for identifying and quantifying client needs and therefore for creating sales opportunities. Regarding critical illness, fact-finds used by agents can be reviewed to ensure that appropriate questions are included to trigger the need and determine suitable cover levels.

Particular areas are:

- *Nationality, Domicile*: When and where does the client intend to retire? Early retirement in another, possibly high-cost, country can have a bearing on cover levels in case of illness.
- *Health*: Not just whether current health is good, but also past and family history, and whether regular check-ups are carried out. A serious illness in the family clearly offers an opening to discuss the financial effects. Someone who has no check-up is perhaps unsure of their current general health and would need peace of mind. Someone who has regular check-ups is aware of the risks.
- *Smoker Status*: Not just current status, also whether any history of tobacco use. Exsmokers are often particularly sensitive to the cancer risk.
- *Children*: Any plans to educate privately, or move onto higher education? What is the total cost and over what period?

- *Property*: Is the mortgage repaid if a serious illness is contracted?
- *Other Liabilities and Debts*: Are these covered in case of a serious illness?
- *Income*: How would this be affected in case of a serious illness?
- *Pension*: How confident is the client of building up a sufficient fund and actually picking up the proceeds?
- *Partnership*: What are the shareholder arrangements in case of serious illness to one partner?
- *Insurance Coverage*: Does the client already have any critical illness cover? If so, what level and how long?
- *Financial Goals*: Does the client require a lump sum in the event of a critical illness?

15

Pricing Elements

PRINCIPLES OF INSURANCE

The function of insurance is to safeguard against misfortunes [like personal losses from disability and death or property losses from fire or windstorm] by having the losses of the unfortunate few paid by the contributions of the many who are exposed to the same peril. Thus, the essence of insurance–the sharing of losses Insurance relies on the law of large numbers to minimize the speculative element and reduce volatile fluctuations in year to year losses.

LAW OF LARGE NUMBERS

The law of large numbers in relation to insurance, holds that the greater the number of similar exposures [*e.g.*, lives insured] to a peril [*e.g.*, death], the less observed loss experience will deviate from expected loss experience. Risk and uncertainty diminish as the number of exposure units increases. Insurance is the antithesis of gambling. Risk is created in gambling. Insurance transfers an already existing risk.

PRICING INDIVIDUAL LIFE AND HEALTH INSURANCE

PRICING OBJECTIVES

Rate Adequacy

To avoid financial problems and insolvency, insurance company rates must be adequate in the light of benefits promised under the company's insurance products. Rate adequacy means that, for a given block of policies, total payments collected now and in the future by the insurer plus the investment earnings attributable to any net retained funds are sufficient to fund the current and future benefits promised plus cover related expenses.

Rate Equity

Equity means charging premiums commensurate with the expected losses and other costs that insureds bring to the insurance pool. The pursuit of equity is one of the goals of underwriting [classification and selection of insureds].

Rates Not Excessive

Rates should not be excessive in relation to the benefits provided. By establishing a ceiling on the rates, this objective is achieved. Competition discourages excessive pricing.

PRICING ELEMENTS

- The probability of the insured event occurring: It is shown by mortality tables in life insurance and morbidity tables in health insurance. The part of risk premium can be calculated by multiplying sum assured with relevant information in these tables.
- The time value of money: The time value of money through rate of interest is the second factor taken into account for calculation of premium. By deducting interest component from risk premium, net premium can be calculated.
- Loading to cover expenses, taxes, profits, and contingencies By adding all these office expenses to net premium, tabular premium can be calculated.
- The benefits promised: The fourth factor is the benefits promised under the contract. A loading in this respect is also included to arrive at the actual premium payable. Tabular premium + benefits promised = office premium.

A favourable experience by the insurer, in respect of the factors, leads to the generation of surplus. The surplus so generated is shared among the eligible policyholders and the owners. An unfavourable experience leads to creation of deficit, which has to be taken care of by the management/owners.

RATE COMPUTATION

- *Yearly Renewable Term Life Insurance*: This plan provides coverage for one year only but guarantees renewal irrespective of the insurability of the policy owner. Premium depends on the rate of mortality. As age increases, premium rate increases. Therefore, there is a possibility that those in good health discontinue the policies because of burdensome premium.
- *Single Premium Plan*: In this system, premium will not increase year after year. Only one single lump sum is collected at the inception to cover risk for the selected period of insurance. The present value of total death claims anticipated to be paid by the insurer over the period of insurance is calculated at a chosen rate of interest. The single premium payable by each policyholder is arrived at by dividing the total value by the number of persons taking insurance at inception. The total fund created by collection of single premiums will be utilized to pay claims year after year.
- *Level Premium Plan*: In this system, premium payable throughout the period of insurance is level or uniform. In this system, reserve

builds up under each policy because the premium charged in the initial years of the policy is more than what is required to cover the death risk. The difference between the face value of a policy and the reserve under the policy is called the 'net amount at risk'.

- *Flexible Premium Plan*: Flexibility of deciding the amount of premium to be paid is allowed by many insurers to policy owners. Ex. Universal life policies. Out of the amount paid, mortality charges and expenses are deducted and balance accumulates and the insurer gives interest credit to the insured.

THE SAVINGS ASPECT OF LIFE INSURANCE

Conceptually, all life insurance policy cash values can be derived in the same way and all evolve for the same basic reason–prefunding of future mortality charges. As a practical matter, however, policies are usually viewed in different ways. With traditional forms of life insurance, the savings element is considered a by–product of the level premium method of payment. Under this, premium is not divisible into risk and saving elements.

With universal life and some other newer policy forms, the savings element is often considered as a more independent part of the policy, specifically designed to build a savings fund from which mortality and loading charges are withdrawn. Under this premium is divisible into risk and saving. The key elements of product pricing are open to the policy owner. The higher the premium the higher will be the cash value.

THE INVESTMENT ASPECT OF LIFE INSURANCE

Unit-linked plans are essentially similar to mutual fund products wherein the premium is invested in various funds in keeping with policyholders' risk appetite. However, the difference in a mutual fund investment is that the money is virtually at call by the customer.

In case of unit-linked insurance plans, it is impossible to predict whether the market will be in an upswing on the day of the policyholder's death or on maturity. The Net Asset Value [NAV] will reflect the underlying value of assets, which in turn is dependent on the movement of the Sensex.

In case of death during the premium paying term or the term of the policy, the sum assured or value of policy fund, whichever is higher, is paid to the beneficiaries. In case of survival up to maturity, the value of the fund is paid out.

The returns on that day [maturity or death] on the plan depend upon the performance of the market, be it equity or debt. So if the fund value falls below amount invested on that day, the policyholder will receive a lesser amount. Hence one can see that the risk here is transferred to the policyholder as nothing is guaranteed.

These plans give an option to the investor to choose between three fund options–debt, equity, and balanced. In these products, premiums can be paid quarterly, half yearly or yearly.

Out of the premium amounts, deductions will be made towards:

- Initial administrative charges
- Investment management charges [there will be an extra charge if the policyholder utilizes the switch over (from equity to debt or debt to balance) option]
- Annual administration charges
- Risk cover and the balance will be invested in a selected fund [debt or equity or balance].

Insurance Companies charge anywhere between 20-35 per cent as upfront charges for their unit-linked plans. So, every time when policyholder makes premium payment, only a part of it is actually invested in the fund of policyholder's choice.

Benefits

- A Unit linked plan providing an opportunity for the discerning investor to benefit from the returns available in the Capital Market without going for direct investment in the capital market.
- Unlike traditional products where investment details and various charges are kept under wraps, ULIPs project all these information upfront.

EXPERIENCE PARTICIPATION IN INSURANCE

Classifications of life and health insurance policies:

- *Guaranteed–cost, Non Participating Insurance Policies:* [without profit]Provide that all policy elements like the premium, the benefits, and the cash values, if any are fixed at policy inception, guaranteed, and make no allowance for future values to differ from those set at inception.
- *Participating Insurance Policies*: [with profits]–Give their owners the right to share in surplus funds accumulated by the insurer because of deviations of actual from assumed experience. The distributable surplus is paid to policy owners as dividends or bonuses. It is in this sense that dividend payments represent each policy's share of accumulated surplus.
- *Current Assumption Policies:* Like participating policies, allow policy values to deviate from those illustrated at policy inception–both favourably and unfavourably–but, unlike participating insurance in which adjustments are based on the insurer's past experience, current assumption policy adjustments are based on the insurer's anticipated future experience. Participating policies take a

retrospective approach to experience participation. In contrast, current assumption policies take a prospective approach to experience participation.

INTERACTION AMONG INSURANCE PRICING ELEMENTS

An interaction exists among the various life and health insurance policy pricing elements. Different facets that enter into insurance pricing–competitive nature, expected termination of contracts, any legal obligations to maintain minimum reserves, level of dividends, inflation, incentives to agency force, level of customer service etc. Insurance pricing focuses on a simulated test of a block of policies.

Asset–share calculation is an example of such simulation of the anticipated operating experience for a block of policies, using the best estimates of what the individual factors will be for each future policy year. It makes clear the differences among cash surrender values [the amount made available, contractually, to a withdrawing policy owner who is terminating his or her protection.], reserves [a higher value measures the company's liability for a given block of policies for financial statement purposes.], and asset shares [the *pro rata* share of the assets accumulated on the basis of the company's anticipated operating experience, on behalf of the block of policies to which the particular policy belongs]. The purpose of this asset–share calculation is to enable the insurer take policy decisions regarding modifications in operations.

16

Underwriting

ORIGIN OF UNDERWRITING

Insurance as a readily recognizable business first emerged in Britain at the end of the 16th century. In fact, Marine Insurance was one of the earliest forms of non-life insurance business that was transacted. Britain's prominent position in the world of sea borne trade created a need for security for commodities that were traded across the great seas. It was in this maritime setting that one of the world's most famous insurance providers Lloyd's of London was born.

Edward Lloyd was running a coffee shop where London Merchants, maritimers and bankers met informally to do business. These financiers wrote their names under the specific amount of risk that they would exchange for a certain amount of premium and in this practice we see the origin of the term 'Underwriting'. Put simply, underwriting is a formal acceptance of a risk for a price which is termed 'Premium'.

The concept of insurance has constantly been evolving and now it is a full-fledged subject. Of the many facets of insurance, underwriting has always been considered one of the most important and therefore critical features. During the 1950s, there were specialists who worked as underwriters and covered almost every type of insurance. The years since then have seen underwriting emerge as an art in it.

The importance of underwriting can be well understood by the fact that even though several activities of insurance company such as marketing, accounting, claims processing etc. , are sometimes outsourced, underwriting is an area over which the company always retains complete control.

DEFINITION

Underwriting can be termed "assumption of liability". It means signing an insurance policy and thereby becoming liable in the face of a specified loss. Underwriting involves the selection of policyholders after thoroughly evaluating all hazards, establishing prices and then determining the terms and conditions of the insurance policy.

The underwriting framework of a company plays a major role in determining the company's standing in the market. The underwriter must aim to generate profits and minimize losses through a well-balanced underwriting policy. One aspect that the underwriter must always bear in mind is that the underwriting must neither be too strict nor too lenient.

If the acceptance criteria are very stringent, then the insurer will miss out on several acceptable businesses and may even face losses because of the expenses involved in cancelling business that the marketing person might have initially agreed to.

This can be remedied by including enough conditions to make the risk acceptable. On the other hand, if the acceptance criteria are too liberal, the insurance company may face substantial losses and be forced to withdraw from a given line of business.

Once the risk involved is deemed acceptable, underwriting then fixes the rate of premium, and subsequently, all other terms involved. There are certain guiding objectives and principles that the underwriter must follow.

OBJECTIVES

Underwriting has three-fold objectives:

- Producing a large volume of premium income that is sufficient to maintain and enlarge the insurance company's operations and to achieve a better spread of the risk portfolio;
- Earning a reasonable amount of profit on insurance operations;
- Maintaining a profitable book of business– that contains all the policies that the insurer has in force.

PRINCIPLES OF UNDERWRITING

Insurance is a concept of creation of a fund of premiums collected from various persons by pooling all of their risks, from which the financial losses of those few who suffer from the insured perils are compensated. The theory of probability, which can predict with a certain degree of precision, the possibility of a certain event occurring that can give rise to a claim provided there is sufficient data on past experience, is invariably the basis on which the concept of underwriting rests.

It follows that a prudent underwriter will necessarily have to build up data on claims lodged and this has to be done on a continuous basis. Further this data base has to be separately compiled for each of the different insurance portfolios–Fire, Marine and Miscellaneous. Having put this practice in place, he should follow certain basic principles before accepting a risk.

The principles that guide an underwriter before accepting a risk are:

- *Selecting Insureds that Fit the Company's Underwriting Standards*: Only those insureds whose actual loss experience does not exceed the loss experience assumed in the company's rating structure will be selected. The rate is based on a low loss ratio. For example, if the expected loss ratio is 20 per cent and a rate is set accordingly, only those insureds will be selected, who can meet the required criteria, so that the actual loss ratio for the group will not go beyond 20 per cent.

- *There should be Proper Balance within Each Rate Classification*: The underwriter must be able to group insureds in such a way that the average rate in the group is enough to pay for all claims and expenses. Therefore, units with similar loss- producing features are placed in the same class and charged the same rate, ensuring that a below average insured is compensated for by an average insured.
- *Charging Equitable Rates*: The rates that apply to one group should not be charged to another group as well. This would mean that one group is unduly subsidising another group. For example, in the case of life insurance, charging the same premium rate for people in the age group of 20-25 years and those in the age group of 50-55 years will result in the younger lot subsidising the older people. This amounts to overcharging and the younger persons will then look out for some other insurance company that has a more equitable system.

THE UNDERWRITING PROCESS

The underwriting process follows a series of stages, at the end of which the status of a risk is decided. It is only after the risk has been weighed and all possible alternatives evaluated that the final underwriting is done.

When a proposal for insurance is received, the underwriter has four possible courses of action:

1. Accept the risk at standard rates
2. Charge extra premium depending on the risk factor
3. Impose special conditions
4. Reject the risk.

FACTORS AFFECTING INSURABILITY

In deciding whether to issue insurance, and if so, on what terms and conditions and at what price, life insurance companies examine several factors to achieve and ensure that rates should be adequate, equitable and not excessive to insureds for insurance coverage.

Life insurance underwriting factors are:

- *Age*: Expected future mortality is highly correlated with chronological age. So age is a key factor in determining the rate an individual is to be charged for life insurance. But it is rarely a selection factor. Proof of age is required only at the time of immediate annuity purchase.
- *Sex*: Is rarely used as a selection factor, but it is routinely used as classification factor with respect to individual life insurance.

- *Medical Spects:*
  - *Physical Condition*: The determinants of physical condition are build, nervous, digestive, cardiovas-cular, respiratory, or genitourinary systems, and glands of internal secretion etc. , which reveal an average expected mortality rate.
  - *Personal History*: Individual's health record, habits, driving violations, and amount of insurance already owned bear his or her expected mortality.
  - *Family History*: Transmission of characteristics by heredity is also important for classification of insureds.
  - *Tobacco Use*: Using tobacco in any form is an important risk factor by itself, causes expected future mortality to be worse than the average, and is a warrant for separate classification.
  - *Alcohol and Drugs*: Excessive alcohol use is associated with higher than standard mortality.
- *Occupation*: The occupation may present environ-mental hazard, the physical conditions risk from accident Because of this, ratings have been reduced or eliminated for many occupations.
- *Hazardous Sports and Avocations*: Scuba diving, mountain climbing, competitive racing and skydiving clearly involve a significant additional hazard to be considered in the underwriting process.
- *Aviation*: The Company may charge an extra premium to compensate for the aviation hazard or this cause of death may be excluded from the policy entirely.
- *Military Service*: The adverse selection involved when individuals are engaged in or facing military service during a period of armed conflict can constitute an underwriting problem.
- *Residence*: The mortality rate in most developing countries is higher than in most developed countries, primarily because of general living conditions. So it will be included in the insurer's premium rate structure.
- *Financial Status and Speculation*: Determining the motivation for the proposed insurance is a primary element in financial underwriting. When motivation is questionable, it is essential to resolve any doubts and establish that the purchase is not speculative.

SOURCES OF INFORMATION CONCERNING LIFE AND HEALTH INSURANCE RISKS

Insurers obtain information about proposed insureds from several sources:

- Application Consists of two parts.
  - Part I of life insurance application contains questions requesting
    a. Information regarding name
    b. Present and past home addresses

   c. Present and past business addresses
   d. Occupation
   e. Sex
   f. Date of birth
   g. Name and relationship of beneficiary
   h. Amount and kind of insurance for which application is being made
   i. Amount of insurance already carried
   j. Driving record
   k. Past modifications or refusal to issue insurance
   l. Past and contemplated aviation activities
   m. Avocations, and plans for foreign residence or travel.
   n. In addition, the company will ask if the life insurance applied for is intended to replace insurance.
- Part II of life insurance applications consists of
   a. Medical history, furnished by the proposed insured to the medical or paramedical examiner.
   b. If the policy is applied for on a nonmedical basis, to the agent, in response to questions regarding illnesses, diseases, injuries, and surgical operations experienced, regarding physician whom the proposed insured has consulted in last 5 years.
   c. Present physical condition.
   d. Use of alcohol, tobacco and drugs.
   e. Individual's parents and siblings, and their present health condition, and the date and cause of any deaths that have occurred.

- *Physical Examination*: Insurance companies routinely use paramedical personnel in lieu of physicians. The frequency of medical examination use and the detail involved are not as great for health insurance applications as for life cases because of expense considerations.
- *Laboratory Testing*: The scope of blood and urine testing for life and health insurance is one of the major source of information regarding applicant's health condition.
- *Agent's Report*: Most insurers request a report about the proposed insured from the agent. If a company does not require an agent's report, it relies on its general instructions to its agents to prevent them from writing applications on persons who are unacceptable risks. If the agent believes the risk is doubtful, he may be instructed to submit a preliminary enquiry. But financial incentive on sale for agents may lead to the principal-agent problem.
- *Attending Physicians Statements*: Are used when the individual application or the medical examiner's report reveals conditions or situations, past or present, about which more information is desired.

- *Inspection Companies*: Life insurance companies often obtain consumer reports from Inspection Company or consumer reporting agency on all persons who apply for relatively large amounts of insurance.
- *Industry Sponsored Databases*: Another source of information regarding insurability in some countries is an industry sponsored database of personal information.
- *Government Records*: These records include informa-tion from civil and criminal courts, property tax records, bankruptcy filings etc. These may be referred to if required.

NEED FOR UNDERWRITING

The need for underwriting arises because of some basic reasons. To avoid adverse selection and certain other hazards, to maintain fair prices and subsidisation and stay ahead of competition.

ADVERSE SELECTION

This term is used for a situation where the insurance applicant presents a possibility of loss that is higher than the average expected from a random sample of all applicants. It arises when the information presented to the insurer and the actual material facts relating to the risk are different.

The underwriter must safeguard against this kind of risk, as otherwise the insurance company would be selling insurance to those whose probability of loss is much higher than the average, at rates applicable to an average risk. This would mean higher than expected losses and hence higher claim payments leading to an increase in premiums. And finally, only those people facing very high chances of loss would find the insurance coverage feasible.

For example, people already suffering from a disease or belonging to the group of high mortality will be eager to claim coverage while those enjoying good health may not go in for insurance. Insurance, as a product, is normally not eagerly bought but mostly sold and if an underwriter senses that there is a perceptible 'eagerness', bordering desperation on the part of the intending buyer, then it is a likely case of adverse selection by the insured.

If the underwriter looks closely at the possible higher risk cases, identifies and blocks the doubtful risks, then such situations can be deterred. Therefore, underwriters must exercise caution while dealing with adverse selection. Along with adverse selection there are certain types of hazards that an underwriter must watch out for.

These are:

- *Physical Hazards*: These are hazards that affect the physical characteristics of whatever is being insured. Any harm to the tangible qualities of the subject matter of insurance can be called a physical hazard. For example: occupational hazards like working in mines.
- *Moral Hazards*: These hazards refer to the defects that exist in a person's character that may increase the frequency or the severity

of loss. Such a character may tend to increase the loss for the company. Ex: killing wife to get death proceeds of insurance.

- *Morale Hazards*: The fundamental postulate of insurance is that the insured should always conduct him as if he is uninsured and that his having taken insurance should not offer him any licence to be any less careless than he otherwise would be. However, if there is a situation of a willful carelessness on the part of the policyholder because of the existence of insurance, then it is a case of Morale Hazard. By such negligence and indifference the possibility of loss is increased. For example, careless acts like keeping the door of one's house open and going out, thereby increasing the possibility of a burglary, or leaving the car keys in the car and increasing the risk of theft are instances of morale hazard.

FAIR PRICING AND SUBSIDIZING

Underwriting helps in determining the expected loss potential of the proposed insured and selecting a price in line with this expected loss. Insureds with an approximately equal loss potential are put into one group and charged the same rate. When the premium paid by some insureds in the group does not correspond to the risk attached to them, the other insureds will have to pay the deficit. That is, those likely to suffer fewer losses will be subsidizing those likely to suffer more losses. This inequity will affect the whole group by increasing the premium rates. Here, the underwriter should be guided by previous records in order to safeguard the company against potential high-risk cases.

COMPETITION

An underwriter can also help an insurance company stay one step ahead of its competitors. Some of the ways this is done is through lower premium rates, innovative marketing strategies etc. The underwriter provides all necessary information and thus helps the insurer make the best possible decisions. For example, in life insurance, suppose the underwriter does a thorough job and studies the research done on mortality and morbidity, the insurer will have a much better idea about the factors that influence mortality and will consequently be able to fix a better price.

This can be better understood with an example. Insurers, despite knowing that chewing gutkha adversely affects health, pay no attention to this fact and do not take it into account while fixing the premium rate. Then one insurance company decides to charge two separate rates for chewers and non-chewers of gutkha, with lower rates for the latter.

As a result the people who chew gutkha will continue to buy insurance from companies with the previous rate, whereas more and more non-chewers will start buying coverage from the company charging lesser rates. If this continues, the other companies will end up providing coverage only to users of ghutka. In the long run, this will prove detrimental to the company, since all gutkha users belong to the high-risk group. This shows how well researched underwriting-which prompted the insurer to charge lower rates, can influence competition and provide benefit to the industry as a whole.

OTHER RISKS

There is also another category, the 'Declined Risks'. These are extra hazardous risks that have been rejected. Yet in certain cases, a premium is fixed after imposing restrictive conditions, clauses and warranties. This is done in order to reduce liability, and the acceptance of such risks is called 'Accommodation'. Ex. War Clause, Aviation Clause

UNDERWRITING AUTHORITY

Underwriting authority refers to the degree of autonomy granted to individual underwriters or groups of underwriters. This authority will differ by position and experience. Different insurance organizations have varying degrees of decentra-lization.

In India, the underwriting authority vests with the insurance company. Post opening up of the insurance sector, some private insurers are decentralizing certain classes of business like travel insurance, where an insurance intermediary is allowed to issue the policy.

THE SCENARIO ABROAD

Specialty lines like aviation and livestock mortality have retained centralized underwriting authority, while some other insurers are delegating a considerable part of their authority to selected brokers. Insurers who follow the decentralization system state that it eliminates duplication and makes the most of the producers' familiarity with local conditions. In return, brokers receive a higher commission rate and a larger share in the profits.

The degree of decentralization permissible depends upon several factors like the line of business involved, the experience and the track record of the producers. There may be insurers who allow their brokers to issue personal lines policies and bill the policyholders. This is certainly a significant amount of underwriting authority. Some other insurers may permit a high degree of authority but restrict policy issuance only to the company, so that control over the brokers' activities is maintained. There are also lines of business where the producer may have no underwriting authority at all. These usually include very hazardous or specialized classes of business.

UNDERWRITING ACTIVITIES

Underwriting activities can be divided into two types:

1. *Line Underwriting*: Where daily underwriting tasks are carried out; the underwriters are usually located in regional offices of the insurer.

2. *Staff Underwriting*: Where the underwriter helps the management in formulating and implementing underwriting policy. They are usually located at the Head Office.

THE UNDERWRITING POLICY

The basic purpose of an underwriting policy is to transform the objectives of the management into rules and guidelines that will direct the company's underwriting decisions. The underwriting policy decides the composition of the book of business. An underwriting policy must take into consideration the following dimensions–the lines of business, the territories involved and the rating plans. Any change in the underwriting policy must be evaluated on the basis of the other dimensions. Changes must also recognise the effects of certain limiting factors that influence the underwriting policy.

These include:

- *The Capacity*: The relation between the premiums written and the size of the policyholders' surplus is called the capacity. It helps to gauge an insurer's solvency. Insurers have limited capacity to write business and therefore they must make the best possible use of what they have. Allocation of capacity is a policy issue that is frequently re-evaluated.
- *Skilled Human Resources*: Insurers require skilled personnel to efficiently market the product, employ loss control efforts and adjust any loss that occurs. The insurer must ensure that there are enough personnel and that they are conversant with the company's policies.
- Insurers must also follow the rules and regulations laid down by the insurance regulator in whose territory they operate. The impact of regulation varies from country to country. They must obtain licenses for writing insurance by individual line within each state, and all rates, rules and other documents must be filed with Government regulators.
- Finally, the availability of reinsurance sets limitations on what the underwriter can write. Reinsurance refers to the contractual relationship by virtue of which, risks are shared with another insurer. It helps in reducing the impact of expanded writings on an insurer's surplus. It also helps in increasing capacity, because the insurer can shift the monetary outcome of a loss and the legal obligations for reserves.

APPLICATION OF THE UNDERWRITING POLICY

Once the underwriting policy is set, it must be communicated to all concerned, as well as applied. Underwriting bulletins and guides are utilised for this purpose. Once the policy is established, underwriting audits are conducted to review the effectiveness of the policy. The underwriting results mirror the efficiency of the underwriting policy. Applying the provisions given in the underwriting policy involves communicating whatever decision has been taken, to the agent. If any modifications are necessary before acceptance, then the reasons for the same must be conveyed to the agent/broker and to any other insurance personnel. Controls must be put in place to ensure that the modifications have been incorporated. The necessary documentation like binders and certificates of insurance must be issued. Also, all information concerning the policy and the risk involved must be documented.

Data about the policyholder including the class, location, risks involved and coverages must be coded, so that the information can be used later. This information will help to follow the progress of the account and notify the insurer in case of losses. Underwriters make use of the underwriting guides to see to it that all information is passed on to relevant members in the company.

UNDERWRITING GUIDES

Underwriting guides outline the ways to realise the objectives stated in the policy. They contain the standards for acceptability and summarise the underwriting authority requirements.

The chief purposes of an underwriting guide are as follows:

- *Supplying a Basic Framework for Formulating Underwriting Decisions*: Underwriting guides identify the principal factors that should be weighed when a particular type of insurance is written. The guides also identify the major hazards associated with any class of business and make sure that these hazards are properly evaluated. Guides also serve as a ready reckoner to the company's underwriting policy.
- The underwriting guide is a means of making sure that the selection process is uniform and consistent. Submissions that are identical in all respects must be treated in the same way. The guides are also a means of informing individual underwriters of a suitable approach to evaluate policyholders.
- Underwriting guides help to unite the insights of experienced underwriters, which will help those less familiar with a particular line of business. The guides contain significant observations that have been gathered on the basis of the insurer's past experiences.
- The guides enable routine decisions to be handled at lower levels of authority and allow the experienced underwriters to concentrate on the more difficult cases. There is a distinction made in the delegation of authority.

Some insurers have detailed underwriting guides that contain detailed instructions on how to handle the various classes. These guides will contain information about hazards, the various alternatives available, criteria used to evaluate a risk, making the final decision and then implementing and reviewing that decision. There are also guides that may not be so comprehensive. Some may contain only the list of classes and acceptable business. Yet others may only contain information that indicates the desirability of an exposure.

RATE MAKING

Rate making, also known as insurance pricing, has an important part to play in the overall profitability of the company. Rate making involves the selection of classes of exposure units on which statistics can be collected regarding the possibility of loss. The underwriter must think about all aspects before deciding on the pricing of a policy.

The rates charged must have three basic characteristics:

1. Firstly, the rate must be high enough to pay for any expenses or losses incurred. This will take a lot of consideration because the actual cost of the policy when it is first sold is not known. It is only when the period of protection comes to an end that the actual cost can be determined.
2. Secondly, the rate must not be too high. Applicants must not be asked to pay rates that are higher than the actual value of their protection.
3. Finally, the rates must not be inequitable *i.e.* , if two exposures are similar as far as losses are concerned, they should not be charged significantly different rates.

There are also certain business considerations that must be met before deciding on the rates charged:

- The system of rating must be simple and understan-dable so that premiums can be quoted promptly. Commercial insurance purchasers should be able to follow how premiums are determined, as this will help them take the necessary steps to reduce their insurance costs.
- The rates must not keep fluctuating *i.e.,* they must be stable. Otherwise irate consumers may look to the government to regulate the rates.
- The rating system must provide the insured with a strong incentive to adopt loss control.
- The rates must change with the changing economic conditions–rates must increase when loss exposure increases.

RATE MAKING IN LIFE INSURANCE IS BASED ON METHODS OF RISK CLASSIFICATION

Once underwriting information about proposed insured has been assembled from various sources, it must be evaluated for selection and classification. It should, Measure accurately the effect of each factor affecting the risk, assess the impact of interrelated factors including the conflicting ones. Produce equitable results; and be relatively simple and inexpensive to operate. Two basic systems are there to accommodate these concerns.

- *Judgment Method*: Under this method the company depends upon the combined judgment of those in the medical, actuarial, and other areas who are qualified for this work to make underwriting decisions. This method is useful when there is only one unfavourable factor to consider for making a decision. When there are multiple factors to consider for making a decision insurers follow the numerical rating system.
- *Numerical Rating System*: The numerical rating system is based on the principle that a large number of factors enters into the composition of risk and that the impact of each of these factors on longevity can be determined by a statistical study of lives possessing that factor. Under this plan, 100 per cent represents a normal or standard risk, one that is physically and financially sound and has a need for the insurance. Each of the factors that might influence a risk in an unusual way is considered a debit or a credit. Ex. If the mortality of a group of insured lives reflecting a certain degree of overweight, or a certain degree of elevated blood pressure, has been found to be 150 per cent of standard risks, a debit of 50 percentage points will be assigned to this degree of overweight or blood pressure. Numerical ratings range in most companies from 75 or less to a high of 500 or more. In most companies, ratings below 125 are considered preferred or standard. Proposed insureds who produce a rate in excess of the standard limit are either assigned to appropriate substandard classes or declined. Use of computers in underwriting is intended to provide consistency, cost savings, and quick turnaround time.

Preferred\ standard\ substandard\ .... \ uninsurable

75 85 100 115 130 150 180.....500 600

Classifying Substandard Risks

The classification of substandard life insurance may be done by charging an extra premium or by other methods for higher than standard mortality. Wide experience of reinsurers and Articles in medical journals is useful to underwriters to seek standard insurance.

Incidence of extra mortality–majority of companies categorize substandard insureds into three broad groups:

1. Those in which the number of extra deaths is expected to remain at approximately the same level in all years following policy issuance.
2. Those in which the number of extra deaths is expected to increase as insureds grow older.

3. Those in which the number of extra deaths is expected to decrease with time.

Methods of rating–the objectives in establishing an extra-premium structure are that it be:

- Equitable between impairments and between classes
- Easy to administer
- Easily understood by agents and the public

Several of these premium structures are:

- *Multiple Table Extra*: Under this method, a special mortality table is developed for each substandard classification that reflects the experience of each, and a set of gross premium rates is computed for the classification.
- *Flat Extra Premium*: This method is used when the extra mortality, measured in additional deaths per thousand, is expected to be constant.
- *Limited Death Benefit*: It is equal to a refund of premiums if death occurs in the first few years.
- *Graded Death Benefit*: It is another form of limited death benefit, with the amount payable increasing in each of the first three to five years, after which the full death benefit is payable.
- *Improvement in Expected Mortality*: Insureds expect reconsideration when an apparent reduction in expected mortality is due to change in residence, occupation, or avocation. To prevent insured persons from withdrawing, companies generally make some provision for handing these improvements. Some companies require a probationary period of one or two years prior to rating removal. This protects the company against the possibility that the insured will return to the former occupation.
- *Extra Premiums*: Most companies offer full coverage to certain impaired risks at an extra premium
- *Modification of Type of Coverage*: This device is useful for cases in which the medical history involves short-term disabilities only.
- *Renewal Underwriting*: It is concerned with the health history of the insured and also changes in occupation, income, residence, or habits, all of which may have made him or her a less desirable risk. With optionally renewable policies, the company has an opportunity to reevaluate its insureds periodically.

SPECIAL UNDERWRITING PRACTICES

Usual underwriting practices are relaxed in several areas. In the process, special underwriting concerns are created.

They are:

- *Non Medical Insurance*: No physical examination is ordinarily required. Medical information is gathered from the proposed insured by the agent who asks medically related questions from the application. Important safeguards built into the nonmedical underwriting rules are limitation on the amount available and a limit on the ages at which the insurance will be issued.

- *Guaranteed Issue Insurance*: If the group is acceptable, the insurance company dispenses with individual underwriting and agrees in advance to accept applications for insurance on all employees who are actively at work. With this arrangement, there is no underwriting of individuals' lives; being actively at work is the only requirement. The mortality experience on these arrangements is higher than usual mortality, as would be expected. To offset the anticipated extra mortality under guaranteed issue plans, many companies pay lower commissions, and either charge a higher premium or classify the policies separately for dividend purposes.
- *Reinstatements and Policy Changes*: When a life insurance policy lapses for nonpayment, the policy owner has the contractual right to apply for policy reinstatement. The owner must pay past-due premiums, plus provide evidence of insurability that is satisfactory to the insurer to avoid adverse selection.
- *Highly impaired risks*: In some cases, individuals with significant impairments have opportunities to obtain insurance at a cost that they can afford, even though the original application may have been declined by one or more companies. These opportunities can be found with companies that specialize in this market.

UNDERWRITING RESULTS

Underwriting results are an indication of the effectiveness of the company's underwriting policy. Statistically, it is represented by the insurer's combined loss and expense ratio. Evaluation of results by the line, territory etc. , will help identify all the problem areas. Besides these, over the years, the entire insurance industry has become cyclical in nature, thus providing industry average performances against which the performance of any insurer can be measured.

The causal mechanism for this cyclic nature of the industry is yet to be determined. Certain factors like inflation, regulation and competition have had a considerable impact. For example, slow regulatory response to requests for rate increase in times of inflation could have been responsible for unsatisfactory underwriting results.

17

Life Insurance Products

TERM ASSURANCE PLANS

NATURE OF TERM INSURANCE

- Furnishes protection for a limited number of years.
- It terminates with no maturity value.
- The face amount of the policy is payable only if the insured's death occurs during the stipulated term.
- Nothing is paid in case of survival.
- Issued for a short period but customarily provides protection for at least a set number of years, such as 10 or 20 years, or to a stipulated age, such as 65 or 70 years.
- It is more comparable to property and liability insurance contracts than to any other life insurance contract.
- Initial premium rates are low compared to other life products because the period of protection is limited.
- Prices of term products of different insurers can be easily compared.
- The term market is more price competitive than the market for cash value policies.
- Usually, term products have no cash values and often no dividends, thus permitting policy comparisons on the basis of premiums.
- Term lapse rates are higher than other policies because these are price sensitive, easily replaceable and only a few penalties for early termination.

FEATURES

Three features applicable to many term life policies:

- *Renewability*: Continuation of the policy for another term without reference to insured's insurability; premiums increase at each interval.
- Convertibility is an option to change over to a cash value policy [whole life or endowment] without reference to insured's

insurability; conversion allowed on attained age method or on original age method.

- Re-entry is the facility to pay lower premium than otherwise if insureds can demonstrate that they meet certain continuing insurability conditions. Insurers use three types of mortality tables.
  - Select [mortality experience of newly insured lives-generally exhibit lower mortality],
  - Ultimate [mortality experience beyond the select years–generally it exhibits higher mortality], and
  - 'Aggregate [includes both select and ultimate] mortality tables.

TYPES OF TERM LIFE INSURANCE POLICIES

LEVEL FACE AMOUNT

- *Increasing Premium*: Yearly renewable term
- *Level Premium Policies*: Life expectancy term based on specific mortality table or Term–to–age–65 [or 70] provides protection for a somewhat shorter period than do life expectancy policies and consequently, have slightly lower premiums.

A cash value often develops during the policy term, increasing for some years then decreasing to zero by policy expiry.

NON LEVEL FACE AMOUNT

- *Decreasing Term Policies*: These policies are commonly used to pay off a loan balance on the death of the debtor\insured. Mortgage protection plan, which clears a mortgage loan when the insured dies. Payor benefit plan [a rider] provides waiver of premiums in juvenile insurance when the parent dies. Family income policy provides monthly income to the surviving spouse.
- *Increasing Term is not Issued as a Separate Policy but Only as a Rider*: Cost-of living–adjustment [COLA] rider provides automatic increases in the death benefit depending on the increase in inflation. Return–of–premium feature provides for return of all premiums in case of death.

USES AND LIMITATIONS OF TERM INSURANCE

- Can be useful for persons with low income and high insurance needs.
- To individuals at the threshold of careers or who started new businesses.
- To indemnify businesses on the death of key employees.
- Supplement to an existing life insurance programme during the child rearing period.
- Can be useful as a hedge against financial loss already sustained.

- For ensuring that the mortgage and other loans are paid on the debtor/insured's death.
- Vehicle for ensuring juvenile education in the case of payor's death.
- Natural for all situations that call for temporary income protection needs.
- It can be the basis for one's permanent insurance programme through a so called 'buy–term–and–invest–the difference [BTID] arrangement. The hope is that the term + the separate investment will out perform the cash value life insurance policy.

The BTID programme may fail in its mission if the individual fails to set aside the planned amounts regularly.

WHOLE LIFE INSURANCE POLICIES

THE NATURE OF WHOLE LIFE INSURANCE

- Whole life insurance is intended to provide insurance protection over one's entire lifetime.
- It provides for the payment of the face amount upon the insured's death regardless of when death occurs.
- Universal life policies can function as whole life insurance if they have sufficient cash value.
- The face amounts payable under whole life policies typically remain at the same level throughout the policy duration, although dividends are often used to increase the total amount paid on death.
- In most policies, the gross premium also remains at the same level through out the premium payment period with some exceptions.

WHOLE LIFE AS ENDOWMENT OR TERM INSURANCE

- Terminal age in all mortality tables–100 years. The company pays the policy face amount to those few persons who live to the terminal age–as if they had died.
- It is also referred as 'endowment–at–age 100 policies'.
- Actuarial principles same as ' term insurance'. Hence also called 'Term–to–age–100'.

WHOLE LIFE CASH VALUES

- All whole life policies involve some pre funding of future mortality costs.
- Cash values are available to the policy owner at anytime by surrendering the policy.
- Loans can be obtained on interest. [up to the policy's cash value]
- Loan is deducted from the gross cash value when death claim is payable.

- Policy loan may, but need not, be repaid at any time and is a source of policy flexibility.

WITH PROFIT AND WITHOUT PROFIT WHOLE LIFE POLICIES

- Most whole life insurance policies are participating.
- A significant proportion is non-participating, but with some non-guaranteed element.
- Dividends actually paid may exceed illustrated dividends when investment returns are high.
- In India it is known as with and without profit policies.

TYPES OF WHOLE LIFE INSURANCE POLICIES

- Ordinary life insurance
- Limited payment whole life insurance
- Current assumption whole life insurance
- Variable life insurance
- Modified life insurance
- Enhanced ordinary life insurance
- Graded premium whole life insurance
- Single premium whole life insurance
- Indexed whole life insurance
- Special purpose life insurance

Ordinary Life Insurance

Ordinary life insurance also known as 'straight life', 'continuous premium whole life', 'whole life'–provides whole life insurance with premiums that are payable for the whole of life.

The features of ordinary life insurance are:

- Permanent protection at a relatively modest annual outlay.
- Cash values normally increase at a fairly constant rate, reaching the policy face amount at age 100.
- Early years cash values are low because high costs of policy sale, commission, underwriting and other administrative expenses.
- Flexibility in this product–'vanish pay' [possibility of no further payments by the policy owner through accumulated dividends and paid up additions] and 'premium deposit rider' [policy owner deposits amounts to pay future premiums].

Uses of ordinary whole life insurance are:

- Offer greater flexibility and value.
- Useful to accumulate savings via life insurance.
- Outlays can be relatively modest because level premium payments for the entire duration.
- Enjoy favourable income tax treatment.

Limitations of these policies are:

- Life policies are costly for those whose life insurance need is less than 15 years. It is also costly for persons whose careers are just beginning because their incomes would not permit purchasing such long term insurance policies.

Limited–payment Whole Life Insurance

The features of limited payment whole life insurance are:

- The policy remains in full force for the whole of life but premiums are payable for a limited number of years only, after which the policy becomes paid up for its full face amount.
- It is contractually guaranteed, never to require premium payments beyond the stated premium payment period. There is no such guarantee with 'vanish pay' policies.
- It contains the same non-forfeiture, dividend, settlement options of ordinary life policy.
- The extreme in limited–payment life insurance is the single–premium whole life policy.

Limitations of these policies are:

- It is not well adapted to those whose income is small and whose need for insurance protection is great.
- This policy is fit for many business insurance situations.

Current Assumption Whole Life Insurance

The features of current assumption whole life insurance are:

- It is referred to as interest–sensitive whole life and as fixed premium universal life.
- In cash value determination this policy uses changing money interest rates and current mortality charges.
- *Two versions*: Low premium version and high premium version.
- Flexibility in premium payments and maintaining death benefits.
- It is a blend of old and new [universal life] [control and flexibility].

Limitations of these policies:

- Unlike universal policy, it will lapse if a required premium is not paid. Hence it gives the discipline to pay flexible premiums.

VARIABLE LIFE INSURANCE

It is also called unit linked life insurance, the features of these policies are:

- It could help offset the adverse effects of inflation on life insurance policy values.
- 'Separate account'-distinct pool of investments–acts as a mutual fund.
- The policy cash values are directly related to the investment performance.
- Regardless of the investment performance, the death benefit is guaranteed.

- Cash values are not guaranteed [passing investment risk to the policy owner].
- Policy loans are to be made available of 75% of the cash value at a fixed or variable rate of interest.
- It is appealing to those who desire whole life insurance at a fixed, level premium and also the potential for important equity type gains [losses].

Limitations of these policies are:

- It is riskier than other policies.
- Regulations require greater disclosure than other policies.

Modified Life Insurance

The features of modified life insurance are:

- Premiums are redistributed over a period of time
- Lower during the first few years
- increase in later years.

Enhanced Ordinary Life Insurance

The features of enhanced ordinary life insurance are:

- Dividends are used to provide a level coverage at a lower than usual premium
- Face amount reduced after a few years and dividends are used to purchase deferred paid-up whole life additions.

Graded Premium Whole Life Insurance

The features of Graded Premium whole life insurance are:

- Premiums begin at a level that is 50% or less than those for comparable ordinary policies.
- Premiums increase annually for a period of 5 to 20 years and remain level thereafter.
- Cash values evolve slowly than ordinary policy
- More akin to YRT policies.

Single Premium Whole Life Insurance

The features of single premium whole life insurance are:

- A large single premium is paid
- Mortality and expense charges deducted annually from the cash value
- Wealthy older persons purchase it

Indexed Whole Life Insurance

The features of indexed whole life insurance are:

- Face amount increases with increases in the inflation.
- Insurance company bills the policy owner each year, if policy owner assumes the risk.

- Not to require evidence of insurability for these increases.
- If the policy owner declines in any year to purchase the increase, no further automatic increases are permitted.

Special Purpose Life Insurance

- Special purposes–synonymous with industrial insurance and home service insurance.
- Family policy
- Juvenile insurance
- Pre need funeral insurance

Insurance covering multiple lives:

- Survivorship life insurance or second-to-die life insurance–pays death proceeds on the death of the second [last] insured.
- Joint life insurance or first–to-die insurance–promises to pay the face amount of the policy on the first death of one of two insureds covered by contract.

UNIVERSAL LIFE [U. L.] INSURANCE

- *Origin and Growth*: Though the concepts upon which UL is based are 100 years old, the credit of conceiving of UL as a product goes to George R. Dinney of the Great West Life, a Canadian insurer in 1962 and1971.
  - The high interest rate environment in mid '80s influenced initial high growth rate of UL.

NATURE

- Flexibility in premium payment [whatever amounts, whatever times] even skip after making an initial minimum premium payments, the provided the cash value will cover policy charges.
- Adjustability of death benefit.
- Superior value through reduced distribution costs.

CHALLENGES

- Agents resisted the commission structures.
- Many companies failed to secure adequate margins because of lower than expected sales.
- Administrative costs are high.
- Uncertain cash flows have proven a challenge in the operation of a UL policy.

OPERATION OF UL POLICY

- Similar to CAWL [current assumption whole life] policies.
- Differ from them in that neither the premium level nor the death benefit is fixed.

- Mortality charges based on insured's attained age.
- UL policies levy high first year surrender charges.
- The cash value less surrender charges yields the policy's cash surrender value.
- The process [flexible premium–expense charges–mortality charges + interest = cash value] is repeated for third, fourth and later periods.
- If the cash value at any time were insufficient to sustain the policy, it would lapse without further premium payments.
- No further premium need be paid, however, if the cash value is sufficient.

UL PRODUCT DESIGN

- *Death Benefit Patterns*: UL policies offer two death benefit patterns [level death benefit pattern and a level net amount at risk (NAR)]. From these two the purchaser selects one. Of course, the pattern may be changed at any time, but, in the absence of a change request, the selected pattern will be followed during the policy term.
- *Premium Payments*: UL policyowners pay premiums of whatever amount and whenever they desire, subject to company rules regarding minimums and maximums.
- *Policy Loadings*: Identifiable loadings are imposed on UL policies in one or both of two ways: 1. Front end loads and 2. Back-end loads. [Front-end loads are first year expenses, commissions, mortality margins, marketing etc. and Back-end loads are surrender charges]
- *Mortality and other Benefit Charges:* Mortality charges are deducted each month from UL cash values. Most UL mortality charges are indeterminate and differentiated. Interest credits and loadings also must be factored into the analysis [other than mortality charges].
- *Cash Values*: Cash value is simply the residual of each period's funds flow. It results from taking the previous period's ending cash-value balance [if any], adding to it any premium paid, subtracting expense and mortality charges, then adding current interest credits to the resulting fund balance. The result is the end-of-period cash value. UL policies also permit policy owners to obtain policy loans on the security of the policy's cash values. The surrenders must be for at least a minimum amount and may carry a processing charge. The policy death benefit is reduced by the exact amount of any partial surrender. [To avoid adverse selection]. Policy surrender involves a surrender charge.

USES OF UNIVERSAL LIFE INSURANCE

- A single UL policy can serve the needs of a family throughout their life cycle.
- A UL policy can be used, as can most other cash value policies.
- It can be used in virtually every circumstance in which a whole life policy could be used.

LIMITATIONS

- Flexibility in premium payment may lead to poor persistency and consumers may lose money.
- Undue emphasis on current interest rate, to the exclusion of other potentially important elements such as expense loadings, mortality charges, and surrender charges.

VARIABLE UNIVERSAL LIFE INSURANCE

It is also called flexible premium variable life. It is a combination of flexible characteristics of universal life with the investment flexibility of variable life.

Nature of Variable Universal Life Insurance

- Same regulations as VLI [Variable Life Insurance].
- Flexibility in premium payments + option of increasing or decreasing the policy death benefit.

Uses:

- Useful for those persons who desire to treat their life insurance policy cash values more as an investment than a savings account.

Dangers:

- If separate account investment results are not favourable, the policy's cash value could be reduced substantially and the policy could require substantial additional premium payments.

OTHER FLEXIBLE PREMIUM POLICIES

Adjustable Life [AL] Insurance:

- Level premium
- Level death benefit life insurance policy
- Assumes the form of any traditional term or whole life policy.
- Offers the policy owner the ability, within limits, to change the policy plan, premium payment, and face amount.
- AL policies require certain minimum annual premium payments.
- In some respects they are similar to fixed premium policies.

FLEXIBLE ENHANCED ORDINARY LIFE

- Combination of whole life, term and paid-up additions in such proportions as to allow the policy owner to establish a comfortable premium level, within limits, and to adjust the policy amount, also within limits.

ENDOWMENT INSURANCE

Unlike term policies Endowment policies promise not only to pay the policy face amount on the death of the insured during a fixed term of years, but also to pay the full-face amount at the end of the term if the insured survives the term.

CONCEPTS OF ENDOWMENT INSURANCE

Mathematical Concept

Endowment Insurance = Term life insurance + pure endowment [to pay the face amount if the insured dies during the period + to pay the maturity amount only if the insured is living at the end of a specific period, with nothing paid in case of prior death]

Economic Concept

Divides endowment insurance into two parts:

1. Decreasing term insurance
2. Increasing savings
   - The savings part of the contract is available to the policy owner through surrender of the policy.
   - The increasing savings feature is supplemented by decreasing term insurance, which, when added to the savings accumulation, equals the policy's face amount.

An endowment policy has the following features:

- Endowment plans promise protection from risk in the event of death of the insured during the policy term as well as an assured sum upon the maturity of the policy. In this type of policy the maturity of the policy is usually chosen to coincide with the retirement of the person.
- These policies are issued for specific terms chosen by the proposer who can choose the duration of the policy which may be 10, 15, 20 or 30 years. Where the duration is short the premium involved is higher.
- It is to be noted that whether the assured meets a premature death or not the full amount of the policy has to be paid by the insurance company provided the premiums have been paid as stipulated in the policy.
- The endowment amount at the end of the term can be used to
  - Purchase an annuity policy for getting a stream of monthly pension for the rest of his life.
  - For parking the money in some investment to generate returns.
- These policies are eligible for loans within the surrender value of the policy.
- If a person wants to meet expenditure like his children's education and marriage, he can go for this plan since he is entitled to the proceeds under the plan on maturity of the policy. The term can be selected to suit these contingencies.

TYPES OF ENDOWMENT POLICIES

- Single premium endowment policies

- *Retirement Income Policy*: The amount payable at death is the face amount or cash value, which ever is greater.
- *A Semi Endowment Policy*: Pays upon survival.
- *Modified Endowment Policy*: Provides for payment periodically.
- *Deposit Term*: First year premiums were set to be higher than renewal premiums.
- *Juvenile Endowment Policies*: Designed to cover child's education, marriage, and independence.

OPTIONAL BENEFITS AND RIDERS

- *Disability Benefits*: A common practice is to attach riders that provide certain benefits in the event of the insured's disability. The two most common disability benefits are
  - Waiver of premium
  - Disability income
- *Accelerated Death Benefits*: This provision involves the payment of all or a portion of a life insurance policy's face amount prior to the insured's death because of some specified, adverse medical condition of the insured. It typically takes one of the three forms.
  - Terminal illness coverage
  - Catastrophic illness coverage
  - Long-term care coverage.
- *Accidental Death Benefit [Double Indemnity]:* This provision may be added to most life insurance contracts, which provides that double of the face amount is payable if the insured dies as a result of an accident. The expression accidental insists that both the cause and result of the death must be accidental.
- *Guaranteed Insurability Option*: It was developed to permit young individuals to be certain that they would be able to purchase additional insurance, as they grew older, regardless of their insurability.
- *Cost of Living Rider [COLA]:* This rider can be useful when one's needs for insurance are expected to change over time in approximately the same proportion as changes in the cost of living.
- *Additional Insurance Coverage*: Attaching term riders to basic policies enhance the total death benefit.

The practice of these benefits to insurance contracts permits flexibility in adapting basic plans to individual needs.

CHILDREN'S POLICIES

- These are a type of *money back plans* to get an accumulated value at the end of a certain period (when the child attains majority). Some plans provide options to the buyer to withdraw lumpsum amounts in periodical installments say every 2, 3, 4 or 5 years after a deferment period. This scheme is designed to provide finance to incur expenses related to the child's education or for helping him to make his livelihood by setting up/starting his profession/business when he grows up. Parents or the legal guardian can also take out a policy on the life of their children from their birth.

- The risk cover generally commences when the children attain the age of 12, 17, 18 or 21 years of age (known as the date of risk) and it is vested on the child on attainment of his/her majority.
- Until the child attains majority, the ownership of the policy rests with the parents, who have to pay the premium regularly.
- One important point to note here is that a child's policy should be considered only after the major income earner of the family has been adequately insured. This is because a children's policy is quite useless if the primary breadwinner of the family dies. In the event of his death, the policy may lapse, as the child may not be in a position to pay the premium. To take care of this contingency it is possible for the proposer to avail the premium waiver benefit by paying additional premium from inception.
- The policy has two stages
  - The first stage covers the period from the date of commencement of the policy to the deferred date that is the date under which the risk commences under the policy. No loans are granted under the policy during the deferment period and no risk of death is covered until the child attains the prescribed age as per the policy contract. If the child dies during the deferment period, the policy stands cancelled and the amount paid under the policy by way of premium without any deduction is refunded to the proposer.
  - The second stage covers the risk period.

WOMEN'S POLICIES

Women are exposed to as many risks as their male counterparts. They are required to perform in the work place as well as fulfill their obligations towards family. If a female member in a home dies it is very difficult to compensate her position by her dependants. So, it is advisable for women from every socio economic environment to purchase a woman's policy to safeguard against the risk of her demise.

These policies provide funds for the purpose of education, marriage or sickness. With guaranteed loyalty and loyalty additions during the policy term period these policies have been tailored to encourage women to save for their own safety and security. Survival benefits can be claimed as per requirement.

Insurance for handicapped dependants:

- It provides for insurance cover that provides for monthly payments for a specific period after a covered illness or injury occurs. Insurance must be purchased prior to illness or injury.

- Under this policy an individual or a member of a HUF can take cover on his own life to provide for a payment of the lump sum and an annuity to the handicapped dependant.
- It provides a way for protection of income and maintenance of standard of living of the policyholder and his family.

COMBINATION PLANS

The life insurer has to satisfy various needs of policyholders. Sometimes traditional policies like Whole Life and Endowment needs to be combined, including the annuity element so as to meet the requirements of certain policy holders, who would be covered for maximum risk, with not much provision for maturity element. The Jeevan Mitra Policy of LIC fulfils such needs. Here, the basic sum becomes payable on maturity, but on death twice the sum assured becomes payable. In case of accidental death, one more sum assured becomes payable.

Recently, LIC launched a triple cover Jeevan Mitra, where the death cover is 3 times the basic sum assured. In case of death by accident, four times of the basic sum assured becomes payable. Insurance is limited only to the premiums paid if death occurs due to natural reasons within six months of the policy's first year and during the later part of the year, the cover is provided at half of the sum assured.

INTEREST SENSITIVE PRODUCTS

Interest sensitiveness is a feature of all savings scheme. Due to inflation, interest rates have become volatile and the rupee is depreciating steadily. Life insurance products are also exposed to interest rate risks and often life insurance salesmen learn from the market that life insurance return is not attractive. To counter these problems, insurers have come up with the following to compensate for the low return. By providing extra benefits, accruing to the policy every year in the form of additions, on a predetermined scale or a rate.

By providing a periodical return of a portion of the sum assured without reducing the death cover during the initial years of the policy or at the end of the term. A policyholder can exploit the benefits of the investment climate prevailing during that time and put the refund money in investments with higher returns.

LIC's Jeevan Chayya Plan (a Children's policy) is an interest sensitive scheme where the sum assured is returned during the last four years of the policy in four equal annual installments. The death cover is for double the sum during the currency of the policy.

Investment oriented policy holders usually go for such policies. Since, the insurer gives periodical repayments of the sum assured to the insured, he does not grant a loan within the surrender value of the policy.

WITH PROFIT AND WITHOUT PROFIT POLICIES

WITH PROFIT POLICIES

- These are participating plans in which the policyholder is entitled to participate in the profits or surplus of the insurer.
- The surplus is determined through the periodical valuation of assets and liabilities as per statutory requirements.
- The surplus is usually distributed in the form of bonus, declared after such a revaluation and is paid along with the contracted amount.
- These plans are very popular in India, because a majority of them purchase life insurance policies for savings purposes.
- The premium rate charged for these policies are higher than that of "Without Profit" Plans.

WITHOUT PROFIT POLICIES

- These are non-participating plans in which the policyholder does not receive a share of the surplus of the insurer.
- The rate of premium is lower for these policies than that of With Profit Plans. Investment plans
- The premium proceeds of the policy are invested by the insurer in the capital markets and other market oriented instruments. The returns are not predictable and they fluctuate depending upon the market conditions. However these policies promise higher returns than other policies.

Plans:

- Bima Nivesh double and triple cover of LIC
- Bima Plus (a Capital market linked plan) of LIC
- Lifetime pension plan of ICICI Prudential (a pension plan)
- Unit Linked policy of UTI

Unit Linked Policy of UTI

It is a unique investment scheme from Unit Trust of India. This policy offers higher rates of return to policyholders and at the same time reduces interest and mortality guarantees offered by traditional products.

These products enable policyholders to:

- Choose a means of savings vehicle.
- Have greater amount of flexibility than traditional products by offering very little limitation on premium payment and withdrawal of money.
- Avail tax rebate under Section 88 of the Income Tax Act and get a tax-free dividend and benefit of longterm capital gains after maturity.

Some other features of the policy are:

- Yield is quite high if entry is at a younger age and it declines gradually with the increase in age of the policyholder.

- The maximum target amount is restricted to ₹ 75,000.
- It is available in two term periods, 10 and 15 years.
- It provides numerous advantages to the policyholders in the form of life insurance cover at a fairly low rate, accident cover, decent rate of returns and tax benefits under Section 88.
- Insurance is limited only to the premiums paid if death occurs due to natural reasons within six months of the policy's first year and during the later part of the year, the cover is provided at half of the sum assured.
- A maturity bonus of 5% and 7.5% is also granted on the 10 and 15 year plans respectively.
- Life and accident covers are not granted to minors under this plan.
- It has no nomination facility.

19

Claim Settlement

CONCEPT OF CLAIMS

Concept of claim with reference to the insurance contract differs from the angle of the parties to the contract. The insurer is under an obligation or responsibility to perform the contract as per the terms of promise made. The insured is in an advantageous position once the premium as demanded by the insurer is paid. The payment of insurance premium and acceptance of the contract by the insurer creates contractual obligation upon the parties to perform some of the duties before or after the claim is made or on happening of event or the loss is suffered by one of the parties to the contract.

MEANING OF CLAIM

Claim is a right of the insured to receive the amount secured under the policy of insurance contract. It is the consideration of the insurance contract. It is a promise made by the insurer to pay the compensation to the insured on happening of some uncertain event resulting in loss or damage to asset insured. It is the pecuniary interest in the insurance contract. It is the insurance amount that is incorporated in the policy document of insurance contract. The claim is a right of the insured in all classes of the insurance contract.

The payment of consideration is linked to the insurable interest of the insured. The insurable interest of the insured or the beneficiary under the insurance contract makes the insurance contract a valid contract. The claim payment and compensation payable as indemnity to the insured are related and are synonyms in the claims management of the insurance policy. The payment of premium is one set of promise whereas promise to pay for the loss suffered by the insured is the second set of promise and form reciprocal promises and considerations for one another.

Claims are to be paid either to the insured or the nominees of the insured by the insurer under the agreement or the terms of the contract of insurance. The important terms of the insurance contract and payment of the insurance claims are the payment of insurance claim either on happening of event or on the date of maturity.

CLAIMS DEPARTMENT

The claims department is one of the key departments in an insurance company.

The claims department has the following functions to perform:

- To provide customers of insurance and reinsurance companies with a high quality of service, so that the company is able to differentiate from the rest of the companies. This can also be viewed as a unique selling proposition of a company. This role of the claims department gives a long-term edge to the company and hence is referred to as the *strategic role.*
- It is the claims department that monitors the claims and sees that whether the benefits of insurance exceed the costs of claims. This role is referred to as the *cost-monitoring role* of the claims department.
- The claims department has to see that the expectations of the customers are met with regard to the speed, manner and efficiency of the service. This is called the customer *service role* of the claims department.
- It is the responsibility of the claims department to meet the standard of service, to keep up to the customers' expectations and still operate within the budget. This is the *managerial role* of the claims department.

Both the quality of service and cost of claims is the responsibility of the claims department. The department has to look after the proper mix of the two. The cost of claims must not exceed a given level in trying to render a very good service to the customer. So the claims department should work with due diligence to balance the two parameters. The department must be able to find out the difference between fake and genuine claims.

In trying to create a good public image, the cost of claims should not be overshot. The importance of cost of claims in the insurance industry cannot be undermined. At any point of time the cost of claims should not exceed the available resources to pay the liabilities. If such a situation arises then the insurance company is technically insolvent. So estimation of future liabilities is just as important as control over the claim payments. As the claims department is in direct touch with the customer, the quality of service has to be ensured by the department.

The management of claims is a very daunting task for an insurance company. The claims department has the sole responsibility of managing claims. Claims management by far is the most complex issue in an insurance company. It involves a variety of specialized tasks, which only specialized people can perform. Various disciplines it involve are marketing and sales, study of human behaviour, finance, control systems and business strategy making. The management of so many disciplines into a single department makes the job of persons more difficult. The presence of so many specialized people in a single department will obviously lead to formation of groups. A healthy relationship within the groups is required. The people in the claims department should have good interpersonal skills. If the employees in the claims department are not able to work in harmony customers will not get the kind of quality in service.

So it is important from the departments' point of view to have sufficient number of people as managers so as to simplify job and proper human resource systems in place so those persons are recruited whose philosophy goes with the mission and vision of the organization. It has become imperative for the claims department to provide quality service to the customers so that the corporate goals are achieved. The claims department in effect acts as an interface between the customer service quality and insurance company's objectives. It has to be given proper weightage and motivation so that the business as a whole functions well.

NATURE OF CLAIMS AND REQUIREMENTS IN THE SETTLEMENT OF CLAIMS

The procedure for handling of claims varies according to the types of cover, the amount of claim whether it is a personal or commercial claim. Claims process is the procedure of handling claims and differs from case to case.

Basically, the following are the different types of claims which come up before an Insurance Company:

- Maturity Claims and Survival Benefits
- Death Claims
- Accident and Disability Claims and
- Annuity Payments

Settlement of claims under life insurance policies depend upon the nature of a claim, eligibility to policy moneys, proof of the happening of the event insured against, proof of title, etc.

MATURITY CLAIMS

Payment of Maturity Claims is by far the easiest to manage. These include benefits payable during the period of assurance called *'Survival Benefits'* under certain types of policies popularly known as 'Money Back' policies.

Payment in these cases is easy because:

- There is no need on the part of the policyholder to prove the happening of the event
- The policyholder is alive so Proof of Title does not pose any problem, and
- The Insurance company need not await any claim from the policyholder and take initiative to settle the claims expeditiously.

At the beginning of every calendar year, the Data Processing Department of a Branch Office generates on the computer a list of policies under which maturity and survival benefit payments will fall due during the next financial year. This list is prepared due month wise in strict policy number order. 7Of late, due to the introduction of software package for claims, this list also provides information regarding the premium status of each policy and also the actual claim amount payable including Vested Bonus, Interim Bonus and Terminal Bonus. These lists are again of two types–one in respect of Maturities where the contracts are to be terminated and the other in respect of survival benefits under 'Money Back' type of policies which continue to be on the books even after the payment of the benefits.

The reasons for initiating action in advance in this area of operations are several. The speed of settlement of claims is very important in building up the image of the insurance company. Maturity and Survival Benefit payments are due on particular dates and the aim is to ensure that the moneys due are received by the respective policyholders on those due dates. If they receive such payments on the very dates they are due, the Insurance Company would have fulfilled its obligations.

The policyholders would feel very happy and satisfied at the service rendered. It is also a great boost to the field force because they can approach the respective policyholders for converting a part or whole of the claim amount into premium for another policy and/or to canvass a new life insurance policy for one of the family members or close friends of the policyholder. From accounting point of view also, it is a good and prudent practice because the claim amounts, which are liabilities for the company, are cleared expeditiously.

One more reason for initiating action early is the presence of a large number of policies in the list of maturities which have lapsed after acquiring paid-up value. The time lag between the dates of lapse of these policies and their respective dates of maturity is always considerable. In many such cases, it is not unusual that the policyholders might have changed residence, information about which will not be available with the insurance office.

Hence, by initiating action at least three months earlier to the maturity dates, the insurance company will have sufficient time to locate the policyholders and arrange payment of the moneys due to them. The requirements for settlement of these claims are very simple.

They are:

- A Discharge Voucher to be sent in advance
- Policy Document
- Any Deed of Assignment, if the same was executed on a separate Stamp Paper.

As the policyholder is alive, obtaining these requirements poses very little problem. A few problems are likely to arise when a Policy Document is misplaced. Usually, in such cases, the Corporation settles maturity claims on the basis of an Indemnity Bond to be executed on a Non-Judicial Stamp Paper of the value of ₹ 100 by the policyholder along with a surety of sound financial standing. While settling survival benefits, however, the corporation insists on issue of a duplicate policy because the contract continues even after the payment of the survival benefit.

DEATH CLAIMS

Life insurance is basically for providing financial security to the families of deceased policyholders. Death claim settlement naturally assumes very great importance in the total operations of any Life Insurance Company. Despite several problems encountered, still Life Insurance Companies struggle to efficiently and effectively attend to this function. Unlike in Maturity and Survival Benefit Claims, the Policyholder is not alive. This itself poses many problems.

Broadly the problems in settlement of Death claims are:

- Obtaining satisfactory Proof of Death, and
- Obtaining satisfactory Proof of Title

These two requirements are independent of each other. It is necessary for an insurance company to decide first whether any liability lies in a death claim. This not only depends on the proof of the happening of the event, *i.e.* death but also the status of the policy as on the date of death. It is necessary to verify whether the policy in question is in force or in a reduced paid-up condition.

In these cases, some money becomes payable. But there may be cases where the policy had lapsed without acquiring any value. It is also necessary for the office to verify whether any claims concessions or administrative concessions are applicable or whether the claim can be considered on ex-gratia basis. Cause of death also assumes importance. If it was suicide, it is to be considered whether it was within one year from the date of the policy. If it was accident, it is to be verified whether Accident Benefit becomes payable.

Once liability is admitted, the office will have to verify the position of title to the policy moneys and arrange payment to the persons legally entitled to receive the same. The Life Insurance company is not expected to know about the death of a policyholder unless the same is intimated by the claimants. Any action can therefore be initiated only after receipt of such intimation.

The letter of intimation should contain certain particulars:

- Policy number and name of the life assured. These two should match; otherwise the policy number must be wrong.
- Date of death, on which depends the status of the policy and amount payable.
- Name and address of the claimant as requirements are to be called from them. Usually, the death intimation should be sent by the nominee or assignee or some one near and dear to the deceased life assured. If the intimation is received from a stranger, the office should be careful to verify as to why a stranger should be interested in the policy moneys.

Once a proper intimation is received, the insurance office will process the same to know whether anything is due at all under the policy. This usually depends on the status of the policy on the date of death. A calculation of the claim amount will be made and requirements are called for from the claimant. If there is a valid nomination or assignment under the policy, duly registered in the books of the insurance company, requirements will be called for from such nominee or assignee only and not from the claimant.

In considering a death claim, it becomes necessary to verify the duration of the policy, *i.e.* the time elapsed from the date of commencement of risk under the policy to the date of death. Normally, if the duration is two years or less, such a claim is considered as an 'Early Claim'. If the duration is more than two years, such a claim is considered as a 'Non-Early Claim'.

This becomes necessary because of application of Section 45 of the Insurance Act, 1938, which is otherwise called 'Indisputability Clause'. This provision of law is of great significance and it was incorporated in the Insurance Act as a protection to policyholders and their claimants.

The clause reads as under:

- "No policy of life insurance, after the expiry of two years from the date on which it was effected, be called in question by an insurer on the ground that a statement made in the proposal for insurance or in any report of a medical officer, or referee, or friend of the insured, or in any other document leading to the issue of the policy, was inaccurate or false, unless the insurer shows that such statement was on a material matter or suppressed facts which it was material to disclose and that it was fraudulently made by the policyholder and the policyholder knew at the time of making it that the statement was false or that it suppressed facts which it was material to disclose. "

The importance of the principle of Utmost Faith has already been discussed in the stage on 'Legal Framework'. It is, therefore, redundant to discuss the same again here. To ensure that the insurance companies do not go to unreasonable levels and repudiate liability under a policy invoking the principle of utmost good faith, the Insurance Act provides protection to the policyholders and the claimants under Section 45.

To avoid liability under a policy of life insurance two years after the policy was effected, the life insurance company will have to prove:

- That there was suppression of facts by the life assured,
- That what was suppressed was a material fact, and
- That such suppression was done intentionally with a view to defraud the insurance company.

The onus of proof of all the lies on the insurance company only. The indication that when the death of a policyholder is within two years after the policy was effected, the company can avoid the liability after proving suppression of material facts by the life assured at the time of taking the policy.

It is not necessary to prove whether such suppression was intentional or unintentional in such cases. The said provision in the Insurance Act refers to the period elapsed from the date on which the policy is effected. But a typical and different situation arises when a policy lapses due to non-payment of premiums and subsequently revived. The question arises whether the duration of the policy should be reckoned in such cases from the date on which the policy was effected or from the date on which it was revived.

The legal provision, *i.e.* Section 45 indicates the former but is silent on the latter. The Life Insurance Corporation of India treats revival of a lapsed policy as a Novatio, *i.e.* a New contract and so applies the provisions of Section 45 of Insurance Act to a case where death of the policyholder takes place within two years from the date of revival of the policy. In one case, the Supreme Court set aside the repudiation of liability made by the LIC of India on the grounds of suppression of material facts by the life assured at the time of revival of his lapsed policy as not coming under Section 45.

The point is debatable. If the Section does not apply to cases of revival of lapsed policies, then there is always a possibility of policyholders taking policies on their lives, immediately lapsing the same and get them revived just when they are on death bed by suppressing facts about their health. If the Life Insurance companies have to assume liability and cannot dispute the same, it will be against public policy.

The duty of disclosure of material facts by the applicant is not limited only to the statements made by him in the Proposal Form. It continues till the date of acceptance of the Proposal by the Insurance Company.

The following extract from the declaration made by the proposer at the bottom of the proposal is significant:

- "And I hereby declare that if after the date of submission of the proposal but before the issue of the First Premium Receipt any change in my occupation or any adverse circumstances connected with my financial position or the general health of myself or that of any members of my family occurs or if a proposal for assurance or an application for revival of a policy on my life made to any office of the Corporation has been withdrawn or dropped, deferred or accepted at an increased premium or subject to a lien or on terms other than as proposed, I shall forthwith intimate the same to the Corporation in writing to reconsider the terms of acceptance of assurance. Any omission on my part to do so shall render this assurance invalid and all moneys which shall have been paid in respect thereof shall stand forfeited to the Corporation".

This condition is also called 'Continued Insurability' condition. It, therefore, becomes necessary for the insurance company, when they receive an intimation of death of a life assured, to verify the duration of the policy, *i.e.* from the date of commencement of risk or date of revival of the policy to the date of death. If the cause of death is such that it can be only a long duration disease, it leads to the suspicion of suppression of material facts about the health of the life assured in cases where the duration as mentioned is two years or less. For this reason, the requirements to be called for in cases of Early Claims are to some extent different from those needed for considering Non-Early Claims.

The Life Insurance Corporation of India calls for the following requirements in cases of death claims:

- Death Certificate in original issued by Municipality/Corporation/ Revenue Officials in the form Prescribed by the Government.
- Claimant's Statement: here the claimant furnishes information:
  - About the deceased life assured, his/her age, date of death, cause of death, place of death, if hospitalized during a period of three years earlier to death, details of the same;
  - Details of the claimant–name, address, how related to the life assured, in what capacity claim is being made and
  - Details of any other policy/policies of the life assured so that all claims can be considered together.
- Statements from the hospital/nursing home where the life assured had treatment for terminal illness in which the hospital/nursing home authorities furnish information about the life assured, his/ her address, date of admission, date of discharge/date of death, time of death, reasons for admission, primary cause of death, secondary causes, duration of illness, whether treated in the same hospital/nursing home at any time earlier for any ailment, if so details; whether treated by any other doctor earlier, if so details, etc.
- Statement from the Doctor who attended to the diseased life assured last; the identification of the life assured, how long the doctor treated him, for what ailments, whether the doctor is the usual medical attendant of the life assured and, if so, for what ailments he treated him etc.
- Statement by a gentleman who is not related to the deceased life assured and who is not interested in the policy moneys, who has attended the Burial/Cremation of the deceased life assured–particulars of the life assured, how long had he known him, any relationship, when did he see him last alive, date, time and place of death, cause of death, whether the body was cremated or buried, date, time and place of cremation/burial etc.
- If the deceased life assured was an employee of any organization, a statement from the Employer furnishing details of the life assured, date of joining service, designation, date last attended duty, date of death, details of any leave availed on grounds of sickness during the period of three years earlier to the date of commencement of risk up to date of death, medical benefit facilities, if any, availed by

the deceased life assured–copies of leave letters, medical certificates submitted for sanction of sick leave, copies of medical prescriptions and bills produced for settlement of medical benefits, etc.

- In case of death due to unnatural causes like accidents, suicide, etc. the following records are called for:
  - First Information report of the police
  - Panchanama report/police inquest report
  - Postmortem report
  - Chemical analysis/forensic report in cases where postmortem is not conclusive about the cause of death
- In very rare cases, Police Final Investigation Report

Specimens of some of the reports obtained by LIC of India are enclosed. In addition, an Investigation Report by one of the officials of the Corporation into the genuineness of the claim is also called for. Where death is due to unnatural reason. Where a claim to consider Double Accident Benefit is received also the reports mentioned at No. 7 are called for.

For considering Non-Early claims, some of the above many not be necessary. A few cases arise where it may not be possible for the claimants to obtain and submit Original Death Certificate issued by the concerned authorities. In such cases alternative proofs also are considered.

Here are a few examples:

- *Death in an Air Crash*: Where there are no survivors, the list of passengers as per the records of the Airlines Company can be accepted as an alternate proof of death.
- *Disappearance on Board a Ship*: The logbook maintained showing the list of passengers on board the Ship when it sailed off a particular port and similar list after it reached the next port–if the name of the passenger appeared in the former register but not in the latter, it should be presumed that he fell into the sea and drowned as there can be no other way of explaining the disappearance.
- *Presumption of Death*: As per Section 108 of the Indian Evidence Act, 1872, if a person has not been heard of for seven years by those who would naturally have heard of him had he been alive, there is presumption of law that he is dead. Here also what is presumed is death of the life assured but not the date of death. Hence the date of the order of the court declaring presumption of death is taken as date of death.

On receipt of the requirements, the Insurance office decides whether there is any liability or not. In cases where the office could obtain documentary evidence of suppression of material facts by the deceased life assured at the time of taking the policy or at the time of revival of the lapsed policy, the liability is repudiated. Where the liability is admitted, the office proceeds to the next step *viz.*, verifying the title to the policy moneys.

EVIDENCE OF TITLE

There are different kinds of evidence of Title to Policy moneys. The simplest of these are Nomination and Assignment effected as per Sections 39 and 38 respectively of the Insurance Act, 1938.

Nomination

Nomination under Section 39 is naming of a person or persons to give a valid discharge to the insurance company and receive policy moneys in case of death of life assured during the period of the policy. Nominee can only receive the moneys. In case of survival of the life assured till the date of maturity, nomination will be ineffective. Nomination can be done by making suitable entries in the proposal to the policy in which case it will be incorporated in the text of the policy. Otherwise, it can be done by an endorsement made on the back of the policy by the life assured. But this will be effectual only if it is communicated to the Insurance Company and got registered in their records.

Nomination can be done only by a Policyholder under a Policy on his own life and not otherwise. For example, when a policy is assigned to a third party, the latter cannot nominate because the policy is not on his life. Similarly, if a parent obtains a policy on the life of a child, the child cannot nominate any one till he attains age of majority because during minority he is not the owner of the policy though the policy is on his own life. After attaining majority, the child can nominate. Nomination can be done in favour of one or more persons. But those nominees who are alive on the date of death of the life assured only will receive the policy moneys. For this reason, while nominating more than one person, the life assured should not indicate shares of the policy moneys for individual nominees.

Nomination can be in favour of a minor, in which case, the life assured can appoint an appointee to receive policy moneys on behalf of the minor nominee in case of the death of the life assured during the minority of the nominee and before date of maturity. During the lifetime of the life assured, he/she can deal with the policy in whatever way he/she may desire and the consent of nominee is not necessary. Nomination once made can be changed by the life assured at his will at any time but before the policy matures for payment.

Nomination once made is automatically cancelled by:

- Cancellation/further change of nomination
- Assignment in favour of a third party—in case assignment is done in favour of the insurance company for a loan out of surrender value of the policy, then nomination will not get cancelled
- A Will.

Nomination should be normally in favour of some one near and dear. If a stranger is named as a nominee, there may be a suspicion of absence of insurable interest. In a Joint Life Policy, normally there is no need for nomination because, in case of death of one life, policy moneys become payable to the surviving life. However there can be a joint nomination providing for a particular contingency, *viz* the simultaneous death of both lives in a common calamity.

Even in such cases, there can be a presumption of law, for example Section 21 of Hindu Succession Act, 1956 reads as follows:

- "Where two persons have died in circumstances rendering it uncertain whether either of them, and if so which, survived the other, then, for all purposes affecting succession to the property, it shall be presumed, until the contrary is proved, that the younger survived the older."

Even where there are rival claimants, the Supreme Court ordered in a case that the Life Insurance Corporation should pay the policy moneys to the Nominee under Section 39 of the Insurance Act, provided the nomination is effective and there is no injunction order from any court of law.

Nomination is an instrument, the insurance law created, to secure an immediate payment of the policy moneys by the insurer, without prejudice to the decision on the question as to who are entitled to succeed the estate of the deceased life assured.

Proceeds of the policy do not vest in the nominee though they are payable to the nominee in the event of the death of the holder of the policy. They do not, by virtue of nomination under Section 39 alone, become a part of nominee's estate before or after the policy matures.

Assignment

Assignment of a policy of life insurance, under Section 38 of Insurance Act, 1938, is a transfer of the property contained in the policy by the assignor to the assignee. Unlike a nominee under Section 39, Assignee under Section 38 has all rights under the policy not only to receive the policy moneys when they are due but also to deal with the policy in any way he desires without the consent of the assignor.

A policy of life insurance is a property. Hence, like any other property, it's owner can deal with it in any way he/she likes. But transfer of a policy of life insurance is covered by Section 38 of Insurance Act, 1938 but not the Transfer of Property Act. Where the Insurance Act is silent about any particular feature of transfer of a policy, the provisions of Transfer of Property Act, 1882 are applicable.

To assign a policy, the assignor should be the holder *i.e.* owner of the policy. It means that the policy need not be on his life. It also means that a person who is an assignee under a policy of life insurance can further assign it to any other person, for which act he need not obtain the consent or concurrence of the original assignor. However, the assignor should not be a minor. A child cannot, during his minority, therefore, assign a policy on his life to another.

Assignee can be anybody including a minor. In case of death of the assignee, the property will devolve upon his/her legal successors. There can be more than one assignee. In case of the death of any one or more assignees, the policy moneys will have to be paid to the legal heirs of the deceased assignee/assignees.

Assignment is transfer of property. So it cannot be effected till a policy is issued. It can be effected by an endorsement on the back of the policy or on a separate stamped deed. It is effective the moment it is done in one of the methods and duly signed by the assignor and witnessed. But as against the insurer, it will be effective only if it is got registered by the insurer in their records. But, where there are more than one assignment, the priority of settlement of claims by the insurer depends on the date of receipt of notice of assignment along with the policy document carrying the endorsement or the stamp deed by the insurer. Notice of assignment can be given either by the assignor or the assignee or any one authorized by them.

Sub-section (1) of Section 38 of Insurance Act, 1938 mentions that an assignment can be made 'whether with or without consideration'. But all assignments without consideration are not valid. Assignment for natural love and affection between parties standing in the near relation to each other is valid. But in any other case absence of consideration may render the assignment invalid.

Both absolute and conditional assignments are recognized under the Act. An absolute assignment transfers to the assignee all right, title and interest of the assignor in the policy to the assignee. The policy vests in the assignee absolutely and forms part of his/her death. A conditional assignment also creates an immediate vested interest in the assignee but such interest is liable to be divested on the happening of the contingencies set out in the assignment. A gift cannot be made by a Mohammedan subject to a condition. However, a conditional assignment of a life insurance policy by a Mohammedan would nevertheless be valid under the Act.

As already stated, the insurer's task is very easy in settling a death claim under a life insurance policy, if there is a subsisting, effective nomination or assignment. The only problem, in respect of a nomination, is when the nominee is a minor at the time of the death of the life insured and there is no appointee appointed under Section 39 or the appointee is incapable to act. In such cases, the insurer can settle the claim only in favour of the legal heirs to the estate of the deceased life insured.

MARRIED WOMEN'S PROPERTY ACT

It is also possible that the policy was taken under Married Women's Property Act, 1874. In such a case, there will be neither nomination nor assignment.

Section 6 of the said Act states as under:

- "A policy of insurance effected by any married man on his own life, and expressed on the face of it to be for the benefit of his wife, or his wife and children, or any of them shall ensure and be deemed to be a trust for the benefit of his wife and children, or any of them according to the interest so expressed, and shall not, so long as any object of the trust remains, be subject to the control of the husband, or to his creditors, or form part of his estate. "

The object of the law is to enable a married man to provide for his wife and children and to create a trust in their favour. The term 'married man' includes a widower or a divorced man. Similarly the word 'children' means issues in the first generation, that is sons and daughters and will not include grand children. But it includes 'adopted children' in case of any one whose personal law permits adoption.

The beneficiaries may be given equal or specified unequal shares. In the event of beneficiary who has a specified share of interest, such share would go to his or her legal representatives in case of the death of the beneficiary. It is also possible to provide that the benefit under the policy shall go to the beneficiaries jointly or the survivors or survivor of them.

A trust may also be created in favour of wife and children as a class. In such a case, the benefit would go to the person who at the death of the life assured shall become the widow of the assured and those of the children by any marriage and whenever born, who shall survive him. However, this facility of beneficiaries as a class is not applicable in respect of Mohammedans because as per their personal law, a gift to a person not yet in existence is void. Hence a Mohammedan can create a trust under the provisions of MWP ACT only in favour of wife and/or children who must be named and who must be existing at the date of the policy.

The procedure to create a trust under the said act is very simple. The policyholder should, at the time of proposing for insurance, indicate that he wishes to take the policy under Section 6 of the MWP Act. He should not however nominate any one under Section 39 of Insurance Act. He will have to complete an Addendum to the proposal.

The form of addendum depends upon two factors, *viz.* the type of beneficiaries–named or as a class and the nature of trustees–individuals or corporate bodies like Banks. There can be one or more trustees but they must be capable of contracting as per the provisions of the Indian Contract Act. Their consent, however, is essential to act as Trustees. They should signify their assent by subscribing their signatures in the Addendum to the proposal for life insurance.

The life assured can give other specific powers to the trustees to raise any loan on the policy for the benefit of the beneficiaries or reserve to himself powers to appoint new trustees in case the appointed trustees become incapable to act or die. Once it is decided to accept the proposal, the insurance company issues the policy document showing on its face that it is taken under 'MWP ACT'.

Where, therefore, the policy is under the said Act, in case of payment of policy moneys, either on the death of the life assured or on maturity of the policy, the insurance company will have to make the payment to the Trustees appointed. If no trustees are appointed by the life assured then payment is made to the Official Trustee of the State. Thus a valid discharge for payment of the policy moneys is obtained by the insurance company from the Appointed Trustees or in their absence the Official Trustee of the State. It is for the Trustee/s later on to pass on the benefits to the beneficiaries according to the terms of the Trust.

In the absence of a valid nomination or assignment or a Trust under the MWP Act, the title to the policy moneys will have to be proved to the satisfaction of the insurance company in one of the following ways, A Probate of the Will if the life assured died testate:

- Letters of administration
- If the life assured died intestate, a Succession Certificate from a competent court of law specifically mentioning the policy of life insurance and the amount payable thereunder.

A will is the disposition of one's property to take effect after his death.

As per Indian Succession Act, 1925:

- 'Will' means the legal declaration of the intention of the testator with respect to his property which he desires to be carried into effect after death.
- 'Probate' means the copy of a will certified under the seal of a court of competent jurisdiction with a grant of administration to the estate of the testator.
- 'Executor' means a person to whom the execution of the last will of a deceased person is, by the testator's appointment confided.
- 'Administrator' means a person appointed by competent authority to administer the estate of a deceased person when there is no Executor.

'Probate' is granted only to an Executor appointed by the Will. The Life Insurance Company will have to act as per the Probate while settling death claims.

Where:

- The deceased has made a Will, but has not appointed an Executor, or
- The deceased has appointed an Executor who is legally incapable or refuses to act, or who has died before the testator or before he has proved the Will, or
- The Executor dies after having proved the Will, but before he has administered all the estate of the deceased, a Universal or a Residuary Legatee may be admitted to prove the Will, and Letters of Administration with the Will may be granted to him of the whole estate, or of so much thereof as may be unadministered.

A Residuary Legatee is the one who is designated by the testator to take the surplus or residue of the property after distribution of the other bequests. The Executor or Administrator, as the case may be, of a deceased person is his legal representative for all purposes and all the property of the deceased person vests in him. A life insurance company should, therefore, make payment of the policy moneys on the death of the life assured to the Executor of Administrator.

A Succession Certificate may be applied for under Section 372 of the Indian Succession Act in respect of any debt or debts due to the deceased or in respect of portions thereof, of the securities to which he is entitled. A policy of life insurance, especially where the policy is for a definite sum, comes within the definition of 'debt' and a Succession Certificate can be granted with respect to it.

Succession Certificate is not granted in those cases where Probate or Letters of Administration are necessary under the Indian Succession Act. Where a Succession Certificate is granted, it is conclusive as against the persons owing such debts specified therein. It shall afford full indemnity to all such persons as regard all payments made in good faith in respect to such debts to the person to whom the certificate was granted. The insurance company will pay the policy moneys to the person holding a Succession Certificate. The Hindu Succession Act, 1955 provides for the devolution of the property of a Hindu.

The Class I legal heirs of a male Hindu dying intestate are son, daughter, widow, mother, children and widow of each predeceased son, children of each predeceased daughter, children and widow of each predeceased son of each predeceased son. Similarly the Act defines the Class II, III and IV legal heirs. The heritable property devolves firstly upon the first category and if there is no Class I legal heir then upon the second category and so on.

The property of a female Hindu dying intestate shall devolve upon sons and daughters (including children of any predeceased son or daughter) and the husband (Class I heirs) and failing them upon other classes (Class II, III and IV legal heirs). The Act also contains rules for distribution among the members of the class entitled to succeed to the estate.

The Mohammedans are governed by their Personal Laws, for example, the first class legal heirs of a Male Muslim are Widow, Sons and daughters, Father and Mother. If he has no sons then, Widow, Daughters, Father and Mother, Brothers and Sisters. A situation may arise when in respect of a policyholder, there is neither Nominee (or nominee is a minor and there is no Appointee) nor Assignee; neither he left a Will.

In such cases, it will be possible for the insurance company to settle a death claim on the basis of a Succession Certificate obtained from a Court of Law. But this will be a long drawn process. The very purpose of life insurance is not served if there is delay in providing the much needed financial assistance to the bereaved family of the life insured. Hence LIC of India has evolved a process by which strict legal proof of title is waived under certain circumstances. There should be a request from the legal heirs of the deceased life assured to waive production of strict proof of title. In such a case, all the legal heirs have to submit an affidavit declaring their names, relationship to the deceased life assured, etc.

On receipt of such affidavit, the office will consider waiver sought for subject to the following conditions:

- The life assured should have died intestate, *i.e.* should not have left a Will,
- There should not be any dispute among the legal heirs,
- There should not be any other property of the deceased life assured for which the legal heirs have to approach a court for a Succession Certificate.

The office will decide to waive proof of title. They will settle the claim in favour of the legal heirs (Class I, Class II or Class III) on the basis of an Indemnity Bond duly executed by all the legal heirs along with a Surety of sound financial status.

Irrespective of whether there is a valid proof of title or it is waived, a valid discharge has to be obtained by the insurance company before the payment is made of the policy moneys on the death of the life assured. A discharge form duly filled and completed by all the legal heirs and duly witnessed will have to be submitted to the company. The policy document will also have to be submitted along with the discharge voucher. On receipt of these requirements, the insurance company will arrange payment.

A situation may arise when the legal heirs are not able to produce the original policy document as the same might have been lost or misplaced. In such cases, the insurance company insists upon an Indemnity Bond duly executed by all the legal heirs along with a Surety of sound financial status. This Indemnity Bond is different from the Indemnity Bond obtained for payment of the policy moneys waiving strict proof of legal title.

ACCIDENT AND DISABILITY BENEFIT

We shall now turn our attention to settlement of Accident and Disability Benefit claims; first, Accident Benefit:

- Death should be due to Accident, *i.e.* by External, Violent and Visible means. Death must be directly due to the accident and there should be no intervening cause. For example, if a person meets with an accident, admitted to hospital, develops Gangrene due to his Diabetic condition and then dies, it is not taken as death due to accident because there is an intervening cause *viz.* , Diabetes.
- Death should take place within a specified period of time after the accident. As per the rules of LIC of India, this period is 120 days.

- Proof satisfactory to the insurance company should be submitted. Usually the requirements called for are
  - First Information Report
  - Panchanama or Police Inquest Report
  - Postmortem Report.

  If Viscera was sent for Chemical Examination, then the Report of the Forensic Laboratory is also called for. These reports indicate the cause and circumstances of death, whether it is accidental in nature, etc.
- The policy must be in full force at the time of death. Policyholder should have availed of the Accident Benefit by paying the necessary additional premium. He must not have been aged 70 years and above at the time of death.
- None of the exclusions should apply for consideration of sanctioning accident benefit in a case. There are also several exclusions in considering granting Accident Benefit. The life assured should not be under the influence of any intoxicating liquor, drug or narcotic at the time of the accident. The accident should not be because of the life assured being engaged in an activity which is a Breach of Law. The accident should not have happened when the life assured is involved in war or war like operations, or when the life assured was flying in an aircraft other than as a passenger, or in police or police like operations, he must not have been engaged in hazardous sports like car or motor cycle racing, mountaineering, steeple-chasing, hangg-liding, sky-diving, scuba-diving, or the life assured making an attempt to commit suicide.

Subject to all the conditions being satisfied, the insurance company decides to allow the extra benefit. The benefit is generally paid along with the normal liability under the policy. There are two types of Disability Benefits. One is waiver of premiums and the other is payment of an income to the life assured apart from waiver of premiums. The exclusions mentioned in respect of Accident benefit are equally applicable to Disability benefits also.

In addition, disability itself is defined as permanent loss of two limbs due to accident, by amputation or other wise. The life assured should not be in a position to pursue the same occupation he was engaged in earlier to the accident. The proof of disability should be satisfactory to the insurance company.

Usually, the following requirements are called for:

- First Information Report of the Police
- A declaration from the life assured explaining the details of the accident and the treatment undergone and the type of disability suffered.
- Records of the Hospital where treatment was given.

- A statement from the Hospital about the extent of disability, whether permanent or temporary, details of any surgery performed, the percentage of disability, etc.

The insurance company considers granting the disability benefits to which the policy is eligible. This leaves us with the subject of 'Payment of Annuities'. Payment here depends upon the type of annuity and also the mode of payment of pension chosen by the annuitant.

The common rule is that before an annuity vests, the entire purchase price must have been paid by the Annuitant to the insurance company. If it is an immediate annuity, the entire purchase price would have been paid in a single installment.

In this case, the payment of annuity commences immediately, the first installment becoming due exactly one payment interval later, *i.e.*, if monthly payment of pension is chosen by the annuitant, the first annuity will fall due exactly one month after the receipt of the purchase price.

So is with the other modes of payment. If it is a deferred annuity, then all the installments of premium falling before the deferred date should have been received.

In such a case, payment of annuity commences exactly one payment interval after the Deferred Date. Irrespective of the type of annuity (except annuity certain), evidence of survival of the annuitant will have to be submitted to the insurance company at periodical intervals. In case of a Joint Life or Joint and Survivorship Annuities, when one of the annuitants dies, proof of death is to be submitted to the insurance company.

It is usually the practice of insurance companies to obtain advance vouchers from annuitants and send cheques in advance for a period of six months or one year. This avoids the administrative work of issuing cheques every month to all the annuitants.

CLAIMS MANAGEMENT SYSTEM AND ORGANIZATIONAL STRUCTURE

The effectiveness of the claims management is dependent on two important elements such as well defined structure of claims department and well defined working of the department. The effective working is again related to quality of services, timely settlement of claims, avoiding of litigations, cost effective settlement, retention of customers and customer relations management.

To achieve these objectives the information of the insurance business should be accessible, the information received or the settlement of the claims should be economical, the information received should be compact and should provide all the information required for the purpose of making some decisions. The management system should contain some facility of cross references and settled precedents.

The claims management system is effective only when it is able to make timely decisions on the following elements:

- Decision relating to the use of information technology. The decision will be related to the extent of use of computers in place of human workforce, cost factors of establishment, sharing of information which is stored by the servers or the computers of certain individual department such as marketing, under-writing, staff and public relations department with that of the claims management.
- Decision relating to the use of services of outsourcing, particularly for the settlement of claims. The outsourcing refers to either having an agreement with some technically skilled persons for their services whenever the need arises, or hire services of the people at the time of requirement.
- Using of intermediaries is another area where the managerial decision is required. As such the organization may be required to use the offices of some persons like agents, staff, professionally skilled and licensed personnel like loss assessors or surveyors or loss adjusters for the settlement of the claim.
- Customer relations management is one of the important factors of the organization. The satisfied customer relations not only improve the business of the organization and avoid complications and complexities in claims settlement. A number of consumer disputes can be avoided by having effective customer relations.
- Decision-making relating to costs of claims is also an important element of the claims management. Costs of claims enquiry, costs of intermediaries, costs of the outsourcing, costs of litigations and settlements, costs of claims due to delay such as interest payments, are to be considered while making decisions relating to costs. Estimation of costs, allocation of funds for claims payments, budget and control of claims fund, analysis of costs, decisions to avoid some of the costs or expenses relating to claims payments, making reserves, planning of claims reserves, designing of reserves of catastrophe claims and bulk claims, reserves for expected events, resources planning to meet the need of claims payments, auditing of claims payments are some of the areas where expert managerial decisions are to be made.
- Management of resources of the organization and allocation and use of the available resources is another important functional area of the management. It is very much important in claims management. Forecasting the budget for claims payment, existing and future claims, establishment of reserves, reserves for unexpected claims and catastrophe claims are the areas where the decisions have to be made. Thus, claims management is having an important role to have

concentration on planning of the management system and organizational structure of the insurance company to provide effective services and deliver services on faster mode.

ROLE OF INFORMATION TECHNOLOGY IN CLAIM SETTLEMENT

ADVENT OF THE INFORMATION TECHNOLOGY IN CLAIMS MANAGEMENT

Information technology involves the use of computer systems, digital electronics and telecommunications to store, process and transmit information. In the context of claims management, it involves storage, processing and transmission of information relating to settlement of insurance claims. IT plays an important role in the present insurance and reinsurance scenario. Its role is expected to be further strengthened in the coming future.

The insurance companies are expected to harness new developments in claims management. This results in better distribution channels to policyholders, effective service to customers and reduction of operating costs. The IT strategy encompasses the whole of insurance organization. All the information generated in various fields will expedite and increase the quality in claims management.

E-BUSINESS AND CLAIMS MANAGEMENT

Features of Insurance claims:

- The number of insurance transactions entered into everyday is numerous. Today, there are a number of insurance companies and a lot more are expected to come up. Every business and every individual has insurance of one type or the other. There are a number of insurance products in the market. All these result in greater claims transactions to be processed.
- Some of the insurance products such as commercial insurance involves more than three to four insurance companies. As a result there is a complexity in the method of risk distribution and other parameters.
- A large number of transactions are handled by brokers and other intermediaries. This results in the complexity in claims settlement, increases the necessity of maintaining records, updated information, and important data and analysis of data.
- The insurance process has become so complex and involves a number of steps. It involves loss adjuster, legal experts, witnesses, etc.
- The requirement of investigating is largely felt due to increase in fraudulent, repeated and exaggerated claims.

- The need for reinsurance also adds to complexity in claim.
- The insurers are faced with new challenges, new issues as a result of increase in the number of products.

Advantages of an IT system in claims management:

- *Elimination of Duplication*: Once all the details regarding the insurance policies issued are entered into the electronic data entry systems, the data can be stored and becomes available to multi-use. Thus it eliminates duplication of both the data and the effort.
- *Reduced Paper Work*: In such a system the files are created electronically. Supporting documents, images of damages and reports of loss assessors can also be stored electronically. This eliminates the necessity to maintain a number of files manually and expedite the settlement process.
- Electronically communicated information leads to quicker communication of the origination of risk, the occurrence of loss etc.
- Electronic authorization, accompanied by payments made through central settlement system results in expediting the claims payment.
- The use of electronic funds transfer. This leads to faster settlement of claims.
- It helps in reducing administration costs. As paper work decreases the need to maintain piles of stationery decreases.
- Faster agreement of valid claims and faster settlement of claims leads to a greater satisfaction of the insured. This adds to the goodwill of the insurer.
- An automated check against fraudulent, exaggerated and repeated claims.
- Expediting payments to be made to brokers, intermediaries, loss adjusters, etc.
- Information on fingertips for decision making purpose is available.

Disadvantages:

- There may be an adverse effect on the cash flow position, as the claims settlement is expedited but the premium collections and the reinsurance recoveries may be delayed.
- IT systems are more suited to standardized insurance products. They are less suited to big, more complex liability claims and non-standardized insurance claims.
- These systems are less flexible, difficult to operate.
- IT is rapidly changing and the pace is so fast that even experts in this field are finding it difficult to cope with. This results in hardware and software products becoming obsolete in ridiculously short periods of time.
- Difficulty may arise in finding the right type of personnel to handle the systems and data.

- The use of electronic communication coupled with a centralized claims function results in a biased approach to the delivery of services.
- The cost of installation and operating a system are heavy.
- The application of the system must be accompanied by a review of claims procedures and practices. This also involves increased cost and work.
- A powerful, flexible and adaptable computer system is valuable but not a substitute to experienced people.
- Physical control over records and assets is critical. The concentration of data processing assets and records also increase the loss that can arise from computer abuse or disaster.
- Changes in technical and business environment will pressurize the need to upgrade the systems and processes which entails expenditure.
- The claim management should be continually reoriented to changing priorities and changes in software technology or it shall not serve the purpose.
- Security and safety of data, information and the system are necessary to ensure success, which is lacking today.

The success of a claims management system depends on the satisfaction of the insured/customers. The ultimate customer is the insured or potential customer who may be attracted to the insurance company by its state of art claims service. Therefore before designing an IT system for claim management customer's expectations are to be taken into account. Both commercial and personal customers today are more aware of their needs, knowledge of how the market works and are more determined to get what they want.

The insurance industry till today has overlooked the expectations of its customers in designing of claims management systems. It now tends to deploy modern technology to stream line operations and generate economies of scale. In the designing of the systems a careful quantification and documentation of the expectations of the consumer is required for the success of IT in claims management.

CLAIM SETTLEMENT

ROLE OF CENTRAL GOVT. IN CLAIMS SETTLEMENT

In view of the economic importance of the insurance sector the Central Government concerns with protecting the interest of the consumers. The Central Government in the year 1993 also set up a Reforms Committee to examine the structure of the insurance industry and especially examine areas relating to expenses, customer services, claims settlement and resolution of disputes.

The dynamic role of the Central Government in claims settlement is summarized hereunder:

- The Central Government shall make policy statements relating to payment of claims. It shall fix norms for disposal of claims and fix time period for particular activities.
- The Central Government shall scrutinize the reports submitted by the insurers and the IRDA relating to payment of claims, amount reserved for the purpose of settlements, amount of claims unsettled, amount of claims unpaid, total of claims applications pending processing and settlements etc. The Central Government shall direct the IRDA to investigate and report on the pending claims or investigate delay in settlement.
- The Central Government shall in general or in a particular case direct the insurance companies to improve upon their claims settlement machinery or speed up the process and quality of claims settlement.
- The Central Government, if it feels that it is necessary to do so can make amendments to the existing laws to facilitate and smoothen the claims settlement process.
- The Central Government shall control and improve upon social insurances and welfare insurance business and shall also monitor the working of special insurance programmes such as rural insurance etc.
- The Central Government shall depending upon the circumstances and requirements appoint the Claims Tribunal for the purpose of settlement of Claims and specify the jurisdiction for the purpose of their functioning.
- The Central Government shall appoint or remove officials for the purpose of achieving expeditious settlement of claims. It shall also withdraw the licenses of insurers who fail to adhere to its directions in respect to settlement of claims.
- The Central Government shall provide for alternative dispute resolution methods such as Arbitration, Mediation, or Negotiation, and Conciliation to provide a nonlitigatory solution to claims settlement.
- Make laws binding on the insurers and other authorities responsible for settlement of claims.
- The Central Government has been instrumental in the appointment of Ombudsman claims.

All the methods employed by the Central Government prove that it indirectly expedites the process of settlement of claims. In the Consumer Protection Act, 'facilities in connection with insurance' has been specifically included within the scope of the expression 'service'. A complaint relating to the failure on the part of an insurer to settle the claims of the insured within a reasonable time and the prayer for the grant of compensation in respect of such delay shall fall within the jurisdiction of the Consumer Redressal Forum constituted under the Consumer Protection Act.

ROLE OF OMBUDSMAN IN CLAIM SETTLEMENT

'Ombudsman' is a Scandinavian term, which means an 'entrusted person' or 'grievance representative.' An 'Ombudsman' is an office constituted by the Constitution, or by the action of a legislature, or Parliament. An Ombudsman receives complaints from the aggrieved persons, investigates, recommends action and issues report on the outcome of an investigation. Individual policyholders take their complaints up with the insurer's senior management and then, if necessary, with the Ombudsman. The reluctance of the public to go for arbitration has led to the establishment of Ombudsman as a machinery for settlement.

An Ombudsman helps speed up independent settlement of dispute. The Ombudsman receives references in relation to complaints, disputes and claims made in connection with or out of policies of insurance. It is a machinery which facilitates satisfactory settlement or withdrawl of claims, by way of award or such other means. The office of an ombudsman is established for the protection of the rights of the insured (being individual) against the insurer (company). The Central Government has been conferred the power to frame rules by the Insurance Act, 1938. To exercise such power the Central Government has framed the Redressal of Public Grievances Rules, 1998.

These rules provide for the appointment of Ombudsman. Customer service is one of the major areas of concern for the Government. As a part of this exercise, steps have been initiated to set up the Ombudsman for further control over personal life insurance claims of both Life and Non-life sectors. By a notification in the Official Gazette, the government notified the Ombudsman Scheme on November 11, 1998 for the expeditious settlement of insurance claims.

The "Ombudsman" can also act as a counselor and mediator, for matters within the terms of reference, if requested to do so by the insurer and the insured. An Ombudsman scheme is presently set up in 12 centres in India. Four have been set up in metropolitan cities like Delhi, Mumbai, Kolkata, and Chennai and others in some major cities like Lucknow, Hyderabad, Bhopal, Kanpur, Bhubaneswar, Bangalore and Chandigarh. The jurisdiction of each Ombudsman is defined and fixed by a notification.

Scheme of Ombudsman

Complaints of the following types come within the purview of the Ombudsman's consideration:

- Repudiation of liability under claims.
- Delay in settlement of claims.

- Any dispute regarding premiums paid or payable in respect of the policy.
- Any dispute regarding the legal construction of the policies in relation to a claim; and
- Non-issue of insurance document to customer after receipt of premium.

Role of Irda in Claim Settlement

In exercise of the powers conferred by clause (zc) of sub-section (2) of section 114A of the Insurance Act (4 of 1938) read with sections 14 and 26 of the Insurance Regulatory and Development Authority Act, 1999 (41 of 1999), the Authority in consultation with the Insurance Advisory Committee, hereby makes the following regulations namely:

- A life insurance policy shall state the primary documents which are normally required to be submitted by a claimant in support a claim.
- A life insurance company, upon receiving a claim, shall process the claim without delay. Any queries or requirement of further documents, to the extent possible, shall be raised all at once and not in a piecemeal manner.
- A claim under a life policy shall be paid or be disputed giving all the relevant reasons, within 30 days from the date of receipt of all relevant papers and clarifications required. However, where the circumstances of a claim warrant an investigation in the opinion of the insurance company, it shall initiate and complete such investigation at the earliest.
- Subject to the provisions of section 47 of the Act, where a claim is ready for payment but the payment cannot be made due to any reasons of a proper identification of the payee, the life insurance company shall hold the amount for the benefit of the payee and such an amount shall earn interest at the rate applicable to a savings bank account with a scheduled bank.
- Where there is a delay on the part of the insurer in processing a claim for a reason other than the one covered by sub-regulation (4), the life insurance company shall pay interest on the claim amount at 10% p. a. effective from the date of submission of all information and papers.
- Every insurer shall set up a proper grievance redressal machinery at its Divisional/Regional/Zonal/Head Office/Central Office, headed by a senior executive not having any direct responsibility for underwriting or settlement of claims.

Every insurer shall place before its Board of Directors at least once every quarter, statistics of:

- The number of claims intimated during the preceding quarter;
- The number of claims settled during the quarter;

- The number of claims outstanding at the end of the quarter;
- analysis of the claims paid by duration elapsed from the date of loss, namely, 0-6 months, 6-12 months and more than 12 months together with explanatory observations regarding delays in settlement in each case;
- analysing claims outstanding by duration, namely, 0-6 months, 6-12 months and more than 12 months.

Role of Consumer Protection Act in Claim Settlement

The insurer to bring profit to his company makes every possible attempt to lessen liability by invoking the agreement clauses of the policy, the terms and conditions of the policy, the nature of occurrence of the event to see whether it is covered under the policy or not, the payment of premium etc. The insurer invariably looks at facts and figures, whether material or non-material to the policy to find an excuse and repudiate the claim made by the insurer. True, the investigation and review of a claim is necessary so that no claimant gets an amount more than what he should be indemnified with. But this practice of the insurers has adversely affected the uneducated and the innocent. That is the reason why there is a Consumer Protection Act.

The insured is the only person who will be approaching the consumer protection machinery for the settlements of the claim because of the following grounds:

- The difference of services,
- Delay in services, *i.e.*, settlements of claims and payments,
- Not providing information required as the consumer of product,
- Not hearing to the consumers and helping them in the claim applications filing, and
- Taking advantage of innocence and helplessness conditions of the consumer and rejecting the policy payments.

The insurer wants to avoid the payments to reduce the liability on a pretext of some failures or non-performances of conditions required to be performed by the insured. However, the provisions of consumer protection provide life to the insured in the settlement of grievances of insurance claims.

Claims Review Committee

The Life Insurance Corporation of India settles a large number of death claims every year. Only in case of fraudulent suppression of material information will the liability be repudiated. The number of death claims repudiated is, however, very small. Even in these cases, an opportunity is given to the claimant to make a representation for consideration by the Review Committees at the Zonal Office and the Central Office. As a result of such review, depending on the merits of each case, appropriate decisions are taken. The claims Review Committees at the Central and Zonal Offices have among other members a retired High Court/District Court Judge.

Consumer Protection Machinery

The redressal mechanism as set up under Section 9 of the Consumer Protection Act, 1986 consists of a three-tier jurisdiction system. There are forums at district level called the District Forums; the ones at State level called the State Commissions and at the national level called the National Commission.

FUTURE OUTLOOK

The insurance industry has grownup to become a veritable institution, with over 6000 insurance companies worldwide collecting $ 800 billion in premiums each year and holding assets with an estimated value of $ 2.7 trillion. Among the various insurance companies are those that offer general insurance coverage including health, automobile, homeowners, life and disability, etc. , and those who specialize in one or more of the aforementioned types of insurance. With the deregulation of the banking and brokerage industries, large conglomerates have been formed that offer every imaginable financial service.

It is now common for these large corporations to offer a variety of insurance plans. In this regard with a large consumer base it becomes necessary for any provider of insurance services to have claims management staff and support systems. With more stringent regulations in place, it will be difficult for insurance companies to repudiate claims for every other reason.

Information technology is helping the insurance companies to manage claims. Many softwares for insurance claims have hit the market. A popular one among them is Claims Management Systems (CMS). It is called Managing, Organizing and Documenting Every Loss (MODEL). This software is developed by Scott Insurance.

The highlights are:

- Automatic completion of state required forms
- Internal claims management training
- Adjuster-to-adjuster claims planning and oversight
- Physician-to-physician medical reviews
- Organization of all information in one place
- Conversation/event documentation
- Internal/external claims information communication
- Progress tracking
- Follow-up for timely return to work, closing or settling claim
- Entries for workers' compensation, property, general liability and automobile claims.

A study reveals that the costs of claims are increasing at an annual rate of three times the rate of inflation. In such an environment it becomes imperative to have a claims management department to monitor and control the costs.

19

Contract Law

This stage considers some of the basic elements of contract law and highlights legal issues addressed in the Uniform Commercial Code. The stage concludes by looking at a sample contract and identifying general questions that apply in most sales situations. In the context of producer marketing associations, buyers are often an organization in which producers are members, such as a cooperative, LLC, or some other type of grower network.

While you might assume because you are already a stakeholder in the group you do not need to worry about protecting your own personal interests, this is not true. This sense of security means producers often enter into marketing agreements with their organizations without much concern over the terms of the contract. Unfortunately, this may be the wrong thing to do because the contracts establish enforceable rights and obligations for both parties.

Your sales relationship with the group results in you having two different roles with the organization. In one sense, you are concerned with the success of the group and are willing to contribute towards this goal. It is reasonable to expect you may even need to make some occasional sacrifices for the organization. In another sense, however, if the organization is having difficulty, your interests may no longer align with the group's. You may be left with unpaid bills or a crop you cannot market.

Desperate times call for desperate measures, and although the association may not want to take advantage of a provision in a contract that is against your interests, it may have no choice. On the other side of the coin, you may assume because you are a member you do not need to be concerned about meeting all of the requirements of a contract. You should not make this assumption.

The organization is counting on you to supply a certain type of product to meet its own obligations with buyers. If the organization suffers losses because you breached the agreement, it may have little choice but to try to shift those losses to you. Depending on how your group is organized, the people who run the business have a duty to do what is best for the organization, even if that means it might injure some of its members. This is not to suggest you should shy away from working with a joint producer association. Rather, you should enter into any agreements with your eyes wide open and recognize what real risks and responsibilities you have in relation to the organization.

To understand the risks and responsibilities involved in the buyer-seller relationship, you need to know the rules of the game. This stage looks at some of the law that affects the business sales relationship between farmers and buyers. It examines basic contract law and the Uniform Commercial Code. Other types of contracts, such as loan documents and insurance policies have already been addressed in other stages.

INTRODUCTION\

Black's Law Dictionary defines a contract as "[a]n agreement between two or more parties creating obligations that are enforceable or otherwise recognizable at law. " For purposes of this stage, we are concerned with agreements to buy and sell some type of agricultural product.

CONTRACTS 101

You should be concerned about contract law because it determines how parties to the contract will need to keep the promises they make. Although very few contracts ever end up in court, if the parties to a contract disagree on something and are unable to resolve the disagreement, they may have to resort to the judicial process. This means that as the parties negotiate a contract, they need to consider how a judge might ultimately interpret it.

For a contract to be enforceable, it must involve:

- *Competent Parties*: A court will not uphold a contract entered into by parties the law does not believe have the capacity to take on such a legal responsibility, such as minors or people who are mentally incapacitated.
- *A Legal Subject Matter*: A court will not uphold a contract requiring anyone to do something illegal.
- *An Offer*: An offer occurs when a party communicates the intention of doing something if the other party does another specific thing. Either the buyer or seller can initiate an offer so it could occur when you approach a cranberry cooperative with an offer to sell your cranberries for a certain price, or if they approach you with a form contract to sign.
- *Acceptance*: Acceptance occurs when a party communicates a willingness to be bound by the proposed agreement. When dealing with a written contract, this usually means when the offeree signs the contract.
- *Consideration*: Each party to the contract must provide consideration for the contract to be binding. Consideration is something of value or a promise to do, or not to do, a certain act in the future. In a

contract between a producer and an LLC that processes and sells honey, the producer's consideration could be the promise to deliver a certain amount of honey while the LLC's consideration could be the promise to pay a certain amount per pound.

The Drake Agricultural Law Center has published an entire book on this subject by Professor Neil Hamilton titled *A Farmer's Guide to Production Contracts*. The book broadly discusses all of the issues involved with agricultural sales and service contracts—everything from entering into the contract, performing under the contract, getting paid, and resolving disputes. The book analyses a number of different types of contracts involving vegetables, livestock, and grain. In a part on the basics of contracting, Professor Hamilton provides twelve rules to consider when entering into a contract.

The following list is taken from those rules and is slightly modified with some of the special issues involved with joint producer relationships:

- Remember the first rule of contracts–whoever wrote the contract took care of himself. Although you might be a member of the group with whom you are contracting, you still need to make sure the terms are fair and your interests are protected. The people representing the organization will take care of the interests of the group; it is your job to take care of your own interests.
- Read and understand any contract before signing it. Because the words in the contract will be enforceable in the future, you need to understand what you are promising to do and what you can and cannot hold the other party responsible for. If the contract is relatively large or involves a long duration, you should consider having your attorney go through the contract with you to make sure you understand all of the provisions.
- Know that complying with contract terms is required before you have performed under the contract. To receive a premium for raising organic vegetables, you will need to certify they are organic. If you are unable to deliver the amount or type of product you promised, you may need to go out into the market to find replacement products, otherwise, you might open yourself up to a lawsuit for breach of contract. Because of this, you will want to make sure you are able to live up to the promises you make in the contract or be willing to pay the consequences.
- Never assume your failure to perform a contract will be excused. If the buyer is damaged by your failure to perform under the contract, assume you will have to make amends. If you think you will not be able to fully meet your obligations under the contract, it is usually best to let the buyer know so both of you can deal with the situation. For instance, before planting, you promised to deliver 1000 pounds of blue potatoes to your cooperative but your crop was wiped out because of a late freeze. You should inform the coop that you will

not be able to deliver the potatoes. The buyer might know about a good substitute source for the potatoes and be able to acquire the product for much less cost than you would be able to. You may still have to pay for any cost difference for the substitute potatoes, but you will not have to pay as much.

- Know the other party's financial situation and performance history. This is especially important when you are not paid immediately for your product because in this case you become a creditor for the buyer. If the buyer experiences serious financial problems after you deliver the product, you may never get paid. This situation is partially dealt with for livestock with the statutory trust in the Packers and Stockyards Act and for fruits and vegetables with the PACA trust in the Perishable Agricultural Commodities Act.
- Weigh the advantages of the contract in terms of higher prices against any increased costs or risks. This suggestion is especially important in niche and specialty markets. Although you usually receive a higher price for the products, you will usually face greater costs or risks as well.
- Remember proposed contracts are always subject to negotiations. Many contracts dealing with the purchase of agricultural goods appear to use fixed "boilerplate" language. But all contracts are negotiable before signing; nothing forces you to sign the contract until you are satisfied with the deal. An important thing to keep in mind is you have much greater power to negotiate changes in the agreement before the contract is signed than after, so make sure you are satisfied with the agreement before signing.
- Make sure any changes to the contract are made in writing. Although it can be difficult to change a contract after it is signed, shifting conditions can persuade both parties it is in their best interest. To ensure the changes are enforceable, the new terms need to be in writing and signed or initialed by both parties.
- Do not rely on oral communications made by the buyer, either before the contract is signed or during the contract performance. If your agreement ever has to be interpreted in court, the court will most likely rely only on the written language in the contract itself. Courts usually refuse to accept evidence of oral agreements that goes against the contract language, and most contracts include a similar restriction. Because of this, you will want to get in writing any agreements important to you. If you are unable to do this, then make sure to keep copies of any documents, such as letters, payments sheets, and checks you can use to show what was agreed to.
- Keep good records of your performance. You never know when you will need to prove you have lived up to your end of the bargain. Keeping good records is the only way to do this. This is especially

true when a crucial part of the contract requires you to raise your product in a certain way. Whether this means not using antibiotics, raising organic tomatoes, or treating your animals in a certain way, if you have records indicating you have done what you promised, you can avoid headaches in the future.

- Do not hesitate to ask questions when you do not understand what is happening. The best time to ask questions about what you are promising to do is before you promise to do it. For example, if your contract with a wholesaler requires you to certify your operation with a third party certifier, make sure you understand what this will entail. To make sure you understand the terms of the contract, you can ask questions of the buyer or your advisors. To make sure you understand the concepts in the contract, ask other people such as extension officers or others who are growing products under similar contracts.
- Stay in touch with the other party to the contract. Regular communication with the buyer will help prevent misunderstandings about the contract or about what is required to satisfy the contract requirements. Open lines of communication will help both parties make sure that each is doing what the other party understood they would do.

THE UNIFORM COMMERCIAL CODE

The rules governing contracts traditionally came from common law, meaning the law that is produced on an ad hoc basis by courts. When the courts came up against a novel problem, they look at what they have done with somewhat similar issues in the past and craft a new rule for the new problem. From then on, when the same set of circumstance arise, the court will follow its precedent.

Because different courts and jurisdictions evolved in various directions, different states handle the exact same issue in various ways. This can lead to confusion for people who do business with firms in other states. To avoid this confusion, policy makers in the U.S. decided to create a set of common rules for commercial law. The result was the Uniform Commercial Code (UCC).

All of the states have adopted a version of the UCC. The laws can differ from state to state, but states generally do not vary from the major themes in the UCC. The UCC deals with a number of subjects related to commerce, such as leases (Article 2A), warehouse receipts (Article 7), and secured transactions where a lender obtains a security interest in goods (Article 9).

This part will focus on the UCC article that covers sales, Article 2:

- *Applicability*: Article Two deals only with sales and does not deal with contracts for services, such as production contract that pays a farmer for raising livestock or vegetables owned by someone else.

- *Statute of Frauds*: To prevent people from lying about non-existent contracts (that is, committing fraud), the UCC has adopted the statute of frauds to encourage people to write down their agreement. Under the UCC, a contract for the sale of goods for a value of $500 or more needs to be in writing to be enforceable. The writing, however, does not need to be a formal contract and it only needs to be signed by the person against whom enforcement is sought.

A contract can also be reached if the agreement is between merchants and one of the merchants sends a writing confirming the agreement and the other merchant does not object in writing within ten days. For example, assume a sugar beet LLC contacted you in the spring about purchasing your entire crop of beets in the fall. You agreed to the price and other terms over the phone. Within a few days, you receive a letter from the LLC that outlines the details of your agreement.

If you are a merchant, this can be enforced against you as a contract, although you never actually signed the document. If you do not agree with the terms as written, then you have ten days to send a written response to the LLC. If you are not a merchant, then the letter could not be enforced against you as a contract.

WARRANTY OF MERCHANTABILITY AND WARRANTY OF FITNESS FOR A PARTICULAR PURPOSE

The UCC assumes or "implies" two types of warranties in sales contracts. The first deals with a warranty of merchantability which means the goods should be "fit for the ordinary purposes" for which the goods were intended. This implied warranty applies only if the seller is a merchant. Importantly for those who prepare food, the implied warranty of merchantability applies to food sold for consumption on or off the premises. (UCC § 314). If someone is injured by consuming the food, the question is whether the food "was not reasonably fit for eating" and whether the injured person can prove the defect caused the injury.

The second type of implied warranty is the warranty that the product is fit for a particular purpose. (UCC § 315). This warranty arises where the "seller at the time of contracting has reason to know the particular purpose for which the goods are required" and that the buyer is relying on the special skill or knowledge of the seller to supply these goods. For example, if you are selling apples to a group you know produces organic apple cider and the group is relying on your knowledge as an organic apple grower, you will probably breach your warranty if you deliver apples that are not organic or have significant traces of insecticide.

REMEDIES RELATED TO A BREACH

The UCC provides a number of possibilities for a party to a contract who incurs costs because of a breach. If a seller breaches a contract, the buyer can cancel the contract and keep what has already been paid. The buyer can also seek substitute products and sue the seller for the extra costs incurred. If the product involved is hard to replace, then the contract may provide liquidated damages, which are fixed damages of a reasonable amount in relation to the actual harm caused by the breach. When a buyer refuses to purchase the products as promised under the contract, the typical remedy is for the seller to find another buyer for the product and charge the original buyer the difference between the contract price and the price actually received. With some specialty or niche products, finding a suitable buyer in a timely manner might be almost impossible. Nevertheless, in general the seller has a responsibility to make a good faith effort to limit the amount of damages.

EXAMPLE CONTRACT

When someone sells something on the spot or cash market, the seller attempts to seek bids from a number of buyers to receive the highest market price possible. When someone is using a more formal contract to market goods, they should also determine whether they can receive a better deal. This means comparing the contract with other similar contracts. This simple idea can be a challenge for farmers raising specialty crops or commodities because similar contracts may not exist. For those who raise commodities, some contracts include confidentiality clauses that prohibit people from sharing the contents. Some states, such as Iowa, prohibit these types of clauses in livestock contracts, but most states allow the provisions.

Even in states where confidentiality clauses are prohibited, there usually is not a formal clearinghouse to provide farmers an idea of what contracts have been offered and accepted. This means that the market for contracts may not be very transparent. This lack of transparency can be an even bigger problem in specialty and niche contracts because no similar contracts may exist. When considering entering into a contract in this type of market, you may need to be creative in determining what types of provisions the contract should include. Contracts can be simple one-page documents setting out the most basic provisions of the agreement, or they may go on for pages attempting to consider every possible issue that might arise in the sales arrangement.

Set out below is an example of a shorter contract that considers most of the essentials of a contract for the sale of a specialty or niche product. It is presented not as a form contract to be used, but simply as a way of raising issues you should consider when drafting or entering into your own contract.

CONCLUSION

This stage introduces the general legal framework of contract law. If you enter into contracts with a producer marketing association, these rules will apply just as if you were dealing with an outside party. By becoming familiar with how contracts are interpreted and enforced, you can help ensure a smoother relationship between members and the association.

Index